PLEASING
GOD

Kay Smith

THE WORD
FOR TODAY

P.O. Box 8000, Costa Mesa, CA 92628 • Web Site: www.twft.com • E-mail: info@twft.com

Pleasing God
by Kay Smith

Published by The Word For Today
P.O. Box 8000, Costa Mesa, CA 92628
Web site: http://www.twft.com
(800) 272-WORD (9673)

A special thanks to Janette Manderson, Sarah Yardley, and Shannon Woodward.

TABLE OF CONTENTS

FOREWORD

YOU WERE CREATED TO PLEASE GOD.

Philosophers through the ages have failed to grasp the very basic purpose of our existence. "Why am I here?" Yet, the Word of God has a ready answer, if they would but listen. It is found in Revelation 4:11:

> Thou art worthy, O Lord, to receive glory and honor, for Thou has created all things. And for Thy pleasure, they are and were created (KJV).

This Scripture makes it clear that each one of us exists to bring pleasure to God. But many reject this truth and fight against it. They choose instead to live for their own pleasure. And God gives them that choice. He will not force anyone to live to please Him. But since God designed us for that very purpose, we will always have an emptiness until we choose to bring Him pleasure. There will always be that haunting awareness that life must be more than what we have yet experienced.

Someone once asked a very wealthy man just how much it takes to be satisfied, and he answered, "Just a little more." That's the problem with living to please yourself. You set your goal and think, *If I just had this, I would be satisfied.* But then when you attain that goal you find you need something more.

There's a better way to live. We can live to please God.

How does one do that? What is the secret of pleasing the Father? Jesus gave us the answer in John 6:38 when He said,

> I have come down from heaven not to do My own will, but the will of Him who sent Me.

There's the key. Rather than seeking your own will, set it aside in order to do the will of the Father. Living to please God brings many wonderful consequences. As Solomon said,

> When a man's ways please the LORD, he makes even his enemies to be at peace with him (Proverbs 16:7).

Paul encouraged us,

> Walk worthy of the Lord, fully pleasing Him, being fruitful in every good work and increasing in the knowledge of God (Colossians 1:10).

The apostle John told us another great benefit:

> And whatever we ask, we receive from Him because we keep His commandments and do those things that are pleasing in His sight (1 John 3:22).

When we live to please God, we have peace with our enemies, we have fruitful lives, an increased knowledge of God, and even our prayers are more powerful and effective.

For the last sixty years, I have had the privilege of watching my wife, Kay Smith, live out these principles to please God. Over time, she has been a blessed helpmate in our ministry. Kay was the first to reach out to the hippies of the 60s. Her prayers and her tears laid the foundation for our church, Calvary Chapel. Since that time, Kay has been the cornerstone of our prayer ministry. And Kay began one of the most successful women's ministries in the country, teaching countless numbers of women how to live to please and honor God.

I pray that you will take this message God has given Kay and let it take root in your heart. The life that pleases God is the only life in which you'll find peace, contentment, and fulfillment. It's a life rich with blessing, purpose, and meaning.

May God bless you as you live to please Him.

> We urge and exhort in the Lord Jesus that you should abound more and more … how you ought to walk and to please God (1 Thessalonians 4:1).

~Pastor Chuck

1

HOW TO PLEASE GOD

EVERY YEAR ON MY BIRTHDAY, I take a moment at the beginning of the day to read what I call my birthday Scripture.

> Indeed, You have made my days as handbreadths, and my age is as nothing before You; certainly every man at his best state is but vapor (Psalm 39:5).

I think it's good to remind yourself of this truth. But lately, God has been impressing on my heart the verse that comes just before that one.

> Lord, make me to know mine end, and what is the measure of my days, that I may know how frail I am (Psalm 39:4).

In the marginal reference of my Bible, just to the side of the phrase "how frail I am" it says, "what time I have." In other words, this verse is asking, "Lord, make me to know what time I have." *The Living Bible* says it this way, "Lord, help me to realize how brief my time on earth will be." That's what David was praying. He was asking God to let him know the length of his days.

Don't you wish God would do that? I do. I wish God would just tell me exactly how long I have left on this earth. "Kay, you have ten days" or "You have ten years." Or even "You have five minutes." Yet, God is sending signs and warnings to us all the time—signs that tell us we really don't have very much time left on earth.

SIGNS OF THE LAST DAYS

Take a moment to turn to 2 Peter 3, where God describes for us what the world will be like in the last days. We read that men will scoff at God and walk after their own lusts. They will willfully forget that God is the Creator of the heavens and the earth. But then read what it says in verses 11 and 12:

> Therefore, since all these things will be dissolved, what manner of persons ought you to be in holy conduct and godliness, looking for and hastening the coming of the day of God, because of which the heavens will be dissolved, being on fire, and the elements will melt with fervent heat?

The word "dissolved" is used twice in this passage. God is clearly reminding us that all the things we're hanging on to will eventually be burnt with a fervent heat. Nothing will last—except our eternal souls. Only the work that we've done for Him—that is not wood, hay, and stubble, but pure gold—will stand the test of fire. This is God's warning.

Nature is another of God's warnings. Volcanic eruptions, mudslides, wildfires, floods, earthquakes, hurricanes—all are God's way of showing us that we are not in control. And these signs tell us we are in the last times.

Economic instability is also a warning sign. The price of gasoline is at an all-time high, with no signs of ever returning to a reasonable cost. And have you had to buy a pair of shoes lately? I think of all the mothers with three or four children who have to find a way to buy school shoes. It's not easy to make ends meet these days.

War, of course, is a sign of the last times. Jesus said,

> For nation will rise against nation, and kingdom against kingdom. And there will be famines, pestilences, and earthquakes in various places. All these are the beginning of sorrows (Matthew 24:7-8).

Our own country is at war right now in the Middle East. Israel is on a constant state of alert and has had several skirmishes in the past few years with the Hezbollah in Lebanon. North Korea has been testing nuclear missiles off their western coast. Iran is suspected of having nuclear bombs or having the capability of producing nuclear bombs, and they've made no secret of the fact that they would like to destroy both Israel and the United States. You would have to be completely oblivious not to see that we are almost at the end of this world as we have known it.

God has never destroyed a society without first warning that society. Back in the days of Noah, those in his community watched him build that ark for over a hundred-year period. During that time, Noah preached righteousness and warned them repeatedly that the flood was coming. The same is true for us today. God is warning us that destruction is coming.

WHAT DOES GOD WANT?

Within that passage in 2 Peter 3 there is a question, one that should be uppermost in the minds of committed Christians during these last days: "What manner of persons ought you to be?" In other words, since our time here is short, what does God want me to do? If I have twenty years left, or only a few months, or a few weeks … or a few hours, what does God want me to do with the time I have left?

Put another way, if Jesus came for His church right now, what would you want to be doing? Would you want to be praying? Witnessing? If Jesus came and you were bathing your babies or cooking dinner or working in an office, what should be the attitude of your heart?

As more and more prophecies have been fulfilled over the years, the awareness that the Lord could come back for His church at any moment has stirred me to ask those questions. And from reading that passage in 2 Peter 3 it seems clear to me that we are to be diligent, pure, and holy. We're to live in such a way to please the heart of God. What exactly does that mean? What does it look like to live with God's pleasure uppermost in your mind?

I was once told a story that illustrates this kind of attitude very well. Ramona Jensen, a YWAM missionary, was once invited to speak at the Evangelical Sisterhood of Mary in Darmstat, Germany. At that time, Ramona was twenty-eight years old. When she arrived, a woman in her sixties greeted her and immediately asked to carry Ramona's luggage. Ramona said, "Oh no, let me do it," but the woman replied, "It would please me to do it." The older woman then picked up Ramona's suitcase and carried it up to the registration hall. As they walked together, she began conversing with Ramona about her favorite things. What color did Ramona like best? What flower? What did Ramona like to drink? What was her favorite Scripture?

The older woman then introduced Ramona to those in the hall as she quietly excused herself. Ramona filled out her registration and talked a bit with her new acquaintances, and after a while she was taken to her room. When Ramona walked in, she found that someone had gone before her and prepared everything with her delight in mind. Her favorite colored towels hung on the towel rack. A vase on the table held her favorite flowers. Next to the vase, her favorite drink—a steaming pot of tea. And framed and hanging on the wall was her favorite Scripture, written out by hand. But it didn't stop there. When she went down to dinner that night, Ramona had no trouble finding her place at the table, because around her plate was a ring of her favorite flowers and chocolates. Just as she sat down to eat, the others in the room stood up and began to sing to her, "*The Lord bless you, Ramona.*"

Ramona was blessed the entire weekend. And just before she left, her hosts gave her a little booklet. As she was reading it on the plane, Ramona realized why she had been treated so graciously—not because she was Ramona Jensen. The Evangelical Sisterhood probably treated all their speakers—in fact, probably all their guests—in just that same way. Ramona understood that they did it to please the heart of God.

TO PLEASE GOD

To please someone means to delight, to satisfy, or to gratify. When our aim is to please God, then we begin to weigh all our actions in the light of whether or not those actions are pleasing to Him. And this is not something we do just out of obedience. We do these things out of an attitude of love. There is a big difference between the two. If you have children, you know that they can obey you by taking out the trash, while griping all the way. But if one morning the trash has been emptied just to please you, you know the difference—and God does too.

Sometimes we have funny ideas about what pleases God. We don't understand that even the smallest of tasks can bless God if we do them unto Him. Amy Carmichael, who spent the majority of her life serving in India, tells about one particular evening when she was in the orphanage she founded. At bedtime that night, there were five little children still in need of diapering and bottling, cuddling and loving. Another woman was tending to them, but when the chapel bells rang out, indicating it was time for the church meeting, she left the babies, picked up her prayer book, and said, "I must go to chapel now." She then raced out the door, leaving all five babies still needing care. And it was Amy Carmichael herself who stayed behind and fed, diapered, and cuddled and bedded them down. She knew the difference between being obedient and pleasing the heart of God. Doing the thing that was most necessary at that moment—showing His love to those little ones—was what pleased the heart of God.

When I first began to understand this difference, I started wondering, *What if I lived that way all the time? What if I ran everything through that filter—that question of "Does this please God's heart?"* It is not a new revelation, not for me and probably not for you. It's likely that the desire began at conversion and I have lived that way off and on all throughout my Christian life—wanting to please God. You know how it is. One day we really want to please Him, and then another time we gripe over having to be obedient.

I believe most of us are "phase Christians." What I mean by that is we tend to go through phases in our Christian life. Sometimes we're in a phase of obedience. At other times we go through a phase of disobedience. Then there are those phases of discovery where we learn some great truth about God and suddenly everything in life hinges on that one truth. This happened to me when Chuck and I first started out in the ministry—everything was faith. We didn't have any money but

God continually provided groceries for us. And at that time, I thought faith was the greatest thing you could have in your Christian walk. So I tested everybody I met to see if they had faith. It didn't matter to me whether or not they had love or anything else, just faith.

But then I discovered love, and so I went through the love phase. Suddenly that was the only thing that mattered, and that was the thing I tested everyone on. Did they really love one another? Did they really love God? After that it was the obedience phase. And on it went.

After a while I began to understand that our Christian life is a lot like a plant that you bring home and care for. You bring that little plant home and say, "I know what this plant needs more than anything else in the world, and that is water." And so you give it a lot of water. Water in the morning, water at noon, water at night. Well, more plants have been killed by overwatering than just about anything else.

So then you go to the next phase. You say, "Oh, I know what this plant needs—it needs light." So you set it in the sunniest place in the house. Sun is beating down on that plant all day long. Well, a plant that gets too much light gets yellow leaves. Too much light can kill a plant. So then you say, "Soil! That's all this plant needs—good soil."

The truth is, your plant needs all those things—air, water, light, and good soil—but it can't have any one of those things to the exclusion of the others. The real question is, what is the purpose of that plant? The purpose of that plant is to bring pleasure to you and to all who come into your home. The plant's purpose is to beautify your home. No one buys a grubby old weed and brings it home and places it on the center of a table or on the mantel.

FOR GOD'S PLEASURE

The more I pondered on this thought, the more God began to strengthen it in my heart. He confirmed it quite clearly one day when I was walking around the house singing, *Thou Art Worthy.* When I got to the words, "Thou hast created, hast all things created ... and for Thy pleasure, they are created," all of a sudden I realized what that meant. It meant that I was created for God's pleasure. I had to stop and think about that for a moment. I was adopted as an infant, and over the years I've thought so many times of what could have happened to me had God *not* placed me in a Christian home. My life would have been completely different. But He had a plan for me. And that plan was for my life to bring Him pleasure. What an amazing thought—I was made for God's pleasure!

And you are too. You were created to bring pleasure to God. Now, why He chose to do that—to use you and me in that way—I don't know. We may never know, but the Word of God tells us very plainly that we were created for His pleasure.

I was so taken with that discovery that I got my Bible and turned to Revelation 4:11, which is the basis of that hymn. I read that verse in every Bible translation, paraphrase, and amplification we had in the house, simply because it blessed my heart so much. That verse affirmed what God had spoken to me through the words of that hymn—that the way I should have been living all of my Christian life—the way God intended me to live—was to live with God's pleasure uppermost in mind.

> Thou art worthy, O Lord, to receive glory and honour and power: for Thou hast created all things, and for Thy pleasure they are and were created (Revelation 4:11 KJV).

That's been the truth from the beginning. Adam and Eve were originally created for God's pleasure, but they chose to please themselves instead of God, and as a result, their relationship with Him was destroyed. Sin and sorrow became the consequences. The same choice is before each of us. If we choose to please ourselves in place of God, we'll lose the fellowship we could have with Him.

Another confirmation of this truth came one day when I read John 8:29 where Jesus, Who is our example, said, "I always do those things that please Him." I realized that if Jesus was making it His aim to please the Father at all times, then I should make it my aim too.

Then I received a third confirmation while reading a little antique devotional that I keep by my bed. Now, if I were looking for something to demonstrate God's Word for the last days, I certainly would not think to turn to a one-hundred-year-old devotional. But I happened to be looking for a topic for a Bible study I was going to be doing, and so I opened it for inspiration. And as I looked at the first devotion I came to, I asked the Lord, "Shall I share this one?" The Scripture was Colossians 3:23, which says, "And whatever you do, do it heartily, as to the Lord and not to men." There it was again. I thought, *Whatever I do, I am to do it to please the Lord. I'm to do it with joy as unto the Lord, not in order to please men.* Included in the devotion was this little poem:

> "Teach me, my God and King,
> In all things Thee to see,
> And what I do in anything
> To do it as for Thee." [1]

CHRISTIAN LIFE SIMPLIFIED

Not long after I read that devotional, while praying I began talking to the Lord about what He had been confirming to me. "This is the way You want me to live, isn't it, Lord? You want me to live every day with the aim of pleasing You." And then I said, "Oh God, just speak to my heart more about this." And immediately the name Enoch popped into my mind. I stopped praying and I opened my Bible and looked up Hebrews 11, where I knew Enoch was listed among the heroes of faith, and read:

> By faith Enoch was taken away so that he did not see death, and was not found, because God had taken him; for before he was taken he had this testimony, that he pleased God (Hebrews 11:5).

When I was a little girl, I learned that Enoch was a "type" or a picture representative of the church. Noah was a "type" of the Jewish people that would be protected during the tribulation, but Enoch was a type of the church that would be taken up in the rapture. Enoch could easily have lived and been destroyed in God's punishment upon the world when He brought the flood. But in Genesis 5:24, it says, "Enoch walked with God and he was not, for God took him."

Enoch's testimony is that he pleased God. And that should be the testimony of the bride of Christ today—that we live to please God. It should be your testimony too.

One of the best things about living this way—and one of the reasons I think this message is so important for women today—is that it simplifies the Christian life.

Think about what you would do if you were suddenly told that you had to evacuate your home. If some disaster struck and you had to leave immediately, what would you take with you? Would you take your most treasured possessions, or would you take the most practical things?

It's a hard decision. I've thought about this every time some natural disaster struck the area and I've watched scenes of people being evacuated from their homes. I think, *If someone showed up at my door and told me I could grab only one thing, what would I take?* I really like my pillow. It can be hard to find a pillow you like. Or would it be best to take a blanket? Would I rather have clothing for the next day? But every time they show clips from fires or mudslides and I see people evacuating their homes with just a small box of their possessions, I ask myself that question again: What do I grab? The answer I keep returning to is that I'd take photographs of my babies. Everything else can be replaced.

I find the same thing is true in the Christian life. When you think, *What should I be doing?* you can easily be overwhelmed. You might say, "Lord, I should be doing this for You" or "Lord, I should be doing that for You." And everything you come up with sounds good. But it can be complicated when you start making a list full of "I ought to" and "I want to" and "I should be doing" tasks. But if you put just one thing on your list: "Lord, I want to please You," then it's not complicated at all. When you're fixing dinner, you do it to please God. If you're cleaning house, you do it to please God. If you're shopping in the market, or driving your car, or having a conversation, you do all those things to please the Lord. Unexpectedly, you find that you are living the life of Enoch. Wherever you go, people know that you love Jesus, because everything you do is done to please Him. Living this way simplifies your life because it eliminates questions of right and wrong.

Years ago, when going to dance clubs was all the rage, people used to come to me and ask if I thought it was a sin to dance in clubs. The question really wasn't whether it was right or wrong to go out dancing. What mattered then, as well as today, is whether or not it pleases the heart of God. Is that where He wants you to be? It is an individual decision, something you settle with God. Your pastor doesn't make that decision for you. Your friends can't decide that for you. It is between you and God. You must ask, "Lord, would this please You? Will I bring joy to You if I do this?" Living this way simplifies your life because it provides the right motivation for whatever you do.

EXCEEDING JOY

As women, we too often look to other people for praise, recognition, approval, or appreciation. We think if we find that acknowledgment we'll have joy. But true joy comes from pleasing God. Psalm 43:4 says, "Then I will go to the altar of God, to God my exceeding joy: and on the harp will I praise You, O God, my God." I love the way that is worded: "my exceeding joy." God is my exceeding joy. Another translation says, "God, the gladness of my joy." He is the gladness of my heart, and if I want to bring pleasure to Him, then I won't be devastated if someone doesn't give me approval. If my husband doesn't appreciate the things I do, I'm not going to be crushed or angry. We all know how we get when we feel unappreciated. But that doesn't matter if I'm living to please God, because whatever I do is for Him. He is the only One whose approval I want.

This can be a precious lesson for those who are married. I've shared this with the women at my church, and those who have grasped the concept of living to please God have come back to tell me that it has revitalized and revolutionized their marriages. Without an understanding of this principle, women who feel neglected sometimes punish their husbands. Or the wife is the neglectful one, and the husband reacts by punishing her. It can be a vicious cycle. But when you begin to realize that your marriage becomes a way to please God's heart, the cycle stops. You realize that something as simple as cooking dinner or picking up after your husband brings joy to God's heart if you do it unto Him. He is pleased when you show love to your husband, when you do things that show you are willing to be a servant. Not only does that kind of humble spirit bring joy to God, it brings joy into your marriage.

Of course, these things don't always happen overnight. It may be that you prepare a really beautiful meal for your husband and he completely ignores it. What do you do? Do you turn to him and say, "Well, it really doesn't matter whether you like this dinner or not, because I didn't do it to please you. I did it to please God. So there, you cad!" Of course you don't do that. You don't say, "I did this to please the heart of God, so it doesn't matter what you think." Instead, with that beautiful fountain of rejoicing in your heart, you silently pray, "Lord, I did it to please You." And because He is a God of miracles, He has the power to open the eyes of your husband too. He can do it! Just keep doing everything unto the Lord, to please Him alone, and watch what He does in your marriage.

AN INVITATION

This principle applies to all your relationships. Take friendship, for instance. In our friendships, we have what I call the "Emily Post syndrome." Do you know what that is? That's when you invite me to dinner, so that I will invite you back to dinner. Now, woe be unto our friendship and unto me if you invite me to dinner and I don't invite you back, because Emily Post, the queen of all etiquette, said we should drop those friends. I have read that same advice from Ann Landers. We all know that is the social custom. If you want to make new friends, you invite them over for dinner and they invite you back. If they don't invite you back, it is a sign that they don't want to be your friend. Well, I say, "Phooey." Don't you believe it. Jesus gave us a completely different principle in Luke 14:12-14. Read how delightful this is in *The Living Bible*:

> Then Jesus said to His host, "When you put on a dinner, don't invite friends, brothers, relatives, and rich neighbors! For they will return the invitation. Instead, invite the poor, the crippled, the lame, and the blind. Then at the resurrection of the godly, God will reward you for inviting those who can't repay you."

Let me ask you, how long has it been since you invited someone like this to your house for dinner? How long has it been since you reached out to somebody whom nobody else cares about? The world is full of lonely, hurting people. Some of them are unlovely people. And most of us would rather be around only the lovely people. But what did Jesus say? He said to invite the poor and the crippled people into your home.

My husband's dad took this Scripture literally and was always inviting strange people into his home. Dad would meet people on the street who had just gotten out of jail, and he would bring them home for dinner. Chuck said that sometimes he and his siblings would sit wide-eyed at what they heard at that table. But it was beautiful. And it was a beautiful principle that Dad taught Chuck. It left an impact on him.

I want to encourage you to look around and see who needs such an invitation. Don't invite the people that are always being invited. Remember how rotten it felt in high school if you were unpopular? It was terrible. High school can be so traumatic for kids if they are not popular. Well, churches can be the same way. So you be different. You look around, see who is hurting or lonely, and do what Jesus said.

So, was Jesus saying you can never again have your friends and relatives over for dinner? Of course not. He was simply pointing out the attitude of the heart. Are you inviting people over to receive an invitation back, or are you doing it out of love? One motive pleases the heart of God. And it is this way He would have you to live.

LOVE'S DESIRE

Living to please God produces a deeper, closer walk with Him. It gives you the grace to ignore injustice or to bear unkindness. It gives you a desire to forgive. It causes you to forsake those things that God doesn't want in your life. It makes you let go of hatred, bitterness, and jealousy. When you do these things, it shows your depth of love for God.

Jesus told us in Matthew 22:37,

> You shall love the LORD your God with all your heart, with all your soul, and with all your mind.

What does that kind of love look like? I remember when my youngest daughter first fell in love with Brian, who is now her husband. Cheryl had found her beloved. It was marvelous to be around her. Nobody had to tell her how to please him. She was constantly thinking of the food he liked to eat, the color he would like her to wear, and how she should do her hair. She'd come in and ask me, "Do you think Brian will like this?" No one had to teach her to think of him.

Clearly, nobody has to tell a heart of love to please its beloved. Love's desire is to please. And when you have the love for God that you ought to have, you will naturally desire to please Him above everyone else.

SATAN'S LIES

Now, I do need to give you a warning. It seems that the instant you decide you are going to live to please God, Satan comes along and begins putting thoughts in your mind. He will cause you to think things like, *Living that kind of life will be too stifling. I'll be bored. I'll be unfulfilled.* See those for the lies that they are. Satan is the father of all lies. Jesus told us that, "The thief comes only to steal and kill and destroy" (John 10:10). Satan wants to steal this truth from you. He wants to kill your joy and destroy the life you can have if you draw closer to God. And as you walk day by day, Satan will whisper these lies to you. Sometimes he doesn't whisper, though. Sometimes he screams.

And then Satan tries to tell you things that will fill you with fear—"If you live to please God, He's going to send you to Outer Mongolia." Let me tell you, I have walked with the Lord over sixty years and I haven't seen Outer Mongolia yet. In fact, I am privileged to live by the ocean, which I dearly, dearly love. Chuck and I are ocean people. I love living just where I do. I am content and at peace because I'm right where God wants me.

You must realize that God will not require you to do anything that He won't first strengthen you for. He will make you adequate for every situation in which He calls you. I will go so far as to say that if you are in a rotten marriage with a cruel husband who mistreats you, and you choose not to leave because you believe doing so will please the heart of God, then God will give you the courage, the strength, and the beauty of spirit to stay in that marriage. Not only will He strengthen you, but God will also give you a joy in doing it. And He may very well reach your husband through your quiet example.

When we live to please God, we might find ourselves in troubling circumstances and we might be very grieved in spirit, but inside we'll have a joy that nothing else in this world can bring.

DON'T WORRY ABOUT FAILURE

If Satan can't scare you away with lies about unfulfillment or the threat of Outer Mongolia, He will try to defeat you with discouragement. Satan loves to discourage us. He'll tell you what he says to me quite often, "You'll fail." Of course, I will fail. But the Christian life is a life of new beginnings. That's one of the things I love the most about being a Christian. First John 1:9 tells me that when I sin, I go to Him, I ask forgiveness, I repent, He forgives, and I get to start all over again. It is a brand-new page.

When I was in school my teachers insisted we fill in every bit of space on our paper. I hated it, because I usually ended up with a scribbly, scraggly mess. I couldn't wait to get a brand-new sheet of paper—a pretty piece with no scribbles, no mistakes, no eraser marks or crossed-out places. That's what God does every time you go to Him and confess that you've sinned. "God, I failed. I have really messed up my life. Please forgive me. I repent. I turn around and walk the other way. I forsake that sin." When you do that, He starts you all over again.

So don't worry about your failure. Satan would love for you to concentrate on it and spend all your time worrying about it. I have failed many times in pleasing God, and I still fail. I don't please Him every moment, but I'm learning. I'm drawing closer and closer.

When Chuck and I were first married and I started cooking for him, I used to always burn the lima beans. I was taught to cook with hardly any water, and lima beans burn very quickly if you cook that way. But despite those early (and frequent) failures, I didn't quit cooking lima beans. I kept right on cooking and I got better and better at it. I learned what to do and I stopped failing constantly. And so it is with our lives.

Sometimes we don't understand just how God views us. Think about your own children for a moment. What do you do when they come in the door after walking home from school and they hand you that wilted little flower that they picked just for you? Do you take that flower and say, "Oh, what an ugly, wilted thing! Why did you bring me that?" Do you drop that flower in disgust and stamp it under your foot? Of course you don't do that. If you are a good mommy, you admire that little wilted flower. You tell your child it is just the most beautiful flower you've seen all day, and then you put that wilted little flower in a vase and set it right in the middle of the table. You do that because those little eyes are watching. And your response says, "I love you."

Or what about the little crumpled papers they hand you on Mother's Day, the ones that say, "Dear Moth … I lov you." Do you take those and say, "You can't spell right, you rotten, little kid!" You don't do that. You save every one. I have boxes in our hall closet full of "Dear Moth" sorts of letters. You treasure those precious letters. Why? Because they show your child's heart—that they love you and want to please you. You didn't focus on the mistakes they made, or what their little hands wrote. You listened to what their heart was saying.

God is listening to your heart today. He knows whether the attitude of your heart is to please Him. He is not up there pouncing on your failures. He is saying, "Keep trying. Get back up and try again."

LOVING OTHERS

Ann Kimmel told a story long ago about a little boy named Chad. When Chad and his family moved to a new neighborhood, he had trouble making friends. Chad was not well-liked by the kids. Every day after school, his mother would see a group of kids walking by the house chatting and laughing together, but Chad would walk all by himself down the street. It broke her heart.

One day Chad came home and said, "Mom, the teacher told us we are all going to make cards for Valentine's Day. We have thirty-three kids in our class and I want to make one for every kid."

Chad's mother looked at him and imagined how much work that would be. Then she thought about how Chad probably wouldn't get any Valentines back and he would come home brokenhearted. But his little face just glowed. He was so enthused with the idea that she decided she'd better help him do it. So, they went out and bought rickrack and paper and paste and all other sorts of decorations, and they spent days working on those cards.

When Valentine's Day came, Chad went happily off to school with his little bundle of thirty-three Valentines, thrilled that he had one for each kid in the room. When the time came for the cards to be passed around and placed in each student's packet, Chad received one Valentine.

Back at home, Chad's mother was worried about him. Thinking to take some of the sting out of the day, she baked a batch of cookies to have ready for him when he got home from school. Later, as the kids started coming home, she saw a big group of kids come down the street laughing and talking together. Behind them was Chad, walking all by himself—with one little Valentine in his hand. He had his head down. His mother opened the door quickly, thinking that she wanted to get him inside the house before he burst into tears. Chad came into the house, still with his head down, and walked right by her. But when he turned around and looked up at her, his face was lit up. With a huge grin, he said, "Mom, I didn't miss one kid." Chad was so excited with the thought of bringing pleasure to others he hadn't even noticed he had received only one Valentine.

Do you see the application for your life? That's how we are to live in these last days. We want to be so enthused with the love of God that we don't even notice the unpleasant things that otherwise would bog us down.

Father, You gave Your dearest possession out of love for us. May that love so fill our hearts that we would have no other desire than to please You. Cleanse us, purge us, purify us. Drive out every desire from our hearts but that one desire that Enoch had—the desire to please You. And when Jesus returns for His bride, may we be a part of that bride, because our testimony is that we lived to please You.

In Jesus' name we pray, amen.

CHAPTER

2

DOES THIS PLEASE GOD?

SOMEONE ONCE SHARED THE STORY about a little girl whose mother overheard her praying the Lord's Prayer. With her eyes shut tight and her hands clasped together, she asked, "Our Father, which art in heaven, how do You know my name?" What this child was really asking was, "God, with all the people in the world, how could You possibly know *my* name?" I think sometimes even adults wonder about that. But I'm here to tell you that He does know your name—and He loves you.

First John 4:19 says, "We love Him because He first loved us." Once you begin to know God's love for you, you can't help but love Him in return. And when you love God, you want to please Him.

I believe pleasing God is the most important truth I can share, especially in these last days. As I said in chapter 1, God first impressed this matter upon my heart and then confirmed it through a number of Scriptures:

> Thou art worthy, O Lord, to receive glory and honour and power: for Thou hast created all things, and for Thy pleasure they are and were created (Revelation 4:11 KJV).

God is worthy to be praised. All things were created for His pleasure—not just some things, but all things. Jesus, Who is our example, said:

> I always do those things that please Him (John 8:29).

Note that Jesus says He *always*—not just once in a while—does those things that please His Father.

> And whatever you do, do it heartily, as to the Lord and not to men (Colossians 3:23).

No matter how small our task, we can do it joyfully unto God, just to bring Him pleasure.

> By faith Enoch was taken away so that he did not see death, and was not found, because God had taken him; for before he was taken he had this testimony, that he pleased God (Hebrew 11:5).

Enoch is a picture representative of the church. We will be taken, or raptured, so that we will not see the tribulation. Like Enoch, our testimony as the body of believers should be that we please God.

YOUR GREATEST AIM

Pleasing God should be our greatest aim—a goal that simplifies and covers every part of our lives. The question shouldn't be, "Is this thing right or wrong?" The question needs to be, "Is this pleasing to God?"

The ladies in our Bible study know that I am firmly against soap operas. In fact, I've teased them so often that I'd like my epitaph to read, "Kay hated for us to watch soap operas." I'll tell you the same thing I've told them: what you take in with your eyes will come out in your behavior, and then your children will absorb it. Knowing that the end times are at hand, the prophecies have been fulfilled, and Jesus is coming soon to take His bride, do you really want to be filling your mind with soap operas? The question isn't, "Are soap operas right or wrong?" The question is, "Will it please the Lord if I watch soap operas?" And this is unlimited—before you watch any television program, before you walk into a movie theater, before you read a book or a magazine, ask yourself if what you're about to do will please God. Let that thought direct all that you do, for you'll discover many blessings await the woman who lives to please God.

In the early days of our women's retreats, we would hand out little slips of paper with promises from the Bible printed on them. These were promises that had been prayed over and then given out to each woman. At one retreat, the verse waiting for me at Saturday night's dinner was,

> When a man's ways please the LORD, He makes even his enemies to be
> at peace with him (Proverbs 16:7).

And when a woman's ways please the Lord, the Lord makes even her enemies to be at peace with her. Not long after I received this promise, God confirmed it. I'd been involved in an uncomfortable situation in which someone had a little conflict with me. And out of the blue, the person called me up and we were able to talk it out. It was just beautiful! God is so precious and so faithful to fulfill His promises.

If we know that all things were created for God, and the aim of our lives should be to please Him, what keeps that from happening? What keeps me from pleasing God? Some would answer, "Well, I really don't know His will." Others would honestly say, "I just want to do what I want to do." Nine times out of ten that's the real reason. People want to do their own thing.

THE ROOT OF IT ALL

The first step towards living a life that pleases God is learning what He likes and dislikes. Sometimes, the reason we don't fully commit ourselves to pleasing God is because we've got a problem at our very core.

Let's look at plants as an illustration. Houseplants can really beautify your home. But sometimes they have problems. Those problems can be external, like too much light or not enough light, acidic soil, or bug infestation. Other times the problem is in the root. It is invisible. You can give your plant light, air, and water, and you can polish the leaves as beautifully as is possible, but if the problem is in the root none of those external things will do a bit of good. It's not going to be a beautiful plant.

Like houseplants, we too can have a root problem that keeps us from being pleasing. Hebrews 11:6 tells us,

> But without faith it is impossible to please Him, for he who comes to God must believe that He is, and that He is a rewarder of those who diligently seek Him.

Why is it impossible to please God without faith? The second part of the verse explains: "For he who comes to God must believe that He is."

Think about that for a minute. You must believe that He is. You might quickly think, *Okay. I'm glad we got over that. I believe that He is; therefore I don't have any problem. He is God. He is mighty and powerful.* The problem, though, is that James 2:19 says, "You believe that there is one God. You do well. Even the demons believe—and tremble!" A recent poll said that ninety-six percent of Americans claim to believe in God, but it's clear that we live in a secular, hedonistic society. So there must be more to this belief than simply believing that God exists.

GOD IS PERSONAL

Hebrews chapter 11 is one of the most moving and vibrant chapters in the whole Bible. If your faith seems weak, I encourage you to read this chapter filled with the exploits of men and women whose faith in God changed their lives. Through faith they subdued kingdoms, worked righteousness, obtained promises, stopped the mouths of lions, quenched the violence of fire, escaped the edge of the sword, became valiant in battle, and turned to flight the armies of the aliens (Hebrews 11:33-34). One of them built an ark for one hundred years in the middle of a desert. Another had a baby at eighty or ninety years of age. Another took hundreds of thousands of people through a sea believing that God would part the water and make dry land for them to walk. These were people who did not just believe that God is some essence way up in the sky that causes flowers to bloom and the sun to shine. They believed God is personal. A God Who knows all our thoughts and weighs all our actions.

Do you realize that God is aware of everything about you? He is a personal God Who cares for you and is always present with you. He is a God Whose thoughts toward you are more than the sands of the sea. He is a God from Whom you cannot hide—and if you think you *can* hide from God, read Psalm 139.

The world is in turmoil. The newspaper is full of stories about conflicts around the world. Hearing that kind of news, day after day, it would be very easy to feel hopeless if we did not believe in a God Who is near and Who has a plan for our lives. But when you are truly aware of God's presence, it causes a response in your life. And when that realization hits you that He cares for you more than He cares for the sun or the moon or any of the stars in the sky, it affects your behavior. After all, He didn't die for the sun or the moon or a star. He died for you.

Without an awareness of God's love for you and a strong conviction that He is near, you won't care whether you please Him or not. The reason we don't go through life pleasing God as we should is not because there is a shortness of His arms, but because we do not have this continued awareness. And I suffer from it as you do. I am shocked sometimes at how I can start the morning with a devotion and then become so involved in something that all of a sudden the Lord will speak to my heart and say, "Kay, you haven't looked up once and just said, 'Oh Father, I love You.'"

My husband, Chuck, says the definition of ungodly simply means living as though God didn't exist. The ungodly person is saying, "God is not here. He's up in the sky somewhere. He doesn't see, He doesn't know, and He doesn't care—so I can do whatever I want." When your choices and decisions are made without any consideration for what God's will is, it's because you really don't believe He is there.

THE AWARENESS OF GOD

What do you do if you are living as though God is not there? The answer is found at the end of Hebrews 11:6:

> But without faith it is impossible to please Him, for he who comes to God must believe *that He is*, and that He is a rewarder of those who diligently seek Him.

Sometimes it helps to say these things out loud. Say that last part, and ask God to make this real to your heart. It needs to be real to you. If you want to live a life that is pleasing to Him, you must know that *He is there*.

What do you do about this problem of living as though God were absent? You diligently seek Him. You start looking for Him and listening for Him. He promised that He rewards those who diligently seek Him. And how does He reward those who seek Him? By allowing them to find Him.

I've known people who have walked with God for fifty years, yet do not have an awareness that He is near. I've known people who were recently born again who have somehow lost the awareness that God is there. At one of our retreats, we had a young girl like that. She'd been born again and was baptized in the Spirit—yet she was suicidal.

Why? Because she had forgotten that God was there. She had forgotten the One Who was ready to strengthen her, to build her up, and to bring her through the trials—the One Who said,

> When you pass through the waters, I will be with you; and through the rivers, they shall not overflow you (Isaiah 43:2).

Maybe you're one who has forgotten. Maybe your heart is broken today. Luke 4:18 says that Jesus came to heal the brokenhearted. Perhaps you're facing a fiery furnace. Daniel 3:25 promises that Jesus enters the fiery furnace with us. Are you facing waters that look like they could overwhelm you? As we just read in Isaiah 43:2, God promises that He won't let those waters drown you. If you're in need today, the greatest thing you can know is that Jesus is faithful and He is near.

GOD'S FAITHFULNESS

Something remarkable about that promise in Hebrews 11:6—the promise that He will reward those who diligently seek Him—is that God honors that promise even when the ones seeking Him are unbelievers.

My friend, Rose, is a Jewish believer in Christ. I once asked her how she came to know the Lord and she said, "I don't know, Kay. I guess

He just lifted the veil." I thought that was so beautiful. But later she told me her testimony. She grew up in an affluent family in Beverly Hills and always had everything she wanted and did whatever she wanted. She traveled all over the world and even dated Elvis Presley. Eventually she met a man in Mexico who was very wealthy and she became his mistress. He introduced her to the drug life and she went downhill rapidly. Rose began floating around the world without any direction or purpose in life, "like the chaff which the wind drives away" (Psalm 1:4).

One day, as Rose was planning to leave Europe and come back to the United States, she arrived at an airport in London with the four men she'd been traveling with. She didn't know much about them. In fact, she was unaware that these men were trying to smuggle $150,000 worth of hashish into the United States. At the airport, she and the men were arrested. She was high on drugs and alcohol at the time, and although she tried to tell the police that she didn't know anything about the hashish, they didn't believe her.

When the drugs in her system wore off, she found herself in a London jail cell. She looked around and thought, *What am I doing here?* She began to wonder if there was any hope. And then she remembered that her mother used to say to her, "Rose, God will help you. God will help you." Although she was a Jewish mother, that is all she ever programmed into Rose about God. But as Rose was telling me her story, she said, "Kay, I literally got down on my knees in the jail cell and said, 'God, if You are there, help me.' At that moment I had a vision of Jesus Christ." Rose said she knew it was Jesus, and she knew He was the Messiah. She said, "I had never felt such warmth and love in all my life. And I forgot I was in that cell. I just wanted His presence to remain with me forever."

Rose was released from jail with a ten-dollar fine. She returned to the United States, and from that day to now she has been a powerful witness for Jesus Christ.

I know someone else who sought God while an unbeliever. "Jim" (not his real name) was a professional man who ended up losing not just one, but two, families because of his alcoholism. When his second wife took their children and moved far away, he was left feeling completely desolate. Then early one morning, after lying awake all night, Jim said, "I knelt by the side of my bed and prayed, 'I don't know You, God, but I know I can't go on any longer. It's either You or suicide.'" And he said, "I can't tell you what happened, Kay, except that peace came over me and peace came into my heart, and I knew there was a God." Today, Jim is walking with Jesus. It's been over two years and Jim hasn't had a drop of alcohol.

And then there is Julie, a woman I once met at a luncheon. She and I were part of a group of ten ladies who had been seated together at a table. I wasn't aware that she didn't know Jesus, but when the speaker asked how many in the room wanted to commit their lives to the Lord, all of a sudden this lady lit up and accepted the invitation. One of the ladies asked her, "Julie, did you accept Jesus?" Julie turned to the rest of us and said, "You won't believe this, but two nights ago I dreamt that I was going to come to a luncheon like this and a lady was going to say to me, 'Julie, did you accept Jesus?' And that's just what happened. When the speaker asked if anyone wanted to commit her life to Jesus, I did it. And then without realizing my dream, you asked me the very same question I heard in my dream!"

In the first two stories, Rose and Jim sought God when they were in great need. Julie responded because God revealed Himself in a dream. But none of the three knew Him previously. How gracious God is to make Himself known to the lost and then to reward them when they had finally turned to Him.

Those of us who are already Christians can recount story after story of times when we diligently, desperately sought the Lord—and were met by Him. I have faced countless impossible situations where I have sought God, and He has met me every single time.

SEEK GOD DILIGENTLY

How do you seek God diligently? It's not difficult. In fact, there are very simple ways you can begin to do this.

Ask God to reveal Himself to you.

Did you know that God wants to reveal Himself to you much, much more than you've ever desired? He is just waiting for you to ask. And sometimes, God doesn't wait. Sometimes when we aren't looking or asking, God will come and say, "I am here."

One New Year's Eve, my daughter Cheryl and I were driving toward Newport Beach early in the evening. All that day I had been quietly praying, "Lord, as this new year is beginning, please make Yourself more real to me than You ever have." I continued asking Him that as we drove along. About a block from Newport Boulevard and 15th Street, the Lord spoke to my heart and said, "Do not cross Newport Boulevard until every car in every lane of traffic is stopped."

So often when we get those strong impressions, we think, *That's just me. It has to be me—it couldn't really be the voice of God.* I was thinking that very thing, so I decided to put it to the test. I asked, "Lord, could this be You?" And again He spoke to my heart, "Kay, do not cross Newport Boulevard until every lane of traffic stops."

When I reached the intersection, I thought, *Lord, I think it is You, but I'm not sure. But just in case You really are speaking to me, I'm going to creep across Newport Boulevard.* And that's what I did. As I started creeping across, all the cars to the left of me stopped, and to the right every lane stopped. By the time I approached that last lane, I was going so slowly I was nearly stopped myself. And sure enough, a pickup truck came screeching toward the intersection and didn't see the signal. The driver ran the red light, slammed on his brakes, and his truck spun into a full circle. When he stopped, he had missed me completely.

Does God speak to us? Does He make Himself real to us—more real than the air we breathe? Ask Him today. He doesn't just want to be an essence up there in the sky. He wants to make Himself real to you. It pleases God when we come to Him like a child and ask, "God, show me You are there. Reveal Yourself to me." He will do it. As He promised in Jeremiah 29:13, "You will seek Me and find Me, when you search for Me with all your heart."

Search the Scriptures.

Search out those Scriptures that show you He is a personal God. Write them down and put them on the bathroom mirror. If you do that consistently, pretty soon when you look at your mirror you'll see God instead of you, as His Word covers your mirror. Write those verses down and put them in your pocket. Put them on your car seat. Put them on the kitchen window. Put them any place where they'll catch your eye.

Study the lives of those who sought God.

Read any book you can find on the subject—of course, the Bible is full of accounts of men and women who sought God. But there are also good biographies of missionaries and others who have gone before us who knew the secret of depending on God and trusting Him for the impossible. Study the life of Jesus. He came to earth not only to die for us, but also to reveal God to us.

Ask God to speak to you—and then listen.

God is speaking to you all the time. He speaks through His creation and through His Word. He speaks through sermons. How many times have you been sitting in church and the pastor says something and all of a sudden God speaks to your heart and says, "You are the woman." Often, God prompts the pastor to say something that brings comfort to our heart, and we think, *He said that just for me.* Every Sunday after the service, at least one person comes up to Chuck and tells him, "Oh, that sermon was just for me." That person heard from God. Why? Because they had asked God to speak to them, and then they listened.

Sometimes God speaks through dreams. That was how God spoke to Joseph when he was afraid to take Mary as his wife. We read in the book of Matthew that the Lord gave Joseph a dream. God spoke to him again through another dream when He told Joseph to take Mary and Jesus and flee to Egypt, because Herod was going to kill all of the children. And when it was safe to return, God spoke to Joseph through yet another dream and told him they could go back.

The apostle Paul heard the audible voice of God on the Damascus Road. No one else understood that voice. At other times God had spoken to Paul through visions.

Many times when I have needed comfort most, God has spoken to me through His Word. I remember a time when Chuck and I were in Israel. Back at home, our son, Jeff, became very ill with flu-like symptoms that had hit every organ in his body. It was so severe that he nearly died. By the time his physician, Dr. Gainey, called us in Israel, Jeff was already admitted into intensive care.

This was 1976, back when a flight from Israel cost $749. We didn't have the money, but we could have begged or borrowed it from friends. I was ready to come home—but I needed to hear from God.

The morning we received the news, I stayed in our hotel room instead of going on the tour with the rest of our group. I wanted to just spend the day praying for Jeff and for the situation and for an answer from God. I fell asleep praying and awakened with tears on the pillow where I must have cried in my sleep, which has never happened before or since. I remember waking up and saying, "God, I have got to have an answer from You. Please speak to me because I have to know what to do."

And the Spirit of the Lord spoke to my heart and said, "Kay, read the second chapter of Philippians." When I opened to Philippians, the Spirit directed my eyes right to verse 27, which says, "For indeed he was sick almost unto death; but God had mercy on him, and not only on him but on me also, lest I should have sorrow upon sorrow."

I sat there and took a deep breath. God healed Epaphroditus lest Paul would have sorrow upon sorrow.

Right at that time in my life, I was going through another great sorrow and I felt overwhelmed. And when I read that verse, I knew God was saying to me, "I am going to heal Jeff, lest you would have sorrow upon sorrow." How much more directly could He have spoken to me? I got up out of bed, and showered and dressed. When Chuck came in, I said, "Jeff is healed."

"How do you know?" Chuck knows me well enough to know that I don't say those things lightly.

I said, "God gave me Philippians 2:27," and I read it to him.

He said, "I believe you. We'll move on that."

When we went down to dinner, a lawyer who was on the trip with us said, "Kay, I have got to talk to you. God has spoken to me."

I asked him what God had said.

He told me, "You are not to go home. Jeff is healed."

That was confirmation. God spoke to me through His Word and through a godly man on the trip. "Thank You, Lord," I said. "I believe You and that is the way I am walking." Not long after, Dr. Gainey called us back and said, "Jeff is well."

God speaks to us! And so many blessings come to those who are attuned to His voice. I think how differently my life would have gone if we had not heard so clearly from God. I remember Chuck telling about the time he came up Fairview Road and looked at this plot of land that is now home to Calvary Chapel Costa Mesa. Back then, that ten acres cost $300,000. We certainly didn't have that kind of money and nobody was about to bestow $300,000 to us. I remember Chuck looking around and saying, "It is too much, Lord. I can't bear the burden." The Lord asked him very clearly, "Whose church is it, Chuck?" And that's when Chuck realized, *That's right, it is not my church. It's Yours, Lord.*

What if Chuck hadn't been listening? He would have gone through the day full of despair, full of anxiety and fear, wondering, *What are we going to do?* But God had spoken and he listened and was comforted. God loves to bring us comfort. I hope you realize that today. When you are in despair, it is His joy to bring you the comfort you need.

GOD'S FRAGRANCE

One morning I awakened in a deep depression. I knew I needed help, so I prayed, "God, please speak to me today. I have got to have Your help." Opening my Bible, I turned to Psalm 37:5 and read, "Commit your way to the LORD." And I just said, "Okay, Lord, I will." I said it, but I didn't feel any impact. A bit later in the day, I went out to the mailbox and found a little Christian magazine. I opened it up, and on the very first page, the very first Scripture was, "Commit your way to the Lord, trust also in Him and He shall bring it to pass."

Later that day while doing the dishes, I turned on the radio. Guess what Scripture I heard? Three times God spoke to me, and He brought me exactly what I needed to lift that depression. That's how powerful God's voice is. It has the power to lift our mood or change our perspective, no matter how difficult the circumstance.

On Sunday mornings we often sing,

> Speak, Lord, in the stillness while I wait on Thee.
> Hush my heart to listen in expectancy.
> Speak, O blessed Master, in this quiet hour.
> Let me see Thy face, Lord
> And feel Thy touch of power
> Like a watered garden full of fragrance rare
> Lingering in Thy presence let my life appear. [2]

I like the last verse best of all, because I love perfume. And that is the way I want my life to appear.

We sang that song one Sunday morning in the first Calvary Chapel, when we were on Church Street. When the service ended, I came out rejoicing in the Lord. But outside the church, a horrible conflict had erupted, and I began to feel angry. Chuck was handling the situation, so I went and stood under a tree nearby. Suddenly, the fragrance of that tree began to come over me, and the Lord brought back the words to the song we had just sung. *Like a watered garden full of fragrance rare, lingering in Thy presence let my life appear.* The beautiful perfume of God spoke to my heart, and all the anger fell away.

That's what we want. We want to wear God's fragrance wherever we go. We want to communicate His love and His grace to everyone we meet.

Jesus said in John 10:27, "My sheep hear My voice." We are supposed to know the voice of God. If this is an area where you need to grow, tell Him that. "Oh God, I don't think I remember You speaking to me, but I want to know Your voice. I want to hear You speak to me—even when You whisper."

SHARE GOD'S TRUTH

Seek God's face. Listen to His voice. Remember that He is near, and He loves you, and He has a plan for your life. And then, share that truth with those you love. Something that wonderful is too good to keep to yourself! If you have children, tell them that God is with them. Before you send them out the door in the morning, let them know that God will be with them throughout the day—especially when the playground bully picks on them. God will be there when they don't do well in their classes, or when they don't feel popular, or when they're tempted to try all those things everyone else is trying, or when they see or hear things they shouldn't see or hear. Teach them to turn to the God Who goes out the door with them.

Do you have a husband? Before he leaves for work each morning, remind him how much God loves him. Say, "Oh, honey, I was just thinking about how much I love you, and God loves you so much more than I do. When you go to work today, know that the presence of God will be with you every moment, because I am going to be praying for you while you're at work today."

Tell your friends about the God Who is near. Remind them that God is a rewarder of those who diligently seek Him. In this way, you will spur your friends on to good works and help increase their faith.

Can you see now why God said that without faith it is impossible to please Him? Unless you believe He is dwelling within you, you can't move mountains. Unless you believe He is near, you are not going to be able to walk through fiery paths. But if you believe He is there, and you seek Him with your whole heart, and listen for His voice, you will find Him. He will reward you with His presence. And you will begin to live a different kind of life. Your choices will change. Your decisions will change. And you will begin to live a life that brings pleasure to God.

Father, engrave this truth on our hearts. Let us see the importance of knowing Who You are and that You are our personal God. That You care, You watch, You wait. Oh God, engrave pleasing You upon our hearts.

We pray in the name of Jesus, amen.

3

DEAD TO SIN

IF WE WANT TO LIVE a life that is pleasing to God, it means we hold nothing back. It means we consider Him first in all that we do. Sometimes it means giving up the things we'd like to do. And sometimes it means doing things we'd rather not.

OBEDIENCE

Once while waiting at the Medford Airport, my husband figured out that if we changed planes, we could get home twenty minutes sooner. He does this sort of thing to me frequently. So we changed our tickets, ran to the other gate, and barely made it—and in the end, it saved us a total of four minutes off our travel time. Nevertheless, God had a plan.

Traveling can really wear you out. I was very tired. So when an older woman sat down in the seat next to me, all I thought was I really didn't want to talk. But it also crossed my mind that Jesus had put her there beside me. Still, I resisted for a while. I looked at a book, I looked at the fabulous scenery out the window, I looked every which way, but I didn't look at this woman, because I knew what the Lord wanted me to do. It wasn't that I didn't want to witness to her. I was just too tired to talk.

All of a sudden the Lord said, "Kay, isn't it true that tomorrow you're going to be speaking about pleasing Me?" And that was true. I was speaking on this very subject.

"Yes," I answered in my heart. And then I obeyed what I knew He was asking me to do.

"Hi," I said to the woman. "Do you live in Orange County?"

"No," she said, "I live in Salinas."

To be honest, I was so tired I just wanted to say, *Lady, do you know Jesus is coming soon and you'd better get ready and accept Him as your Savior?* But then I pictured myself looking up and saying, "How's that, Lord? Did that please You? Can I go to sleep now?"

I knew that wasn't what the Lord wanted. He immediately brought to mind the Samaritan woman at the well and how much time Jesus spent ministering to her. So, I started really talking with this woman who lived in Salinas. And you know how good the Lord is— He slipped Israel into the conversation. Chuck and I had just been there a few weeks earlier, and as it turned out, this woman's brother and sister-in-law had also just been there.

"Oh, interesting," I said. "Are they Christians?"

She answered very hesitantly. "Well ... ah ... yes."

God is so good to always give us clues. Immediately I knew that they weren't Christians and she wasn't born again. So I said, "Are you a Christian?"

She gave me the same kind of slow, affirmative response.

"Do you go to church?"

She told me she was a Methodist. I was glad to hear that, but there's a difference between going to church and being born again. So I asked her, "Well, are you a born-again Methodist?"

"Am I a what?" she exclaimed.

So I had a chance to say, "You know, the situation in Israel is so bad. We believe that Jesus is coming soon." We had a precious time talking together after that. She didn't accept Jesus right then, but I know that seeds were planted. It wasn't by accident that we sat together. I ended up with a feeling of satisfaction that went beyond my own tiredness and will. I knew that by my obedience, I had pleased God.

What if I hadn't, though? What if I'd just kept staring out the window, or had buried my nose in a book, or taken a nap? How would I have felt? Satan would have loved that. It would have given him an opportunity to say, "Look, Kay, when it comes right down to the bottom line, you don't live what you say." And the truth is, I want to live everything I say. That is a desire of my heart, because that also pleases God.

BEYOND BELIEF

In the last chapter, we looked at Hebrews 11:6, which tells us,

> But without faith *it is* impossible to please *Him,* for he who comes to God must believe that He is.

If you want to please God, you must first believe that He is. But your belief must go beyond believing that He makes the flowers bloom and the sun to shine. You have to believe that He is the God of all power, and the God Who put you on this earth for a definite purpose. He is the God Who is watching you, loving you, caring for you, and tenderly guiding you as much as you allow Him.

That last part is so important. You will never be able to live a life that is pleasing to God unless you have the faith to believe that He is infinitely concerned about you. Because this is so important, this is one of the areas that Satan hammers at us the hardest. He will constantly try to convince you that God is not interested in you, does not watch you tenderly, and doesn't really care all that much about what happens to you.

I urge you to stand up against those lies. So often when hard times come—when you go through the death of a loved one, or encounter problems in your marriage, or when one of your children starts rebelling—that's when your defenses can drop and it's easy to start listening to Satan. You may ask, "God, where are You?" You could begin to believe that He really doesn't care, and then become angry with Him.

It's so grievous to see a Christian who is angry with God. Joy Dawson, a speaker at Calvary Chapel, once said, "How can you be angry with a God Who is all-loving and with Whom there is no iniquity, no sin at all?" Not only is God all-loving, but His thoughts toward you are nothing but good. In Jeremiah 29:11 He states that very clearly.

> For I know the thoughts that I think toward you, says the LORD, thoughts of peace and not of evil, to give you a future and a hope.

God loves you more than anybody else ever could or ever will. You must program this into your brain on a daily basis: "God loves me." Say it using your own name. His love for you will not stop, no matter what you do. Don't think that just because you've sinned that means He doesn't love you anymore. Let me ask you this—when your children sin, do you love them less? No. You might *like* them a little less at that moment, but you don't love them less. Usually the naughtiest child is the one that needs the most attention. Sometimes they misbehave for that very reason—to get a little extra love and attention. Sometimes Christians do the same thing. They misbehave in an attempt to get more attention from the body of Christ.

BEYOND THE FLESH

But just as you continue to love your children when they are naughty—and the church continues to love the ones who misbehave—so too, God continues to love His children even when they go astray. God loves bad little girls and good little girls. The difference is, when we're good we bring joy to His heart. And that's what we want to do.

So first believe that He is and believe that He loves you, because without faith, it is impossible to please Him. And there's one other thing that will keep you from pleasing God. It's found in Romans 8:8, "Those who are in the flesh cannot please God." You cannot please God without faith, and you cannot please God if you are in the flesh. These things actually work together. If you have faith to believe that God is, and that He is dwelling in you, and if you are aware of His presence and believe He is with you constantly, you will not walk in the flesh. You just won't.

This eighth chapter of Romans is a particularly deep passage of Scripture. We are not sailing on the shoreline when we talk about Romans 8. We're plummeting. We're going in the depths. Once you begin to understand the truths in this passage, you'll feel a greater responsibility before the Lord. This is a lesson that is much needed among God's people.

What does it mean to be in the flesh? We know what it means for those who are not Christians, for those still controlled by Satan, who follow their evil impulses and exist in a kingdom of darkness. But what does it mean for a Christian to be in the flesh? My husband defines it as "living with your bodily appetite as the top priority in life." *The Amplified Bible* says it is catering to the appetites and impulses of the carnal nature. And *The Living Bible* says it means following our old, evil desires.

Those who claim to love Jesus but live after the flesh are often called "carnal Christians." But there's a great debate about that. Theologians have argued for years about whether or not it's possible for someone to be a Christian, and yet be carnal at the same time.

It seems pretty clear to me. If you look at the parable of the ten virgins in Matthew 25, you will see that five were wise and five were foolish—five were prepared for the coming of the bridegroom and five weren't. I would call the five unprepared virgins carnal Christians. Instead of focusing on their coming bridegroom, they were walking after their own desires. And that is how the fleshly Christian lives day in and day out—always being led by their own impulses.

ELIMINATE SIN

In England at the turn of the century, Christians gathered for praise and Bible teaching at what was called the Keswick Conventions. Missionaries Hudson Taylor and Amy Carmichael were among those who attended these summer conferences.

In one of the meetings, a minister stood up and said, "I have prayed that I would step on your toes this morning. I want to touch the places in your life that you are holding onto that grieve God's heart, and I want to offend you if I have to ... to break your heart, to get rid of these things [that grieve God]."

That's a good prayer. I am praying that the Holy Spirit will speak to you through this chapter and put His finger on any sin that needs to be eliminated from your life. Conviction can be uncomfortable, but so necessary, especially if you want to live a life that is pleasing to God.

In *The Living Bible*, Galatians 5:19-21 describes living in the flesh this way:

> But when you follow your own wrong inclinations your lives will produce these evil results: impure thoughts, eagerness for lustful pleasure, idolatry, spiritism (that is, encouraging the activity of demons), hatred and fighting, jealously and anger, constant effort to get the best for yourself, complaints and criticisms, the feeling that everyone else is wrong except those in your own little group—and there will be wrong doctrine, envy, murder, drunkenness, wild parties, and all that sort of thing.

We've all been guilty of something on that list. All of us have been led by the flesh in some form or another. But what I'm about to say isn't a general message about sin. I'm now specifically addressing the Christian who is living an inconsistent, yo-yo life. This is the person who is happy in Jesus one day, and so depressed the next that she can hardly walk across the room. One day she has a victory, and the next day she's out of fellowship. One day she's pleasing God and witnessing to others about Him, and the next day she's hanging out where she shouldn't and doing all the things she knows she shouldn't do. This is the person who has placed *self* on the very throne of her life.

That's what the flesh will do if you let it have its way. It's rotten and it will always be rotten. And God knows that. So He came up with a solution, and it's found in Romans 6:6:

> Your old evil desires were nailed to the cross with Him; that part of you that loves to sin was crushed and fatally wounded, so that your sin-loving body is no longer under sin's control, no longer needs to be a slave to sin (TLB).

What that verse tells you is this: you are no longer under the domination of sin. You were once chained and shackled and you couldn't help what you were doing. But that was before you met Jesus Christ. When you received Him as the Savior of your life, He delivered you from sin's powerful hold by crucifying it on the cross. Sin can no longer have dominion over you. God put to death this body of sin that we carry around with us.

ATONEMENT

For some reason, we often neglect this truth. If I asked you to sit down and make a list of all the things that Jesus' death brought to you, you would probably quickly write down "forgiveness of sin, eternal life, justification, redemption, and atonement." But we forget what He did to free us from sin's power. We forget that He destroyed the works of Satan so that sin can never again control us.

Christ's death is what we call a "vicarious atonement." That means He died in our place. I should have hung upon the cross. You should have hung upon the cross. God is through with these bodies of ours—and not our literal bodies, not this tent that we are housed in. I am talking about the sensual evil nature. It was put to death on the cross of Calvary so that it would no longer rule over you and me.

You must recognize this fact. I want you to read and meditate on Romans chapter 6. Ask the Holy Spirit to help you: "God, make it clear. Show me this truth. I need it, Lord." When you finally understand this truth, it will set you free. It was such a liberating revelation for me. Now, when temptation comes, I realize I don't have to succumb to it. Temptation has lost its power over me.

The first thing you must understand is that as a believer in Jesus Christ, your body is a temple of the Holy Spirit (1 Corinthians 6:19). God has a right to rule your life; sin does not. Romans 6:12 says, "Do not let sin control your puny body any longer" (TLB). Don't you love that? It goes on to say,

> Do not give in to its sinful desires. Do not let any part of your bodies become tools of wickedness to be used for sinning; but give yourselves completely to God—every part of you—to be tools in the hands of God, to be used for His good purposes. Sin need never again be your master, for now you are no longer enslaved by sin, but you are free under God's favor and mercy (Romans 6:12-14 TLB).

RECKON YOURSELF DEAD

Sin cannot dominate the born-again believer. Because God wants you to live a life that is pleasing to Him, He will give you the power of the Holy Spirit to *live* to please Him. My flesh, my body appetites could never be pleasing to God, so He put them to death on the cross. And now, as Paul explained, "I have been crucified with Christ; it is no longer I who live, but Christ lives in me" (Galatians 2:20). Jesus, through His death, took the punishment for my sin, but my sinful nature was also put to death on that cross. I am no more in subjection to it. I do not have to obey it. I am no longer a slave to my passions or sinful desires, no longer under its power.

So what do we do? Romans 6:11 tells us exactly what to do.

> Likewise you also, reckon yourselves to be dead indeed to sin, but alive to God in Christ Jesus our Lord.

The NLT clarifies "reckon" this way: "Consider yourselves to be dead to the power of sin...." In other words, we need to say, "I am dead to sin, but alive to God in Christ."

Now, I want to make this very, very practical. When you are tempted by something—whatever kind of temptation is most prevalent in your life—go to the Lord in prayer and you say, "Father, I want to live a life pleasing to You, but Satan and my flesh are in rebellion against You, and they are lying to me. They are trying to cause me to sin and grieve Your heart by making me think I cannot be freed from this thing. But You said in Your Word that I am no longer a slave to sin. The power of sin no longer has dominion over me. Therefore, I yield to You, and ask that Your Holy Spirit do His work in my life to free me from this temptation."

Remember, your body is the temple of the Holy Spirit. He lives within you and His power is available to you.

It really comes down to a question of control. Do you want to be controlled by your flesh, or by the Spirit of God? If you are not continually being filled with God's Holy Spirit, then you *will* walk after the flesh. It's guaranteed. The flesh and the Spirit are antagonistic to one other, warring constantly—and the battle is for control over you.

When you are filled with the Holy Spirit, His power flows from you. Things that used to tempt you are no longer a struggle. In fact, one evidence that the Holy Spirit has taken up residence within you is a change in your desires. You don't want to do those sinful things you once craved. You begin to hate sin—those things that grieve the heart of God.

If you're not there yet, you can begin with prayer. Tell God you want to please Him. Tell Him you want the power of the Holy Spirit in your life. Ask God to break your heart with anything that breaks His heart. And then watch how your desires begin to change.

YOU HAVE A CHOICE

Since God has given you the power of the Holy Spirit and has broken sin's domination over you, the question of who will take control of your life comes down to one word: choice. Day by day, moment by moment, you have the choice of pleasing God or pleasing your flesh. It's the simple choice of being filled with God's Spirit and walking after God's will, or walking the way of the flesh.

Don't ever forget that word. Choice. You can choose to sin or you can choose to please God. The next time you're tempted to give in to your flesh, think about that word. Think, *If I yield to this desire, I am choosing to yield to the flesh. I have a choice.* But the opposite is also true. In that moment, you can choose to yield to the Holy Spirit and walk in obedience.

Some of you who are reading this might say, "Kay, you don't understand. I am still in bondage—real bondage. I don't know what is the matter with me. I just can't seem to walk consistently with the Lord." Yes, you can. There are things you can do—that you are responsible to do—if you're to overcome those sinful desires.

Your first responsibility is to, "Put on the Lord Jesus Christ, and make no provision for the flesh, to fulfill its lusts" (Romans 13:14).

Years ago a woman came to our home and confessed to me that she had a problem with sexual sin. She was extremely promiscuous. The sexual sin was bad enough, but the way she went about meeting men was very shattering to me. She would take tracts from our church, with our name on the back, and go down to the beach pier and pass them out. This was how she met and picked up men.

She said she really wanted deliverance from this lifestyle, so I prayed with her and asked God to free her. But a few days later, she came back and told me she couldn't do it—she couldn't stop. The temptation was too great.

I told her, "I know God gives deliverance. There is no shortage with Him. Tell me what you've been doing."

She admitted that after we had prayed the first time, she left my house, went directly to the church, picked up a handful of tracts, and went back to the pier. And then she succumbed to temptation again.

"Why did you go back down there?" I asked.

She replied, "I thought the Lord wanted me to pass out tracts again."

I told her He didn't. Then we prayed again—and every week for about six weeks. We continued meeting and praying because she kept doing the exact same thing. She just persisted in going down to the pier.

Finally, God told me to share Romans 13:14 with her. When we met that last time, I said, "Look, don't come over for prayer anymore, because I am not going to pray with you. I have three little kids and I can't take any more time from them. It is not doing a bit of good, because you are constantly making provisions for the flesh. You keep going right back to the place of temptation."

Chuck always says that if you are an alcoholic, don't go in a bar to get a Coke. Stay away from the bar. It's like dieting—it doesn't work very well if you go to the market and buy a bunch of goodies for the family. Don't fill your pantry with temptations. I have found that the best way to diet is to put my whole family on a diet, because if I bake cookies it is terrible for all of us. As God has said, "Don't make any provision for the flesh."

If you do not seem able to walk the victorious life in Christ, don't blame Him. He is not deficient in power. Some place along the line you are making provision for the flesh.

NAIL THE COFFIN SHUT

Our next responsibility is found in Galatians 5:16: "Walk in the Spirit and you shall not fulfill the lust of the flesh." Galatians 5:25 adds, "If we live in the Spirit, let us also walk in the Spirit." What does it mean to walk after the Spirit? It means doing those things that please God. And in this instance, what pleases God is for you to mortify the flesh.

> Therefore put to death your members which are on the earth: fornication, uncleanness, passion, evil desire, and covetousness, which is idolatry (Colossians 3:5).

To mortify means to put to death or to reckon as dead. God nailed your fleshly desires to the cross. Your job now is to reckon them as dead.

Dr. J. Vernon McGee used to say that the flesh is forever trying to climb out of the coffin. Be on the lookout for that, and continually render it dead.

The King James Version of Colossians 3:5 says, "Mortify therefore your members which are upon the earth; fornication, uncleanness, *inordinate affection....*" I want to address those two words: inordinate affection. And I'm going to be blunt because it's needed.

As the wife of a pastor, I can assure you that pastors are like any other men—born again, to be sure, and anointed by God for their calling— but for some reason, women have a tendency to fall in love with pastors. It happens all the time. A woman will be sitting in the service and she'll start thinking about how compassionate the pastor seems. Maybe she doesn't have a boyfriend, and she's lonely. Or maybe she's married but her husband doesn't listen to her. So she decides to make a counseling appointment. And here is this godly, loving, compassionate, tender man who listens to her and gives her wise advice—and so what does she do? She falls in love with him.

That's inordinate affection. It's a work of the flesh and a tool of Satan. I want to make this very clear: you can never please God as long as you have inordinate affection for a married person. Untold numbers of ministers are living as miserable, defeated men right now because some woman in the congregation set forth to seduce them and destroy their ministry. They've lost everything. And of course, they are just as responsible for what happened. But the root of this is inordinate affection—and quite often it starts with the woman.

FLEE

Keep yourself from inordinate affection. Do whatever you must to put it to death. Don't allow yourself to start daydreaming about the pastor, or the worship leader, or the married man sitting in front of you. It would be better for you to get up and leave the service than to sit there allowing those evil thoughts to take root. As we're told in 2 Timothy 2:19, "Let everyone who names the name of Christ depart from iniquity."

Abstain, ladies. And what does that mean? It means to deprive yourself. I implore you to do this, just as Peter did in 1 Peter 2:11: "Beloved, I beg you as sojourners and pilgrims, abstain from fleshly lusts which war against the soul." You are only a pilgrim upon this earth. You are a citizen of heaven, not of this earth. Don't give in to those things that war against your soul.

Peter beseeched us to abstain, but Paul comes right out and commands it. "Flee sexual immorality" (1 Corinthians 6:18). In this day and age we have to hit these things heavily, because our society is obsessed with sex. You can't read a magazine, watch a commercial, or sit through a TV show or a movie without being bombarded with sexual images. It's everywhere, and we are not doing enough to shield ourselves from it. We're told to flee, but do we? We sit there, take it in, and then wonder why we are so tempted.

It's particularly hard for those of you who are younger. In his letter to Timothy, Paul doesn't just tell Timothy to flee lust, he tells him "flee also *youthful* lusts" (2 Timothy 2:22a). There are things that tempt a young woman that just don't appeal to me anymore. I am not tempted to take drugs, drink alcohol, or go to clubs. But those things may be great temptations to you. So you're to run. You're to flee. You're to make sure you're not even in a place where those things are done. Instead of chasing after temptation, "pursue righteousness, faith, love and peace with those who call on the Lord out of a pure heart" (2:22b).

HONOR GOD IN THE DETAILS

I don't want you to be tempted, nor do I want you to *be* a temptation. This brings up the issue of modesty. First Corinthians 6:20 tells us, "Glorify God in your body and in your spirit, which are God's." Let me ask you something about the way you dress. Can people look at you and tell you are a Christian? What I'm asking is, do you live to glorify God in *all* ways—including the way you present your body? You may have never thought about that before, but if you really want to be a woman who pleases God, you will honor Him even in these small details. Include Him in all your wardrobe decisions. When you're out shopping for clothes or a bathing suit, stop and ask, "Lord, is this okay with You?"

You have been called to live a holy life. That means you do not live as others do. It means you do all things as unto God, with an eye for pleasing Him.

> Finally then, brethren, we urge and exhort in the Lord Jesus that you should abound more and more, just as you received from us how you ought to walk and to please God; for this is the will of God, your sanctification: that you should abstain from sexual immorality; that each of you should know how to possess his own vessel in sanctification and honor, not in passion of lust, like the Gentiles who do not know God; for God did not call us to uncleanness, but in holiness (1 Thessalonians 4:1, 3-5, 7).

I have never known anyone who grew and matured in Christ and lived a holy life who was not very aware of the truths we've covered in this chapter. The flesh is a mighty foe and there is no instant way to overcome it. It's all a matter of choice—of walking daily in the Spirit, one wise decision upon another.

Remember that God has given all that you need. He has freed you from the power of Satan and given you His Holy Spirit to dwell in you and empower you. But you have a responsibility to choose wisely. If you want to live a life that is pleasing to God, you must choose to count yourself as dead to sin. You must choose to flee temptation. And you must choose to yield yourself to God's Holy Spirit. The life that does these things will be a beautiful, fragrant life.

The choice is yours.

Father, we thank You for what You did on the cross. Thank You for delivering us from the power of sin. We ask that You forgive us for the times we've stumbled and the times we've been unfaithful to You. We long to walk in Your light, Lord. Open our blinded eyes to see these truths. Break our hearts, if need be, that we would be freed from anything that is keeping us from living a life pleasing to You. May the light of the knowledge of Jesus Christ shine upon our hearts. And may we be filled to overflowing with Your Holy Spirit.

In Jesus' name we pray, amen.

4

A PATTERN
FOR CHANGE

I DON'T KNOW IF YOU'RE aware of this, but God's Word is full of patterns. For example, very often, just before God gives a promise, He'll lay out the condition to that promise.

> Fear the LORD and depart from evil. It will be health to your flesh, and strength to your bones (Proverbs 3:7-8).

> Give, and it will be given to you: good measure, pressed down, shaken together, and running over will be put into your bosom. For with the same measure that you use, it will be measured back to you (Luke 6:38).

> Seek first the kingdom of God and His righteousness, and all these things shall be added to you (Matthew 6:33).

The pattern in all these cases is simple: "If you do this, I will do that." I love that. I love knowing that if I apply God's patterns to my life, it will work every single time. It has never failed me once. Every time I choose to obey Him or to focus on Him instead of on my problem, He has brought me relief from anxiety, bitterness, and unforgiveness.

CONDITIONAL PROMISES

The problem is, we're often very ready to claim the promise, but we don't want to meet the condition. We say, "Oh Lord, I want this part of the verse, but I don't want to do that part of the verse." Conditional promises don't work that way. You must be willing to do your part if you want God to do His.

Sometimes, however, you're willing to do your part but you're not sure how. You've made up your mind that you want to live a life that is pleasing to God, but you're not sure how to do that in a practical sense. Here again, God puts a pattern in place that can help you to obey.

Let's say, for instance, that you are fretting about something in your life. Maybe you're being persecuted by a family member or a neighbor or a coworker. No matter what you try, you can't stop thinking about the situation. Even Satan is hassling you by bringing it to your mind constantly, and you can't stop dwelling on it. So you go to your Bible—always the best thing to do—and you turn to Psalm 37 where God says, "Do not fret because of evildoers."

If you quit reading right there, you might be able to stop fretting, but not for very long. That's because you haven't replaced your fretful thoughts with good thoughts. But God knows we need to do both. And so He gives us that pattern in His Word: "Don't look at the problem— look at Me."

Let's look closely at Psalm 37:1-7:

> Do not fret because of evildoers, nor be envious of the workers of iniquity. For they shall soon be cut down like the grass, and wither as the green herb.
>
> Trust in the LORD, and do good; dwell in the land, and feed on His faithfulness. Delight yourself also in the LORD, and He shall give you the desires of your heart.
>
> Commit your way to the LORD, trust also in Him, and He shall bring it to pass. He shall bring forth your righteousness as the light, and your justice as the noonday.
>
> Rest in the LORD, and wait patiently for Him.

The first thing God says in this passage is, "I don't want you to fret." So you say, "Yes, Lord, I see in Your Word that You don't want me to fret. So I will stop fretting." But God is not finished. What does He say to do next? Verse 3 says, "Trust in the LORD." Now you've been given two things to do. Stop fretting, and start trusting in the Lord.

What do you see in the rest of that passage? "Dwell in the land." When I think of dwelling, I think of meditating. Meditate on the Lord. Do you know what happens when you meditate on the Lord? You can't help but begin to delight in Him. And that's verse 4: "Delight yourself also in the LORD." Then it goes on to say, "Commit your way to the LORD," and finally, "Rest in the LORD."

MAKE A LIST

What I like to do is make a list of these verses and carry it with me. If I am downstairs doing dishes and I know I'm going to be fretting, I will prop it up on the windowsill right in front of me. And as I'm doing the dishes I read, "Don't fret; trust, dwell, delight, commit, rest"—and

I start doing it. I make a decision to stop fretting. And then I think, *Lord, I trust in You, so I will commit this to You. You are my Creator, God. You are my King. You are capable and all-powerful. You will take care of this for me.*

And then as I remind myself of all that, I can't help but begin to praise Him. *Oh, God, You are so wonderful! You always take care of me. You always provide just what I need. Even now, as I'm washing these dishes— I've got hot water, and detergent....*

That might seem funny to you, but I was a young girl during World War II and I remember that it was very hard to wash dishes. The soap we had then was terrible, and it wouldn't make any suds. It wasn't fun to do dishes, because I couldn't splash suds all over the place. So I thank the Lord for these wonderful detergents that clean my dishes beautifully, so that I can see my face in them.

And it just goes on from there. I thank Him for the gardenia plant outside my window. I thank Him for the little plants on my countertop. I look around and thank Him for the sun that is shining in the window, and for the fact that I get to live in this area. Then I praise Him just because He is God—because He is marvelous in all His ways and faithful and just and good and righteous and holy and pure and forgiving and full of mercy and compassion. And do you know what happens? I begin to rest, because my mind can't praise God and fret at the same time. And yours can't either.

As you follow these steps obediently—as you lift your eyes from the problem to the One Who is able to take care of the problem—you will receive the release you need, and you will please God.

That's a pattern that will work for you every time. Even if you have to run through that list over and over, all through the day, you will find the rest you cannot find while fretting and stewing.

A PATTERN FOR CHANGE

JAMES 4:1-10

Another pattern God has given is found in James 4:1-10. It's a long passage, and you might be tempted to think, *Oh, I've read that before. I'll just skim it.* But I want to ask that you read it as though you've never seen it before. I pray that God will open your eyes anew to these words:

What leads to strife (discord and feuds) and how do conflicts (quarrels and fightings) originate among you? Do they not arise from your sensual desires that are ever warring in your bodily members?

You are jealous and covet [what others have] and your desires go unfulfilled; [so] you become murderers. [To hate is to murder as far as your hearts are concerned.] You burn with envy and anger and are not able to obtain [the gratification, the contentment, and the happiness that you seek], so you fight and war. You do not have, because you do not ask.

[Or] you do ask [God for them] and yet fail to receive, because you ask with wrong purpose and evil, selfish motives. Your intention is [when you get what you desire] to spend it in sensual pleasures.

You [are like] unfaithful wives [having illicit love affairs with the world and breaking your marriage vow to God]! Do you not know that being the world's friend is being God's enemy? So whoever chooses to be a friend of the world takes his stand as an enemy of God.

Or do you suppose that the Scripture is speaking to no purpose that says, The Spirit Whom He has caused to dwell in us yearns over us and He yearns for the Spirit [to be welcome] with a jealous love?

But He gives us more and more grace (power of the Holy Spirit, to meet this evil tendency and all others fully). That is why He says, God sets Himself against the proud and haughty, but gives grace [continually] to the lowly (those who are humble enough to receive it).

So be subject to God. Resist the Devil [stand firm against him], and he will flee from you.

Come close to God and He will come close to you. [Recognize that you are] sinners, get your soiled hands clean; [realize that you have been disloyal] wavering individuals with divided interests, and purify your hearts [of your spiritual adultery].

[As you draw near to God] be deeply penitent and grieve, even weep [over your disloyalty]. Let your laughter be turned to grief and your mirth to dejection and heartfelt shame [for your sins].

Humble yourselves [feeling very insignificant] in the presence of the Lord, and He will exalt you [He will lift you up and make your lives significant] (*The Amplified Bible*).

That's such a beautiful passage with such a wonderful promise at the end. If you humble yourself in the sight of God, He will make your life significant. I don't believe there is a single woman anywhere who does not want significance. We all want to live meaningful, worthwhile lives.

A STRONG CONFLICT

At the beginning of this passage, James points out the source of conflict in our spiritual walk, and he words it strongly. Our wars and fightings, strife and discord are caused by our lusts. "Lust" means a strong desire of the flesh. We tend to think of lust always in a sexual connotation, but it isn't. Lust is a strong desire for fulfillment that is not of God. Once again, the flesh is causing trouble. And when we are in the flesh, we cannot please God.

The flesh is demanding and covetous. It says, "I want what I want when I want it. And if I don't get it, you're going to see some anger, strife, and discord." It's very easy to see those who are being led by the flesh. They have to be in the limelight all the time and if they aren't, they will cut you to ribbons. But this is in complete opposition to God.

In the last chapter we talked about the fact that your flesh has been crucified with Jesus Christ on the cross and it no longer has the power to dominate you. Jesus gave you the victory over the flesh. He crucified it. But what happens when you forget that your flesh has been crucified? Do you mistreat people? Backbite and gossip? Do you stamp your foot and have tantrums? Do you carry secret jealousies in your heart, secret envies against those who are prettier, or richer, or more intelligent, or more talented?

The flesh is wildly insecure. Our culture knows that and plays on it. Advertisers know the best way to get you to buy their products is to make you feel inadequate without them. Without their product, you can never be all that you ought to be. You won't be as beautiful as you could, or smell as nice as you should.

Not only is the flesh insecure, it's also competitive. The spirit of the world encourages you to compare yourself to others and then try your best to out-do them. Be better than the person next to you. Be richer, prettier, thinner, and smarter. If you aren't richer, prettier, thinner, or smarter, then your flesh starts tearing down those who are. "She is not all that pretty." "That color looks horrible on her." "She's not all that bright."

WHAT DOES GOD VALUE?

Tragically, insecurity so often leads to wickedness. And the truth is, the majority of women in this world have suffered from low self-esteem. A survey of New York's famous models revealed that not one liked her own appearance. Although these women were paid enormous sums of money for being a model of beauty, they felt insecure. Isn't that interesting? It's all because of the world's flawed value system.

What we need is a new value system—a system founded in Jesus Christ. The question should be, what does God value? This is why being pleasing to Him does so many marvelous things in your life. If you are living to please God you won't be consumed with questions of whether you are fat or thin, ugly or beautiful, dumb or smart. Instead you'll be consumed with Him. You'll be significant because you know you are worthwhile to Him. You'll take Psalm 139 to heart and believe that you are fearfully and wonderfully made, and of great worth and value to God.

Sometimes we're not the instigator of jealousy—sometimes we are the victims of it. Occasionally you are put in a position where just because you live, breathe, and walk, you're disliked.

WHAT IS YOUR REACTION?

Quite a long time ago, early in our ministry, we had a church party where everyone was to come in a costume. We didn't have very much money, but I figured I could buy some burlap and make an Indian costume out of it. So, I sewed up a little burlap dress and put on some dark tan makeup. Have you ever had one of those times when you just felt like you looked good? We have them once in a while, don't we? It was one of those times. We went to the party and I was having a great time.

A very close friend of mine came dressed as a clown, and she looked adorable with that big clown mouth painted on her face. As the evening went on, I was laughing and having a good time and being very sanguine. Then I noticed several times that she was just watching me. All of a sudden she walked up with a squirt gun in her hand and squirted me right in the face. The water didn't hurt, but I felt the spirit behind it. I knew it was malicious. I felt a stab in my heart, yet I wanted to be gracious, so I laughed. But later that night, while in bed, I cried in my pillow. I prayed, *Lord, why did she do that to me?* But the Lord said, "It isn't important why she did that. It is important how you react." He stopped me right then and there from allowing my hurt feelings to turn into bitterness. In a sense, He gave me yet another pattern to follow: when you are hurt, love back.

Well, I did that. I continued to love my friend. I even forgot about the party. We moved to another church where Chuck began pastoring, and five years later she and her husband followed us to that church. The four of us went to lunch one afternoon to catch up. She and I were talking when suddenly she turned to me and said, "You know, Kay, I have something to confess to you that has been bothering me for five years."

I couldn't imagine what she felt she needed to confess, but then she said, "Do you remember that party?"

I really didn't. But then she added, "I came as a clown."

Then I remembered.

She said, "You know what? You were so beautiful in that costume, and I was jealous. I just have to confess this to you. For five years I have carried this on my heart."

When a friend squirts you in the face because you look decent one night in your life, you have a right to be angry—at least by the world's standards. But God kept me from being angry or bitter by showing me that pattern: love those who hurt you. It doesn't matter who it is. It might be your husband, your children, or a good friend who hurts you. You might very well be the victim. But God doesn't want you to walk around angry, bitter, and full of unforgiveness. He wants to free you from that hurt so you can have joy and peace.

In the first six verses of chapter 4, James paints a very clear picture of a life in the flesh. And that's the first thing you must do—recognize the source of the problem. Your flesh is obeying Satan instead of God. You must acknowledge that you have a sin nature and then go to God and ask for help.

> Come close to God and He will come close to you. Recognize that you are sinners, get your soiled hands clean; [realize that you have been disloyal] wavering individuals with divided interests, and purify your hearts [of your spiritual adultery] (James 4:8).

Ask God to shine His light on your heart and show you any sin that must go.

THROW OUT THE GARBAGE

Satan's work is always in darkness. He loves to keep us blind about ourselves, because if we don't recognize the truth he can keep us trapped. And Satan loves to deceive us about our own sin, since he knows that our unconfessed sin will hover over us like a black cloud and hinder our prayers. But who among us doesn't sin? How sad to see someone walking about as some super saint with a phony, plastic smile plastered on her face, while deep inside there is the blackness of sin. Remember that Jesus called the Pharisees whitewashed sepulchers, because outwardly they did all the right things, but inwardly they were full of garbage. John wrote,

> If we say that we have no sin, we deceive ourselves and the truth is not in us (1 John 1:8).

If you are not consciously aware of your sin, ask God to search your heart and reveal the truth to you.

James stated his case so strongly in James 4:1-3 that it would be easy to look at that list and say, "I'm not that bad. I'm certainly not a murderer." That's probably true. Maybe there's only a little garbage inside. The problem is, a little garbage—left to fester—can raise a giant stink.

I remember once when I was young and my parents forgot to take the garbage out before we went on vacation. It was just a tiny bit, but when we got home and opened the door, the smell was unimaginable. A little garbage can destroy your life. It's like an infection in your body. Left untreated, it will worsen until it kills you.

So what are those little bits of garbage in your life? Bitterness is one. You might have just the tiniest little root of bitterness, but Hebrews tells us "springing up [it can] cause trouble, and by this many become defiled" (Hebrews 12:15).

Rebelliousness is another bit of garbage. It is just like the sin of witchcraft. What does witchcraft do? It reaches out and puts spells on people. When those who are rebellious come in contact with other people, their sin pulls others away from God instead of moving them towards Him. Rebelliousness is contagious.

GOD'S SWEETNESS

We must be brutally honest with ourselves. We must ask God to search our hearts and put His finger on any sin that must be thrown away. But then secondly, we must recognize God's enabling power. You can behave as you ought to behave. You don't have to walk in hatred, bitterness, or malice—no matter what anybody does to you. God will enable you by His grace to walk in a manner pleasing to Him.

When trials got bad, Amy Carmichael used to look up and say, "Your grace, Lord, Your sweetness for this situation." God has sweetness for your situation, too. Like the prophet Elijah, who poured salt on the bitter waters and turned it sweet, it may be that you need God to sweeten the bitter waters in you. It may mean that He has to put a little salt on your wound and let it sting a bit to purify that area, but if it results in your healing, isn't it worth the sting?

God is all-powerful. He has everything you need to walk in victory. In *The Living Bible*, James 4:6a says, "He gives us more and more strength to stand against all such evil longings." He will give you all the power you need to meet whatever evil tendencies are troubling you.

PATTERN 1: RECOGNIZE YOUR SIN

The only thing that can hinder your healing is a refusal to recognize these ugly attitudes in yourself. That comes from pride. "I am not like that!" Oh yes, you are. We all are. But God does not give enabling power to a person who doesn't recognize the need for it and call upon Him. As James will go on to tell us in verse 9, pride should be the last thing we feel. We're supposed to mourn over our own behavior, but instead, what do we do? We turn and look at someone else's behavior and point with a haughty finger.

Ladies, don't allow haughtiness into your life. And whatever you do, don't allow it into your marriage. How often I've heard a wife say with indignation, "I have a right to feel this way." Of course, you do. In the world's eyes, you have every right to feel that way. You have a right to go to the divorce court too. But a marriage filled with "I have my rights" is a marriage headed for destruction. "He insulted me. He neglected me. He rejected me; therefore, I have a right to feel this way." You may have a right to feel that way, but it isn't pleasing unto God and it isn't healthy for you—and it isn't healthy for your marriage. Not only that, but if you allow yourself to have those kinds of thoughts, then you're very likely also programming that same kind of haughtiness and pride into the little ones who are watching you and who want to grow up to be just like you.

So pride has to go. We need to humble ourselves. What happens when we do? As we read in verse 6b, "God resists the proud, but gives grace to the humble." As long as you go along saying, "I can handle that," you are not going to receive God's grace. It comes to those who are humble. Verse 10 gives us a wonderful promise about this: "Humble yourselves in the sight of the Lord, and He will lift you up."

PATTERN 2: TOTAL SUBMISSION

In the pattern God has for dealing with our flesh, pattern 1 is: "Recognize your sin and confess it to God." Pattern 2 is found in James 4:7: "Therefore submit to God." This is not a partial submission—this is total.

Submitting to God does not require a lot of complicated steps. A very practical way to submit to God is simply make a statement to Him declaring your recognition of the problem. Maybe it's your own bad attitude. Or maybe it's someone else's bad attitude toward you and you're having a hard time controlling your reaction. Just make a statement to God about your utter helplessness to change without His help. In humility, declare your dependence on Him and ask Him to do whatever He must do to change you.

Beloved woman of God—how this pleases the heart of God when you do this! Do you know what you are doing when you humble yourself? You are acknowledging that He is Lord of your life. We sing, "He is Lord, He is Lord"—but do we really mean it? Do we really submit ourselves unto Him? Do we stop and say, "Lord, I am helpless in this situation. Will You handle it for me?"

I've watched some women go through the most awful circumstances but refuse to be broken by them. They stand as straight today as the day their trial began and their battle cry remains, "I'll do it or I'll die!" Sadly, they probably *will* die trying to resist God. They're hurt, bitter, and angry with God, all because they refuse to be broken.

Some of us are like stubborn-spirited children when it comes to discipline. God brings something into our lives that is meant to chastise us so that we learn a valuable lesson. But what do we do? We enter into a battle of wills with God. We stand straight and stiff and say, "I won't cry. I won't be broken—I won't." Listen, the Bible says, "For whom the LORD loves He chastens, and scourges every son whom He receives" (Hebrews 12:6). Don't resist the discipline of your Father. At the first little swat just look up and say, "That is the only swat I want. Do whatever You want in my life." Be broken before Him. Be humble. Submit to Him—and let Him work in you.

PATTERN 3: RESIST THE DEVIL

Pattern 3 is found in the second half of James 4:7, which contains a comforting promise: "Resist the Devil and he will flee from you." We have a wrong perception of Satan, don't we? We tend to think of him as being big and powerful and ferocious, but he is just an angel who was kicked out of heaven for rebelling against God. He is not like God. He doesn't have the power God has. Jesus defeated him on Calvary and he can no longer have dominion over you. And right here in James we're told that if we resist the Devil, he has to flee. But do we resist him?

How we need to meditate on this promise and begin to use it! First Peter 5:8-9 tells us, "Be sober, be vigilant; because your adversary the Devil walks about like a roaring lion, seeking whom he may devour. Resist him, steadfast in the faith." There it is again: resist him. But we're not to fear him. As a matter of fact, Isaiah 14:16 tells us we are going to look on the Devil and say, "Is this the man who made the earth tremble?"

When I begin to have a bad attitude, if I stop and say, "God, in the name of Jesus I resist Satan," he flees. Maybe it is just for a minute and I need to do it again another minute later. But pretty soon Satan is so far gone that the attitude I initially struggled with doesn't even come into my mind anymore. Resist Satan and he will flee.

PATTERN 4: DRAW NEAR TO GOD

After you recognize and acknowledge your sin, submit to God, and resist the Devil, James 4:8 tells what you're to do next: "Draw near to God and He will draw near to you." This is pattern 4. Like a little child climbing into her mommy's or daddy's arms, we need to draw near to God.

Have you ever been around a little baby who is afraid of a dog? What does that baby do? She runs for her mommy or daddy. She runs for that place of safety and clings and pulls until she is picked up and reassured. That's what God does when you draw near to Him. He holds His arms out to you and He says, "I am your shield. I am your high tower. I am your place of comfort. You don't need to worry about anything ferocious. I'll protect you."

I hope that as you read these words, you sense God's loving presence. He is right there with you, right now, ready to take you in His arms and give you the reassurance you need. He is there to comfort you, to care for you, to help you live a victorious life that is pleasing unto Him. Sense His loving presence and respond to Him.

In Psalm 27, David said that he longed to dwell in the sanctuary for two reasons: to inquire of the Lord and to behold His beauty. What about you? When you go into the sanctuary on Sunday morning, do you say, "Lord, I am here this morning to inquire of You. There are some things I need to know as I walk this path, and I need some answers from You today." And then as the Lord whispers through a song or you sense Him in the stillness of the service, do you behold His beauty? Do you respond with worship? "Oh Lord, You are so beautiful, so precious to me. I love You, Lord, and I praise Your name."

It's easy to say, "Praise the Lord!" but we need to really do it. We must learn to praise Him in the language He has given us, and we need to praise Him in the Spirit. Nothing lifts us out of an ordinary day like praise and worship.

I was going through a horrible situation awhile back, and as I was driving to the church it was on my mind. But in the middle of my thoughts, the Lord said, "Kay, from this point until you get to the church you are to do only one thing—praise Me." So that's what I did. And by the time I got to the church I was no longer thinking about that horrible problem, because My eyes were on God and my thoughts were all on Him. I could sense His presence there with me, and He refreshed me.

PATTERN 5: CLEANSE YOUR HANDS

James 4:8b gives us pattern 5: "Cleanse your hands, you sinners; and purify your hearts, you double-minded." Hand cleansing represents the things you do. Heart cleansing represents the things that you are inside.

We don't do this in the church today, but in the Old Testament tabernacle, hand washing had great ceremonial significance. But we could do the same thing right in our homes. Think of how often you wash your hands in a normal day. As you wash your hands say, "Lord, please wash my hands spiritually. Cause me to do only the things that You want me to do. And while I am washing my hands, Lord, purify my heart. Purify it from all the garbage, all the rottenness that is in there. Apply a little soap inside. Cleanse me, Lord."

It's so important to go to God for cleansing. We want to be stable, strong, mature Christians who will influence others and live to please God. If we're double-minded—if we love God but also allow a love of the world to creep in—we need to confess, repent, and be cleansed.

PATTERN 6: GRIEVE OVER YOUR SIN

The sixth pattern comes from James 4:9, which is a heavy verse: "Lament and mourn and weep! Let your laughter be turned to mourning and your joy to gloom." *The New Living Translation* phrases it this way: "Let there be tears for what you have done. Let there be sorrow and deep grief. Let there be sadness instead of laughter, and gloom instead of joy."

When the Spirit of God is at work in your life, you will grieve over your sin. I remember as a little girl watching people walk down the aisles to the altar in the front of our church. Something in the sermon would have really spoken to them, and they would come with tears pouring down their cheeks.

I saw the same thing years ago at an end times conference in Hawaii. The people were so moved by the message that they literally ran to the altar with tears pouring down their faces. They just couldn't get to Jesus fast enough.

Theologian Jonathan Edwards who was a key figure in The Great Awakening once preached a sermon he titled, *Sinners in the hands of an angry God*, which so broke the hearts of those who heard it that they crawled to the altar.

I've been broken like that. Once, when I was harboring a disobedient attitude, God spoke to me and broke my heart. I began to weep before Him over the way I had been behaving. He then brought this poem to mind. It's one I've read again and again, because I never want to think lightly about my sin:

> My God! my God! and can it be
> That I should sin so lightly now,
> And think no more of evil thoughts
> Than of the wind that waves the bough?
> I sin, and Heav'n and earth go round,
> As if no dreadful deed were done;
> As if Thy blood had never flowed

To hinder sin, or to atone.
I walk the earth with lightsome step,
Smile at the sunshine, breathe the air,
Do my own will, not ever heed
Gethsemane and Thy long prayer.
Shall it be always thus, O Lord?
Wilt Thou not work this hour in me
The grace of Thy Passion merited,
Hatred of self, and love of Thee!
O by the pains of Thy pure love,
Grant me the gift of holy fear;
And by Thy woes and bloody sweat
Wash Thou my guilty conscience clear!
Ever when tempted, make me see,
Beneath the olives' moon pierced shade,
My God, alone, outstretched, and bruised,
And bleeding, on the earth He made;
And make me feel it was my sin,
As though no other sins there were,
That was to Him Who bears the world
A load that He could scarcely bear. ³

God does not look at sin lightly, so we shouldn't either. Can you sin so lightly and not even care? God allowed His Son to be nailed to a cross for you—is that not enough to break your heart? Be afflicted over your sin. Let it break your heart, and move you to true repentance.

In chapter 3, I urged you to ask God to break your heart with those things that break His heart. I hope you have asked Him that. If not, now is a good time. He will do it if you ask Him. We want to be sensitive to sin. One of the signs of maturity in a Christian is they are concerned when even the tiniest sin hurts. Christians who are very immature, who are very shallow spiritually, can sin and not care at all. They might say that they shouldn't have sinned, but they don't weep before God. But we want to be mature Christians who bring pleasure to God's heart.

PATTERN 7: HUMBLE YOURSELF

And then finally, in verse 10, we have that beautiful promise: "Humble yourselves in the sight of the Lord, and He will lift you up."

Roy Hession wrote a book called *The Calvary Road,* [4] which, in my opinion, is probably the most penetrating book written, apart from the Word of God. The author said as he began to write, he started to realize he was nothing but a worm that deserved to be trodden upon.

Some might read that and think, *Oh, he has low self-esteem.* That's not low self-esteem. It's just the truth. We all are of infinite worth to God, but when we realize how we have failed Him and how we have grieved His heart, it opens our eyes to our utter worthlessness apart from Him. Everything we have—all our talents and abilities—needs to be brought to the cross and crucified. We must be emptied so that He might pour Himself into us.

Though you might feel very insignificant in the presence of the Lord, He promises that He will exalt the one who is humble. He will lift you up and make your life significant. Just as we discussed at the beginning of this chapter, this is another conditional promise. If you humble yourself, God will lift you up. You can count on it. If you want a significant life, there's the pattern.

LIVE FOR JESUS

In chapter 1 we read Psalm 39:4, where David says to God (and I'm paraphrasing), "Show me what time I have left. Show me how frail I am. Show me how many days I have." As I said, I've asked the Lord to do that for me. Do I have a week or a month? Do I have years? I keep praying this because He hasn't shown me yet. But the one thing that He has said is, "Kay, you don't have very long, so live every moment pleasing to Me." And I don't live every moment exactly pleasing to Him, but I am walking as closely as I can. Now and then, the Spirit taps me on the shoulder and says, "That didn't please God, Kay Smith." And I repent and I start back up again.

James 4:14 reminds us again of how quickly our lives pass. "You do not know what will happen tomorrow. For what is your life? It is even a vapor that appears for a little time and then vanishes away." *The New Living Translation* says, "Your life is like the morning fog—it's here a little while, then it's gone." This earthly life is just a vapor that appears for a little time and then vanishes away.

Listen, all you little vapors out there, let's live for Jesus. With the time that He's given us, let's love Him and bless Him and serve Him. Let's live a life that's pleasing to our God.

Lord, You are our life and we have no life outside of You. We acknowledge that You are our Creator—the One Who gave us life—and apart from You we have no significance at all. I pray, Lord, that the truths of this chapter will find lodging in the heart of each precious woman who reads it. We want to be women who walk in complete submission to You, pleasing unto You in all our ways, and grieving over those things that break Your heart. Touch us in a brand-new way as we have never been touched before. Renew a right spirit within us. Create a new heart within us, a heart of love and desires that are after You.

In the name of Jesus we pray, amen.

5

WALK WITH GOD

I'M CONVINCED THAT FROM NOW until the day I leave this earth, I will continue to learn more and more about pleasing God. That's what I want. I don't ever want to stop learning to please Him. That's my desire for you too.

Paul had that same desire for the church in Thessalonica.

> Finally then, brethren, we urge and exhort in the Lord Jesus that you should abound more and more, just as you received from us how you ought to walk and to please God; for you know what commandments we gave you through the Lord Jesus. (1 Thessalonians 4:1-2).

In our quest to "abound more and more" to that ideal—that ideal where we please God in our thoughts, in our words and in our actions—we want to go back and look more closely at Enoch.

Remember that the Word tells us that Enoch "had this testimony, that he pleased God" (Hebrews 11:5).

So how did Enoch live? What did he do that, for all of eternity, he would be known as one who pleased God? In Hebrews chapter 11, we find two requisites of pleasing God evidenced in Enoch's life. They are not only essential, but are very simple for us to heed. I pray that God writes these precious truths upon your heart and in your mind.

FAITH PLEASES GOD

The first is found in the first two words of Hebrews 11:5: "By faith …" You could almost start with those two words and skip to the end of the verse, picking back up at "he pleased God," because by his faith Enoch pleased God. As we discussed earlier, it is impossible to please Him without faith. We must believe that He is there and that He loves us.

One of the reasons why faith is so important is because faith is the catalyst behind what we do. Our works and our conduct are a result of our faith. This becomes clear as you read through chapter 11 of Hebrews. I hope you take a moment to read it—and read it over and over and over again. I know of no other chapter in the Bible that is more inspiring than this chapter. Look at what faith did in the lives of these people:

"By faith, Noah … prepared an ark."

"By faith, Abraham went out, not knowing where he was going."

"By faith Sarah … bore a child when she was past the age."

"By faith Jacob blessed … and worshiped."

"By faith Moses … chose to suffer affliction with God's people rather than enjoy the passing pleasures of sin."

"By faith they passed through the Red Sea."

"By faith the walls of Jericho fell down" (Hebrews 11:7-30).

When you read about the great exploits these people accomplished by faith, it can't help but touch your heart.

Where does faith come from? It comes from God. Isn't it beautiful that the very thing God desires from us, He gives us? Romans 12:3 says that, "God has dealt to each one a measure of faith." And Ephesians 2:8 tells us very clearly that faith is a gift of God. But we also learn from the book of Romans that we can do something practical to gain more faith. "Faith comes by hearing, and hearing by the Word of God" (Romans 10:17).

If this is news to you—the fact that faith is God's gift to each person, and you can gain more faith by hearing the Word of God—then I encourage you to write these verses down and memorize them. Say to yourself, *I know I have faith because God has given it to me.* The Word of God is steadfast and true and sure. If God said He has given you faith, you can *believe* that God has given you faith.

READ THE WORD DAILY

Now, if faith comes as a gift from God, and increases from hearing the Word, then every time you hear the Word your faith is built up. Hebrews 4:12 assures us the Word of God is "living and powerful," and that means it is alive and it does amazing things in your life.

I read at least one psalm every day, and as I read it I say, "God, this is at work in me." For instance, Psalm 42:8 says, "The Lord will command His lovingkindness in the daytime, and in the night His song shall be with me—a prayer to the God of my life." And I say, "Lord, You have commanded Your lovingkindness in the daytime. I receive that from You, because Your Word is alive and powerful and I am going to experience Your lovingkindness this very day." And I do, because faith is built up in me and His Word works in me. That is why you must read the Word throughout the day, if you can. Keep Bibles all over the house where you can pick them up easily. Take the time to write out Scriptures and place them where you will see them often.

I have three bookcases in my bedroom. On the one across from my bed, I keep a big stack of Bibles. My daughter Cheryl used to tease me about that stack of Bibles. "My, my, aren't we spiritual, Mom!" We would laugh about it, but the reason I have so many Bibles is because I like to look up verses in different translations. That one bookcase happens to be the most convenient place for those, but we keep Bibles all over the house. You can find them in almost any room, because a lot of times when the phone rings, we need a Bible right there and then. Or if I am in the living room and troubled about something, or in the middle of a situation, I don't want to have to go back upstairs to get a Bible. So I love having one within reach.

Now, if God's Word says, "faith comes by hearing, and hearing by the Word of God," and if our faith is built up by hearing and reading the Word of God, then we certainly need to be in His Word. Doesn't that make sense? You have a choice, of course. You can choose to believe God's Word and act on the faith He has given you, or you can accept Satan's lies and believe that you don't have any faith. The choice is entirely yours. But being that the first requisite to please God is to exercise the faith He has given you, you can probably tell which choice I think you should make.

If we go back to the example of Enoch, we can see that his faith pleased God. But what about the second requisite? Genesis 5:22 provides the answer: "Enoch walked with God."

THE WALKING CHOICE

Our Christian life is often described as a journey. We talk about the paths of righteousness, the highway of holiness, and the steps of a righteous man. We walk in the light. We walk in love. We walk in joy. We are told *not* to walk in the counsel of the ungodly. Christian books entitled *The Pilgrim's Progress* and *Hinds' Feet on High Places* allegorize the Christian's journey. We talk constantly about our walk. So when we hear that "Enoch walked with God," this figurative type of speech is familiar to us. But what does it mean in practical terms?

It begins, first of all, with a choice.

I think marriage is a beautiful illustration of what it means to walk with God. When a man asks a woman to marry him, he's asking her, "Will you walk with me all the days of your life?" That woman has a choice. She can say no, or she can say, "Yes. I choose to walk with you."

Walking denotes togetherness, whether you're talking about the relationship between a man and a woman, or a person and God. If you choose to walk with someone, you cannot walk with them and be alone at the same time. Togetherness is implied. You have a choice of learning to walk with God or not walk with God at all. But if you desire to please Him, then you must walk with Him.

To walk with someone means you are aware of their presence. And this is true with God. If you're to walk with Him, you must be continually aware of His presence.

The Practice of the Presence of God [5] is a short little book written by Brother Lawrence. I've read it several times and I recommend that you do too. In this book, Brother Lawrence writes that there was one thing in life he wanted to do, and that was to love God all of the time and with all of his heart. He said he was glad to pick up a straw from the ground if he could do it to show his love and please God, because he had resolved to make loving God the purpose of everything he did.

This is a wonderful goal, and one that we should all take as our own—but it will only happen if we make ourselves consciously aware of God's continual presence with us.

AN INTIMATE RELATIONSHIP

Let's go back to the illustration of a bride for a moment. Picture that moment when the bride is walking down the aisle with her father. There's a symbolism to that walk. She walks down the aisle with her daddy, but she walks up the aisle with her groom. Those two walks signify a change in her relationships. At the end of that aisle, when she says her vows to the man waiting there for her, she will no longer be under her father's authority. Daddy will no longer be first in her affections. That can be very difficult for her parents, you know—particularly for daddy. That walk up the aisle is not just two people taking a stroll—it is symbolic of a brand-new relationship.

In the same way, when we walk with God as Enoch walked with God, we're entering a new, more intimate relationship. In order to keep that intimacy, we must be aware of God's nearness, and mindful of the fact that we belong to Him.

I have found—and I think it is true with most wives—that I am nearly always conscious of the fact that I am married. I can't tell you how, but there's just a constant sense of it. I don't stop and think, *I am Mrs. Smith. I am married.* But unmistakably, I build my life around Chuck's coming and going. Most days now, I go with him to the office and spend the day there with him. But in earlier times, as soon as he left in the morning, I'd go back for my second cup of coffee and would plan dinner for when he came home. Throughout the day my decisions were all made with Chuck's schedule in mind. It's just what I did because I am his wife.

A CONSTANT AWARENESS

Our walk with God should be exactly like that. Because we belong to Him, we should have a constant awareness that we are walking with Him. We should go through our day with an awareness of serving and pleasing Him.

Amy Carmichael had a prayer tower built in her orphanage that she had established to save the young Indian boys and girls from a life of bondage as temple prostitutes. Every hour the chimes in the tower would ring out, and everyone would stop for a moment of prayer in recognition of the presence of God. What she was doing was implanting into those little children a constant awareness of Jesus in their midst.

We have prayer available around the clock at Calvary Chapel. Whenever someone is in great difficulty, they can call the church office at any hour of the day or night and have someone pray with them. In the early days of our church, when we were much smaller, we had a prayer chain, and those on it would each take an hour of the day to lift up those specific needs. We would keep praying until we heard that there was a real victory for that person. Sometimes we prayed for four or five days at a time. Sometimes we did it two and three weeks at a time. But every hour on the hour, wherever we were, whatever we were doing, we would pray for that person in need. What I remember most from those times was how aware we were of the presence of God all through the rest of the hour.

If you are not aware of the presence of God continually, you might try that yourself. You could even do it with your children. Set the timer and say, "When the timer dings we are going to stop for a couple of minutes.

We don't have to pray out loud, but let's just stop where we are and think about God and remember that He is with us." How precious that would be! And if you are a widow or a single person, how precious to form that habit of being aware of God. How can you walk with Him if you are not aware of His presence? You can't.

So often when I was driving, I would just start talking to God. I've found it's a perfect time to have a conversation with Him. Look for those moments when you can acknowledge His presence. Take every opportunity to include God in your life.

WALK AND TALK TOGETHER

Many years ago Chuck and I went to a pastors' conference in Medford, Oregon. My friend, Wendy Fremin, was there too. A luncheon was held for the pastors in one of the local restaurants, and Wendy and I thought we should go also, so that if any of the pastors' wives showed up they wouldn't be alone. But no other wives came, so Wendy and I ate in another part of the restaurant and then took a long walk around the town.

I have known Wendy for a long time and over the years we have eaten many meals together. But I discovered that evening that I really hadn't known her as well as I had thought. Do you know how I got to know her better? It was while we walked together. During that walk, while we wandered around town stopping in all the little shops, I discovered that Wendy liked china cups and that she only had four of them. I discovered that she collected butterfly things for her mom, because her mom loved butterflies. In fact, her mother's love of butterflies was the inspiration behind the *Butterfly* album that Wendy's band, *Children of the Day*, put out in the early years of Calvary Chapel. I hadn't known that before.

I found out so many interesting things about Wendy while we walked together. I saw how she reacted to certain things. I found out some things that pained her and some things that she disliked—all because we took the time to walk together. Once I had all that knowledge, I also had a choice to make. Knowing what Wendy liked and disliked, I could deepen our friendship by doing the things that pleased her, or bring tension into our relationship by doing things that could hurt or displease her.

You have that same choice with God. As you walk with Him and talk with Him, you'll get to know what pleases and displeases Him. He'll sometimes say, "This really pleases Me. I like it when you do this." He will tell you, "I don't want you to do that."

THE JOY OF OBEDIENCE

A friend and I once planned a crafty little scheme to surprise another friend. I thought our plan was very cute and very clever. My fellow surprise-planner and I were laughing and having a good time over our little scheme, but one afternoon while I was preparing to go someplace and I was praying about the day, the Lord spoke very strongly in my heart. He said, "Kay, I don't want you to do that." And I thought right back, *Oh Lord, but it's so funny and it will be so much fun.* Do you ever talk to the Lord like that? I thought, *Lord, everyone will laugh. It will be funny.* But the Lord said again, "Kay, I don't want you to do that. You have a choice. You can please Me, or you can choose not to please Me."

I want to please God. So I told Him that. "Well, Lord, You know I want to please You." And then He said, "You know, Kay, I don't even like the attitude that makes you want to do things like that."

I said, "Oh, You are going to deal with my attitude too, Lord?" Now He was getting down to the deeper motivations of my heart.

So, I didn't do it. I went to my friend and shared with her what the Lord had told me. She knew we needed to obey. And you know what? Pleasing God brought me a lot more joy than I would have gotten from going through with my plan. How could I find joy in something that displeased God? But the only way that I could have heard His voice and learned what pleased Him was by walking with Him. It gave Him a chance to talk to me and it gave me a chance to listen.

During our visits to Hawaii over the years, one of my favorite things to do is to take long walks with Chuck. And when Chuck comes in and says, "Hey, honey, let's go for a walk," the first thing I say—which is so typical of a woman—is, "Okay—where are we going?" I ask because I want to know if we're going to walk on the sand or on the sidewalk. On the sand I go barefoot, and I just want to know what I should wear. God reminds us in Ephesians 6:15 what we are to wear when we walk with Him. We're to have our feet fitted "with the preparation of the gospel of peace." God tells you exactly what you are supposed to wear. I appreciate that. Because with my husband, I want to know where we are going and how I should prepare.

There are two things Chuck hates when we walk together, two things that he absolutely despises. He can't stand shopping, and he can't stand coffee stops. Now, those are two of my very favorite things to do. But you see, because he has chosen to walk with me and I love him and enjoy walking with him, I don't want anything to spoil our walk. I don't ask to go shopping, and I don't ask to go into a coffee shop. When we walk together, I put aside my own desires in order to please him.

Do you do the same when you are walking with God? Do you put aside your own desires to please Him? Do you quit doing those things which would have you going one direction and Him going in another?

This goes far beyond obedience. Can you see the difference? This is the desire to please which can only be born in your heart. You must love somebody to want to please them.

When you love God as you ought to love Him, your desire to please Him will be strong enough to make you put aside your own preferences. If you only know God in the sanctuary, if you only feel His presence on Sunday morning, you aren't walking with Him. Walking with God means a continual fellowship with Him. You simply will not have this desire to put aside your own preferences if the only time you walk with Him is in the sanctuary.

THE PATH GOD CHOOSES

We used to have a dog, Tolstoy, who was a real character. He was big and white and fluffy and adorable, and we were all crazy about him. But he was a pain in the neck to take on a walk. The truth is, I didn't take him on walks—he took *me*. I used to feel like *The Flying Nun* whenever we'd go down the street. He was so strong that he could actually pull me. In fact, I once broke my toe while trying to walk with him. We used to have to put him on a leash and hold the leash very tightly. Do you know why? Tolstoy had his own idea of where he wanted to walk.

On his own, he used to get into a lot of trouble wandering around. He'd cross the street in front of cars. He'd run after a pack of mongrels. If we had let him, he probably would have run with the wrong kind of people, too. He just couldn't keep out of trouble. The dogcatcher caught him once and he had to spend a day and a night in the slammer.

God doesn't leash us. He could, but He doesn't. Instead, He gives you the privilege of free choice. But when you choose to walk with God, you give up the right to wander. He gets to choose the path you walk. But sometimes we have a little Tolstoy in us, don't we? Sometimes the

Lord chooses a path that looks like it's going to be the most boring path ever—or the most scary. But is that so? Not according to His Word. The Bible tells us that He leads us in the paths of righteousness. He leads us beside the still waters. He leads us in the paths that are best for us. How faithful God is in the paths that He has designed for you to take. He even gives us the feet of wild goats to scale the craggy mountains we couldn't climb otherwise. He gives us hinds' feet in high places, so we can get up those steep places. He is with us through the valley. He makes the crooked way straight. He takes us on the most delightful, joyous, marvelous path we could ever imagine.

In Enoch's time the people were very wicked. In Jude 14 and 15, you will read how Enoch prophesied in his times about the wickedness of the people and how God was going to come with ten thousands of His angels to destroy them for their terrible disobedience. And it wasn't that much later that Noah was born and the flood came and destroyed the whole world except for Noah and the people in the ark with him.

You might think, *Kay, it is so hard to walk with God in this day and age. You don't know the temptations and testings.* I really don't think they are all that different from the time when Enoch and Noah lived. If you read what it was like in their day, it was just as bad as it is now. People lived only for pleasure, just as most do now. And certainly in the time of Lot, homosexuality was prevalent. In fact, the cities Sodom and Gomorrah were destroyed because of it. Those were terrible, terrible days to live in. The culture was wicked—just as ours is. But even as Enoch walked with God in his day, you can walk with God today.

A CHANGE IN PERSPECTIVE

Walking with God gives you strength to live in a godless culture, because doing so changes your perspective about what you see. I can read the newspaper and watch a newscast on TV and get so depressed by what I see there. But then when I read God's Word I'm built back up again. I find new hope and a new perspective.

It's just like when we discuss things with our friends. I can have my own ideas about a certain subject and tell my opinion to a friend, only to have that friend say, "Yes, but have you ever thought about this …" and she'll bring in a whole new perspective and help me begin to see the subject in an entirely different way. As we walk with God He will say to us, "But have you thought of this? Have you thought about that? Don't you remember the Scripture? Don't you remember that promise I gave you?" Sometimes He challenges our thinking, and sometimes He gives the precise encouragement we need. "You don't have to be discouraged." "You don't have to be defeated." And so as we walk along with Him, God changes our perspective.

Medical studies have shown that walking can be a cure for depression. A daily walking regimen can reverse certain types of depression. It doesn't happen overnight, but in time, the increased circulation to the brain brings in a fresh supply of blood, balancing the chemicals in the brain. I believe it. I have found that when I am prone to depression, getting out and taking a walk makes a big difference. Especially if I include God in my walk—by reciting Scripture, praying, and just talking with Him about things I see along my walk. There's a double benefit. Not only am I being built up physically, but more importantly, spiritually.

An old hymn I love to sing is *In the Garden*:

I come to the garden alone
While the dew is still on the roses
And the voice I hear falling on my ear
The Son of God discloses.
And He walks with me, and He talks with me,
And He tells me I am His own;

> And the joy we share as we tarry there,
> None other has ever known.
>
> He speaks, and the sound of His voice,
> Is so sweet the birds hush their singing,
> And the melody that He gave to me
> Within my heart is ringing. [6]

There's a special joy we feel when we walk with God. It reminds me of the special joy Chuck and I feel when we take a walk together in Hawaii. Sometimes we play games as we walk along the beach, like deciding that we're going to walk a straight line in the sand no matter what the tide does. Every so often while we're walking in our straight line, the tide will come in and splash all over us, leaving us soppy and wet. It's crazy, but we enjoy it.

In the late afternoons, we usually start out walking away from the sun so that when we turn around, we can watch the sunset as we walk all the way back. Hawaiian sunsets are legendary. The sun is big and orange and it paints both the ocean and the sky bright orange. We share that beautiful scene together, and sometimes we share it silently. We don't have to say a word. I know what he is experiencing and he knows what I am too.

INTIMACY WITH GOD

It can be like that when you're walking with God. You have an awareness of His majesty and His power, and He suddenly seems so precious to you that you can't find words. You can only respond with silence. No words are needed. At times, the sunset has been so beautiful it has caught my breath. Have you ever been in the presence of God when you felt such a warmth and a glow that you could hardly breathe? If you've never experienced a moment like that, He wants to do that for you. He wants you to know the joy and awe of His presence.

Jesus spoke much about joy, and even prayed that we would receive it. He wanted it for us. We should have constant joy, constant wonder. Our day should be full of new discoveries about God. He wants to reveal Himself more and more, but we are so busy walking Tolstoy's path that we wander from Him. We're not in that place where we're able to listen to His voice and notice all the things He wants to point out to us along the path. We lose our awareness of His lovingkindness and goodness and gentleness.

Dr. Donald Grey Barnhouse, founder and editor of *Eternity Magazine*, shared about a trip to Greece with his wife and small child. From Corinth they traveled by train to another small city to see some archaeological discoveries. Once they arrived, they walked a mile and a half to the ruins. The walk was beautiful, and at one point they stopped for a few minutes while his wife and child rested on a large rock. Leaving them, he wandered up a little incline to explore a bit, and as he did he looked over the incline and saw a field of cyclamen flowers. He had never seen cyclamen growing wild before. Knowing how much it would delight his wife, Dr. Barnhouse picked a bunch and brought it back. When he handed her the bouquet, she was breathless with the beauty of the cyclamen. He said from then on, all through the rest of their lives together, every time they saw cyclamen there was a precious sharing of that special memory.

Dr. Barnhouse also recounted a time in the dead of winter when he and his wife were walking together in New York with a friend. Their friend happened to be walking in between them as they passed by a florist shop, where they saw in the window a cyclamen in full bloom. Dr. Barnhouse said he and his wife both saw it at the same time, but the man between them didn't even notice the cyclamen. The two of them looked at each other with a quiet expression of joy, sharing their secret memory without a word.

Do you know that God desires that same intimacy with you? Has that ever occurred to you before now? Because it's true. God wants to have those secret memories with you. You're His bride. He wants to walk through life gathering those intimate moments with you.

YOUR FIRST LOVE

Have you ever had a moment when something caught your eye and it reminded you of some glorious thing God has done for you? Have you ever felt your heart lifted up toward Him in a moment of wonder shared only by the two of you? Do you ever think back to the time you were born again when everything changed so suddenly and so wonderfully? Do that. Remember those moments. If you are going to daydream, daydream about the things of God and return to your first love.

What if a wife were to say to her husband, "I will cook for you and clean for you and I will bear and raise your children, but that is it. There will be no love between us, no joy, no wonder, no intimacy." Sadly, a lot of Christians make that speech to the Lord through their actions. They are willing to serve Him, even willing to go out and make disciples for Him, but that's it. They won't walk with Him. Just as a woman who approaches her marriage with that attitude will never know the full blessing, so too will a woman with that attitude deny herself of a rich, full, glorious relationship with God. If you choose to walk your own path, doing your own will, you will never know the beautiful, wonderful, marvelous walk you were meant to have with God—and you will never be truly pleasing to Him.

I suppose one of the sweetest stories I have ever heard about walking with Jesus is in the poem *Footprints in the Sand,* [7] which tells about a man who, when he got to heaven, looked back over the path of his life. Everywhere he had walked he could see two sets of footprints, except when the path came to a valley. There, through the valley, he saw just a single set of footprints. The man asked the Lord, "Why weren't You with me in the valley? When I needed You most, You deserted me." The Lord spoke to his heart and said, "No, I didn't desert you. I knew you couldn't make it through that valley by yourself, so I carried you."

That is what God does when you walk with Him. In those places where you can't make it by yourself, He picks you up in His loving arms and carries you. I think when we get to heaven and look back, we will all be amazed at how many times God had carried us.

The choice to have intimacy with God is yours. You can look at your walk with Him as one of service, a thing of simple obedience or disobedience—but it can be so much more. It *should* be so much more.

Beloved woman, draw near to God and He will draw near to you. Begin a walk of intimacy today, and discover how exciting, and glorious, and altogether marvelous it can be to walk closely with the One Who loves you.

Father, we desire to know You in the fullness of Your glory. We don't want to be like a bride who holds her Groom at arm's length, allowing only service between them and never intimacy. Help us to see how much more we could have with You. Open our eyes to the joys that can be ours, if we would only place our hands in Yours and begin to walk where You lead us. Draw us, Father. We want to come closer.

In Jesus' name we pray, amen.

CHAPTER

6

A LIVING SACRIFICE

I KNEW A WOMAN WHO went through a very difficult time. And one day during this troublesome time, she said to me, "I know God is punishing me."

"Oh no," I said. "He is not." And then I repeated that. "He is not. I know He isn't."

"How do you know that?" she asked. All I could tell her in response was, "I know my God."

Because I know Him, I know that He's not a God who punishes His children. My God does not operate that way. He chastens those He loves, but He does so to bring them to repentance, and to draw them closer. Punishment drives you away from Him. Punishment is for those who reject God, not for those who love Him.

What do you do when your child stumbles and falls? Do you punish that child, or do you pick him up and love him? It pains me when I see a child fall. As a matter of fact, I get almost angry, because I don't like to see children get hurt—especially when they're mine. One of our little grandkids was playing hide-and-go-seek under the kitchen table, and the inevitable happened. He got so excited that he stood straight up and hit his head. Ouch! It hurt me to see him bump his head.

Our God does not get angry at us when we stumble and fall or bump our heads. He reaches down to us. Don't ever make the mistake of thinking that because life is difficult, it means God hates you or is punishing you. He is not. He is calling you unto Himself. And He's calling you by name.

My husband has a phenomenal memory—especially when it comes to names. You can walk up to him ten years after the last time he saw you, and he will remember your name. But Chuck is only human. Once in a great while, he has a slip up—but not very often. I remember one time when one of our son's old girlfriends decided to test Chuck in this. Chuck Jr. had gone out with Terry for two years, but after they broke up we didn't see her for a long time. She came to church one night, walked up to Chuck and said, "I bet you don't remember me." And he said, "How could I ever forget you, Janine?"

"It's Terry," she said. Janine had been a different girlfriend of Chuck Jr.'s.

But God never makes that mistake. He knows each of us by name. Say that to yourself. "God knows my name." He does! He knows your circumstances, your heartaches, your problems. He knows what you need today. Not only does He know your name, but also He is near to you. He wants to be with you and see you through every trial. Let Him do that. Let Him correct you if you need it. Let Him wash you, redirect you, and then help you back on your feet. There's nothing in the world like a new beginning, and it can be yours whenever you want it. The Word of God says, "His compassions fail not. They are new every morning; great is Your faithfulness" (Lamentations 3:22-23). And we're promised in 1 John 1:9, "If we confess our sins, He is faithful and just to forgive us our sins and to cleanse us from all unrighteousness."

Think about that. At any moment you need cleansing, you can go to God, confess your sin and turn from it and you will be cleansed. How blessed we are!

THE DAY OF ATONEMENT

The Jewish mind cannot comprehend such ready forgiveness. Israel knows of only one day of cleansing, one day when they can find forgiveness for their sins—the Day of Atonement or *Yom Kippur*.

The word *kippur* has two meanings: "atonement" and "pardon for sin." In the Hebrew language, the word for "atonement" means covering. It is interesting that in the Greek, the word "atonement" means something entirely different. It means we are made one with God. It is not just the meanings of the words that differ, however. The very substance of our sacrifice differs from that of the Jews. And though Christianity has its roots in Judaism, you will see that what happened on the Day of Atonement was but a shadow of the greater event that happened on our true Day of Atonement two thousand years ago, when God's Lamb not only covered our sin, but made us one with God.

Leviticus chapter 16 describes what Aaron, the high priest, was to do during that first Day of Atonement. All the details are spelled out there.

And those details involve several references to the words "slaughter" and "blood." Since the temple is no longer standing, Jews today no longer offer animal sacrifices. But because Leviticus 16:31 and 34 say that it is to be a lasting ordinance—they observe the day without the sacrifices. They believe, wrongly, that the expiation for their sins that went on when there was blood atonement continues on today. They believe they have an ongoing atonement and pardon from those earlier blood sacrifices.

Without Jesus Christ—without the reconciliation that He made for us on the cross—there is no atonement for sin. Jesus spanned the bridge for us, enabling us to have fellowship with God. He is our High Priest who intercedes for us continually. So apart from Jesus Christ, there is no expiation for sin. This is why we are so burdened for the Jewish people, because as the prophet Isaiah wrote, they are blind.

Today, the Jewish people believe they can make atonement for themselves through fasting, prayer, and acts of charity during the month before *Yom Kippur*.

FORGIVENESS OF SINS

"What sins does God forgive us on this day?" they ask. It's interesting that the Jewish people feel God only forgives those sins that are committed by man against Him. They don't believe there is forgiveness of those sins man commits against man. Those sins aren't dealt with on this particular day—only those sins committed against God.

Knowing their belief about this, when Jesus was asked to teach the disciples how to pray, He said in the Lord's Prayer, "Forgive us our debts, as we forgive our debtors" (Matthew 6:12). And during the Sermon on the Mount, Jesus taught, "If you bring your gift to the altar, and there remember that your brother has something against you, leave your gift there before the altar, and go your way. First be reconciled to your brother, and then come and offer your gift" (Matthew 5:23-24). Jesus was telling the Jewish people that you couldn't have something against your brother and come into the presence of God and receive this full atonement.

On the Day of Atonement, pardon is asked for all of Israel—but for no one else. They believe that God only forgives the sins of the Jews on this day. It isn't for the rest of the world. One reason why they believe this is that in the *Viddui*, or confessional, many of the sins listed can only be committed by the Jewish people. For instance, if they have violated their dietary laws by eating meat and drinking milk at the same meal, they need forgiveness for that. Those laws simply don't apply to anyone outside Judaism.

On this "Sabbath of Sabbaths," Jews are to afflict their souls—meaning they are to fast from both food and water for a twenty-four hour period. The afflicting of their souls is to heighten repentance. They cannot use any ointment or perfume. They can't bathe or even brush their teeth. They cannot wear shoes or clothing made of leather, which I found to be very interesting. The reason—they don't want to be reminded of their forefathers' sin of worshiping the golden calf. I thought Chuck made a very smart observation once when he inquired about that. He asked, "Do they have to take off all their gold too?" But no, they don't.

In the synagogue it is not a day of gloom, but a day of both solemnity and optimism because they believe their sins are about to be put away from them.

YOUR REASONABLE SERVICE

You may be wondering, *Why is Kay telling me all this about the Day of Atonement?* Well, I want to make a comparison between a sacrifice that is made because you *hope* to have forgiveness, and a sacrifice that is made because you're grateful for the forgiveness you've *already received*.

Jesus was God's Lamb, sacrificed once for all. His death covered all our sins. We don't have to come trembling into the temple and offer an animal for slaughter, hoping to appease God for another year. It's done! Our own Day of Atonement happened two thousand years ago. We're cleansed in God's eyes. No more blood is required. So how should we respond to that? Romans 12:1 provides the answer.

> I beseech you therefore, brethren, by the mercies of God, that you present your bodies a living sacrifice, holy, acceptable to God, which is your reasonable service.

It is our reasonable service to offer ourselves to God as *living* sacrifices. It is a way of thanking God for offering Jesus Christ for our sins, that through Him we have this life. We have forgiveness of sins. We have justification. We have reconciliation. We have redemption and eternal life. As we remember the awful price paid for our sins, how can we do less than want to bring joy to the heart of God Who gave so much for us?

Our highest aim should be to please Him. And that, of course, is the focus of this book. I have personally never studied anything that I have enjoyed sharing with others more than this topic of pleasing God.

What propels me, what motivates me, is the fact that as I look around, I see a deep need in the church. I see so many women not walking the way God intended them to walk. I see women going through hard circumstances, or I see women in pain. I see some women who just don't know how to find the answers in the Word. And I see some who really long to go deeper with God, but they're just not sure how to do it.

This book came from a calling God placed on my heart, and out of the deep love and concern I feel for women who belong to Jesus.

A PLEASING ATTITUDE

Whenever I'm studying a topic while preparing to teach, it seems that God just brings all sorts of things along to give me illustrations. While I was studying for this teaching, Chuck and I took one of our trips to Hawaii. A lot of people back home had told me how glad they were that Chuck and I were going to get away together and have some time to rest. But it didn't turn out like that at all.

For one thing, I didn't feel well. Not only was I really exhausted, but I came down with a strep infection. Then I discovered that Chuck had scheduled a whole bunch of speaking engagements, so we only got out once or twice for a walk—and I've already told you how much I love to take walks with Chuck. So, as the kids would say, "I was all grumped out." I didn't want to do anything, because when you don't feel well, everything just seems to aggravate you. I really wanted to be alone with Chuck but the Lord didn't choose that for me—neither did Chuck. And as wives, don't those sorts of things infuriate us?

Now, right in the middle of the whole thing the Lord said to me, "Kay, you are not pleasing Me in your attitude."

I don't know why, but sometimes when the Lord says something we don't like to hear we mutter back, don't we? And I did. So I muttered back, "Lord, You know this trip was supposed to be like a honeymoon and we are supposed to be alone, spending time together. All the people back home are thinking we are having a vacation, but this is no vacation. We're running all over and seeing all these people...."

But the Lord stopped me. He said, "Kay, that doesn't matter. You are not pleasing Me."

"But, Lord ..." I persisted.

Then He said, "What do you really want to do?"

And I knew. I said, "I really want to please You."

"Okay then, Kay," He said, "Shape up."

So I did. I shaped up and I had a beautiful time. My birthday happened to come up during that trip, and on the night of my birthday, Chuck spoke at a prophecy conference. At the end of his teaching, about 250 people came to Jesus. That is about the zingiest birthday present anyone could ever have. When I saw all those people flooding down to accept Christ, all I could do was praise the Lord for what He had done.

WHAT MATTERS MOST

Pleasing God refines your life. You might feel at times that your children are impossible or your husband is impossible. Every bad thing in your world is the fault of those disobedient children or that stubborn husband. But what you really need is a change in your perspective.

While on this trip we met a couple who had the perfect marriage. Now, I really think mine is super, too. But sometimes you meet people that are so well-matched, they even look alike! This couple was like that. And they were completely tuned in to each other. They both love Jesus with all their hearts. They're both interested in the same things, and their paths walk in the same direction—no tugging or pulling at all. It is an absolutely beautiful marriage.

I would guess that only one out of a thousand marriages is like that. Most marriages are not quite that perfect. Usually two extremely opposite temperaments come together. Each completes the hole that exists in the other—and that is exactly what we need, right? "It's like I needed a slap in the face," we say sometimes. But we rebel and fight against the very things that would cause us to grow in Jesus. The solution to the difficult moments is to look unto Jesus and say, "Lord, how may I please You in this situation?" Believe me, when you do that, it works. All of a sudden it isn't his fault. It isn't the children's fault. It doesn't matter whose fault it is anymore, because all that matters is pleasing God.

I want you to take in that simple truth and let it really become a part of you. I want pleasing God to become such a habit in your life that you would "abound more and more" (1 Thessalonians 4:1). I think it is probably the quickest way to grow—outside of suffering. We grow fast in suffering, don't we? You either grow or you die. But living to please God will do the same thing. If you will allow the Holy Spirit to put this principle in operation in your life, you will grow spiritually—and quickly. Just look unto Jesus and say, "How may I please You in this?"

THE DEEPER LIFE

When I was a little girl, we used to have an expression that we learned from some carnal Christian. If we didn't like somebody we used to say, "I love that person just enough to get into heaven." That's awful, isn't it? But a lot of Christians live that way. They want to walk with God just enough to get into heaven, and that's it. There's no power, no real light in their life. They have a dull, poor witness. They're lukewarm and we know what the Lord thinks of lukewarm Christians. He said He would vomit them out of His mouth (Revelation 3:16). I don't ever want to live like that, and I don't want you to, either.

I don't believe the deeper life is only for some believers. I believe God calls each one of us to a deeper walk. He's given each of us the capacity to experience a rich, full relationship with Him, but the choice of whether or not we do that is left up to us.

People have asked me over the years, "What do you mean by 'the deeper life'? What do I do? How do I begin?"

Well, you start by being born again. Coming to Jesus is the first step, because you can't go out into the deep waters unless you first get on the ship. So you start on the shoreline, and you get on the ship, and only then can you head for deep waters.

In the simplest terms I can use, the deeper life is the life that acknowledges the lordship of Jesus Christ. It's the life that says, "Jesus, You are my Lord. I want to be under Your rule. I'm Your bondslave. I'm committed to You. Take my life, Lord, and have Your way with it."

ROMANS 12:1

Do you know the kind of person who makes that statement? A person who has taken Romans 12:1 to heart. I'm going to write it again here, because we need to read it again. Now, if you've walked with the Lord a long time you might say, "Romans 12:1—I've read it in the past. I read it a few pages ago in this very book. I've heard five hundred sermons on it. I have memorized it backwards and forwards and there is not one thing that Kay Smith can share that will be new to me." Listen, even if all that is true, I want you to read it again—but this time, read it as though you have never seen it before. Ask God to help you with that, and He will.

I, too, have read this particular Scripture many, many times. So when I sat down to study it I said, "Lord, I know this passage well. I'd like to ask You to make it brand-new to me. Would You? By Your Holy Spirit would You just bring out some things I have never seen before and present it to my heart in a special way?" And He did that for me. So let's look at Romans 12:1 with new eyes.

> I beseech you therefore, brethren, by the mercies of God, that you present your bodies a living sacrifice, holy, acceptable to God, which is your reasonable service.

When Paul writes, "I beseech you," he's saying, "I implore, I appeal, I plead, I beg you to do this thing—to give your life over completely to Jesus Christ." Our plunge into the deeper life begins here. As long as you control your own life and refuse to surrender to His lordship, you cannot grow. You just can't. A plant that says, "I'll grow by myself" and refuses sun, air, water and nutrients is a plant that will remain stunted—and will eventually die. You must surrender to the lordship of Jesus Christ if you're going to grow, and not spiritually die.

And how is Paul making his appeal? He makes it on the basis of God's mercies. Ours is a compassionate God. He had pity on us when He saw us absolutely estranged from Him—hopeless, helpless, and eternally lost. His mercy led to the cross, where His Son, Jesus Christ, made a bridge for us—that through Him we could be saved. So Paul tells us to look back at the mercies of God.

THE TEMPLE OF GOD

In the first eleven chapters of Romans, the apostle Paul teaches all that Jesus Christ has done for us. Now Paul says, "I plead with you—after all God has provided for you through the death of His Son—present your bodies to Him," or as *The Amplified Bible* says, "Make a decisive dedication of your bodies." And the word "present" in that verse is the same word used in Luke 2:22 when Jesus was brought into the temple as a baby and presented, or dedicated, unto the Lord.

I love baby dedications. I love to watch as Chuck holds a baby in his arms and presents that child to God. Have you ever presented your own body in dedication unto Jesus Christ? You can do that. You can say, "Lord, I am Yours. I present all that I am." I urge you to do that. In fact, "I beseech you therefore, sisters, by the mercies of God, that you present your bodies...." In the Greek that word for "bodies" means the entire person—the body, soul and spirit.

It is amazing how many people claiming to be born-again believers have never presented or dedicated their physical bodies to God. Instead, ungodliness takes place within what should be the dwelling place of Jesus Christ. "Oh, sure. I am born again. I go to church." But then they go out and commit sexual sin. They use the body God gave them to indulge in all kinds of things that are unbecoming to the temple of God and they think lightly of it. It's a sad, grievous thing.

Beloved woman, I beg you to present your physical body to Jesus Christ—to the Savior who endured pain, and betrayal, and shame, and death on a cross so that you could be His. Don't put anything in that body that would not bring Him pleasure. Don't dress in a way that would not bring Him pleasure. Don't offer your body to any activity that would not bring Him pleasure.

"Do you not know that you are the temple of God and the Spirit of God dwells in you?" (1 Corinthians 3:16). When I consider the fact that God chose to put this treasure in earthen vessels, I can't help but ask, "Why, why, why, Lord, did You ever choose to dwell in these unrighteous, disobedient bodies? And how could You ever take pleasure in these clay vessels?" Yet He did—and somehow He does.

"You are not your own … for you were bought at a price; therefore glorify God in your body" (1 Corinthians 6:19-20). I pray that everyone who looks at you will see a glow about you and know you are a Christian. It's evident in true Christians—it really is. I have spoken to groups where not everyone was a Christian, and I've looked out and seen blackness on some of the faces. One time while I was speaking, I saw a young lady with that blackness over her. It tore at my heart while I was sharing, and finally I felt prompted to say, "There's someone here who is filled with darkness." The young woman began to weep and weep, and after class she came to me and said, "When you started talking about that, I felt like I was clothed in darkness."

The light of Jesus Christ will shine upon the face of a Christian. I continually ask God for that. I say, "Lord, be the health of my countenance. I want people to know. When they look at me, I want them to know that I'm Your child." My son-in-law, Brian, has said that when he first saw Cheryl, he could see a purity about her. He said it was one of the things that attracted him to Cheryl. And I have seen over and over again what Jesus does to the countenance of men and women who had lived dark, hopeless, sinful lives—once He begins living in them, their very expressions change.

So make it your aim to glorify God in your body. And then present to Him your soul—that part of you that is your mind, your emotions, and your will.

PRESENT YOUR MIND TO GOD

Our minds can get so cast down. You must ask yourself, *What am I reading? What am I watching? What am I indulging in my thoughts?* Dedicate this part of yourself to Jesus. Say, "Lord, my mind is Yours. I won't set my eyes on anything that wouldn't please You. I don't want my thoughts to grieve Your heart."

Now, because we are all in process, we are going to fail at this from time to time. We will allow our minds to partake of things it shouldn't. But at that place where the Holy Spirit nudges you and says, "This is not My will for your mind. I don't want you to keep sowing those thoughts in your mind, because you will eventually reap what you have sown in today." That's the moment when you want to present your mind to God. When you sense the Holy Spirit saying, "Please turn off the TV," or "I'd like you to put down that book," or "I'd rather you put away those bitter, mean, critical thoughts," that's when you say, "Yes, Lord, I dedicate my mind to You."

PRESENT YOUR EMOTIONS TO GOD

What about your emotions? Are they under the control of the Holy Spirit? If you're Irish like me, you'd better think about handing control over to God. Otherwise, you're going to have a stroke—or at the very least, high blood pressure.

I tend to be emotional, but my husband is more logical. Together, we're a good combination. Being emotional can be a strength at times, such as when the kids were little and they would bring home their little drawings from school. Daddy would say, "Yes, that is a fine picture." And I'd say that was the greatest picture I had ever seen in my life, even though what they thought was a flower looked more like a turtle to me. But every strength has a weak side too. Sometimes spilled milk on the table and all over the floor could look like a real disaster to me.

Eventually I came to the place where I said, "Lord, I just cannot handle my emotions." And do you know what He said? "Kay, I have been waiting for you to say that. Why don't you just present them to Me?"

I said, "You mean, Lord, that You can take charge of my outbursts and my impatience, and somehow you can work by Your Holy Spirit to give me that divine control that I need?"

He said, "Yes, I can. I can do it if you will present them to Me. You've just never asked Me to take charge of your emotions, Kay."

I realized He was right. I'd walked a long time and never thought to offer God my emotions. Since then, I've offered them to Him many times. I have to do it again and again.

In all this there is a crisis experience, and there is a progressive experience. There is the moment when we say, "Lord, I am all Yours. I give myself completely to You." Our commitment begins to be worked out in our lives, but then as we falter and we stumble, we need to bring our failures to the Lord. We need to say, "Father, I present my emotions to You all over again because I haven't been doing well."

God loves it when we do that. Give your emotions to Him. Let Him control the passions of your heart. I see so many women who have not handed their emotions over to God—with devastating consequences. Their uncontrolled emotions lead them into wrong relationships and cause them to make wrong decisions. They end up going places God never intended for them to go, all because their emotions are not under the control of the Holy Spirit.

Before I married Chuck, I was very much in love with him. Although at the time I didn't know about the need to present my emotions to God, I did pray, "Lord, if Chuck Smith is not the person for me, then I surrender all my emotional responses to You." This was very difficult for me because I was already deeply in love. But I knew if Chuck was the wrong man, it would be disastrous. I'm very happy to say he was not the wrong man.

Paul urged us to surrender our bodies because he realized what you need to know: God will always do the very best for you. He created you and He knows what you need. And one of the things you need is for Him to control your emotions.

Job 5:2 is a good description of uncontrolled emotions. "For vexation and rage kill the foolish man; jealousy and indignation slay the simple" (*The Amplified Bible*). The footnote in this version says, "This was written many centuries ago, but physicians and psychiatrists today are continually emphasizing the importance of recognizing the principle it lays down if one would avoid being among the constantly increasing number of the mentally ill and those killed by avoidable illnesses." What do out-of-control emotions do? They "kill the foolish man ... and slay the simple."

The bitterness, hatred and malice you carry around are killing you, all because you refuse to present your emotions to Jesus Christ. You don't want to give them up to His control. And yet relinquishing them is the healthiest thing you can do. Did you know that every time you're angry or bitter your blood vessels contract and the blood can't flow properly through the body? That's reason enough to present your body to God.

If you have to give your emotions to God fifty times a day, do it. Do it until it becomes a Holy Spirit-controlled habit. Don't spend your emotions on fleshly pleasures. Regardless of the emotions you're dealing with—unbridled passion, inordinate affection, anger, jealousy—dedicate those to Jesus Christ and then rest in the knowledge that He can handle them so much better than you can.

PRESENT YOUR WILL TO GOD

We have a grandson named William. When he was young his daddy said that they were right to name him, "Will I am." He was one strong-willed little guy. The beautiful thing is, when William presented himself to Jesus, that willfulness became used for God's glory.

Let me ask you—who makes the decisions in your life? Are you following your own will, or the will of the Holy Spirit? Romans 6:16 clearly warns:

> Do you not know that to whom you present yourselves slaves to obey, you are that one's slaves whom you obey, whether of sin leading to death, or of obedience leading to righteousness?

The picture this verse gives is yielding your will to either God or Satan. Whatever you do, you are either pleasing God's heart or pleasing Satan. If you please yourself—against God's will—you please Satan. Your choices—in big or small things—matter to God.

WHAT WOULD YOU SACRIFICE?

I grew up in the wrong age. When I was a little girl, everything was about sacrifice, because I lived through the Depression and World War II. Now that I'm an adult, everything is *me, me, me*. I wish it had been reversed so when I was a little kid everything was *me, me, me* and I could turn now to sacrifice.

When Paul speaks of a "living sacrifice" in Romans 12:1, what does he mean? We have to first understand the word "sacrifice." A sacrifice always indicates loss to the one who is offering the sacrifice. If there's no real loss, it is not a sacrifice.

A woman once went to Jesus bringing her costliest possession and poured the contents over His head. As the expensive perfumed ointment flowed over Him, Jesus said, "Wherever this gospel is preached in the whole world, what this woman has done will also be told as a memorial to her" (Matthew 26:13). She gave the costliest thing she had. That's what God asks of you too. What is the costliest thing you could give Him?

In her book entitled *Tomorrow You Die,* [8] missionary Reona Peterson Joly tells of a time she went to Albania with the organization, Youth with a Mission (YWAM). Albania had been the first country in the world to declare itself to be atheistic. They had announced that no religion would be permitted in their country whatsoever. Particularly, they were set against Christianity and banned the preaching of the gospel—a crime punishable by death. When Reona learned of this Christian prohibition, she felt this marvelous, wonderful, glorious burden to take a friend with a tour group and leave Bibles wherever they could throughout this country.

In her hotel room one day, Reona gave a Bible to the cleaning lady who came into her room. Somehow, the local authorities discovered what

Reona had done and arrested her. She was told that by nine o'clock the next morning, she would face a firing squad.

Albania was possessed by Satan at this time, and bent on removing all traces of religion from their country. The government was known to kill priests who refused to renounce Christ by sealing them in barrels alive, and rolling them into the ocean. Reona knew she was in serious danger. When they released her—with a promise to fulfill her execution in the morning—Reona went back to her hotel room believing it was her last night alive.

Standing in her room, this young missionary had two thoughts: *If this is to be my last day of life, how should I spend it?* And, *What will I find difficult to leave behind?*

Let me ask you the same question. Not counting your loved ones, what do you find difficult to sacrifice in your life? What would you find hard to give up, should God ask you to leave it behind?

When we think about being a living sacrifice, we need to keep in mind that a person who offers a sacrifice gives up all rights to that offering. Once a sacrifice was laid on the altar in the temple, the one who offered it left it there. They didn't return to it. That offering had been devoted to God for His exclusive use—forever. And that needs to be our attitude when we present ourselves to Jesus Christ. We no longer belong to ourselves. Everything that was ours is now His. It means that God has the right to do with us whatever He wills.

THE JOY OF PLEASING

Ours is a narcissistic, self-exalting society. The deceitful propaganda constantly thrown at women today is, "Look out for yourself. Consider yourself before anyone else. If your husband is in the way, get rid of your husband. Why stay married out of obligation? That's no reason to stay. If your kids are in the way, get rid of the kids. Don't let anyone come before you."

But what did Jesus say? "If anyone desires to be first, he shall be the last of all and servant of all" (Mark 9:35). What did Paul exhort us to do? "Let nothing be done through selfish ambition or conceit, but in lowliness of mind let each esteem others better than himself" (Philippians 2:3). What is the Holy Spirit asking of us? "Present your bodies a living sacrifice, holy, acceptable to God, which is your reasonable service" (Romans 12:1).

So what does sacrifice mean to you today? Maybe it means staying in a difficult marriage. Your heart may be broken today over the way your husband treats you. But if you stay in that marriage with the thought of pleasing God, and willing to sacrifice all that you are to be obedient to God, He will bless you beyond anything you could imagine.

A woman who has learned the secret of pleasing God can get through anything. She can endure a bad marriage. She can serve those who are ungrateful day after day. I've known women in the most disastrous circumstances demonstrate a joyful heart. I have seen them reaching up, praising and thanking Jesus, all because they've learned the joy of pleasing God.

FOR YOU, LORD

I once heard about a Christian in the military who found himself in a horrible situation. He hated his job, and disliked his military brigade because of their vile behavior. One day while lying on his cot thinking about how much he despised his life, the Lord asked him, "Would you be willing to stay here and continue suffering for Me?" *For Me ... for Me ...* The man couldn't get those two words out of his mind. But then he changed those words to *"For You,"* and he said, "Yes, Lord, I can do it for You." And those two words changed everything for him. He said that every time he faced something that looked hard or even impossible, he'd say, "For You, Lord. For You." Life was no longer about pleasing others or being pleased—it was now all about pleasing God.

One of the hardest things to overcome is that situation where you've clearly been wronged. The other person is absolutely at fault and you are absolutely innocent. "Right" is on your side. But have you ever considered this is also *right* where sacrifice comes in?

A retreat speaker once told our women that when you've had a break in a relationship, regardless of who did what, you're to go to that person and say, "If I have offended you, will you please forgive me?"

Why is it that whenever you hear something about forgiveness and reconciliation, the face of that one person whom you really don't want to think about pops up on a six-foot screen right in front of your face? I saw that face—the face of a woman who had wronged me. She lived far from me, but I knew I would be seeing her soon. I said, "Lord, You know she did wrong to me. Do You really want me to go to her and say 'If I have offended you ...' when really, Lord, SHE is the one who is wrong?"

To my relief, I heard the Lord say, "No, you don't have to." A sweet feeling of peace came over me and quieted my spirit.

But about a week before I was to see this woman, I began to feel uneasy. We'd be together for several days, and I knew it would be tense. So I began to pray very desperately. "Lord, there's tension between us, and I don't like tension."

He said, "It is all right, Kay. I will take care of it."

I thought, *Oh, praise the Lord.* I prayed some more and read my Bible.

Maybe it was all the verses that kept coming through my mind, but I began to pray, "Lord, no matter who is right in this circumstance, I really do want to please You."

And I felt as though the Lord said, "If you really want to please Me, then just wait on Me. I will show you what to do."

I waited on Him all week, and it was glorious. I was so excited to see what the Lord was going to do that I floated through that week. And then finally, when the time had arrived, I found myself face to face with this woman. I said, "You know, I feel there is some tension between us."

"Yes, there is tension," she acknowledged.

I went on. "We're going to be together for the next few days and I can't go on with all this tension."

She agreed.

And then, without any warning, out of my mouth came the words, "If I have offended you ..." I thought, *Where did those words come from?* But the moment I spoke them I felt this bouncy joy.

The woman said, "As a matter of fact, you have."

In the flesh, my natural reaction would have been to defend myself. But instead, I stood there and told her I was really sorry.

Then she said, "It really wasn't you. It was your friends who offended me." That was hard to hear. As strange as it sounds, it hurt me worse than if I had been the one to offend her.

We stood together and talked things out, and it turned out to be a precious, beautiful time. But the most precious moment came when I went back to my room and I heard the Lord say, "Kay, you have pleased My heart."

Sacrifice is always a choice. God will not force you. But if the deepest desire of your heart is to please Him, you will choose to make whatever sacrifice He asks of you. And He will make something beautiful out of your obedience.

A while after this conversation, that same woman and I were praying over a painful situation in her family and we began talking about grudges. I said, "I am just not a grudge holder." And she said, "I know that—and I appreciate it." Something of Jesus had shone through, because I wanted to please the heart of God.

You know, we tend to think of hate as being the opposite of love. But that's not true. Selfishness is the opposite of love. Selfishness breaks up relationships because it demands its own way. We live in a narcissistic culture where selfishness is not only permitted, it's encouraged.

Resist that message, beloved woman. Listen instead to the Holy Spirit within you, Who wants to so transform your life that all who meet you will see the shining love of Jesus within you.

Lord, so often we want to keep little rooms for ourselves, little hidden places in our hearts where we can indulge self. But God, when we think of Your mercies, Your greatness, and Your goodness in giving Your Son, Jesus, for our sins, how can we do less than give back all that we are to You? It is such a meager gift in comparison, but it is all we have to give.

Stir us to the very depths, Lord. Show us where we're holding back. Teach us to present our whole being to You. And then, have Your way with us, Lord. May we be living sacrifices through whom You shine, that we would reveal You to a dying world.

We want to please You, Father. May it begin at the altar.

In Jesus' name we pray, amen.

7

LOVE NOT
THE WORLD

WE WERE AT THE AIRPORT getting ready to board our plane for a trip when a man glanced over at Chuck, then shot a look again, and his face just lit up. Walking over, he said, "Oh, it *is* Chuck. It is you!" He told us he had been going to Calvary Chapel Costa Mesa for four years, but was now moving to Sacramento. He said, "Every Sunday for these last four years I have wanted to come up and say hello to you, but I would see the line and change my mind—or I'd get scared and just walk the other way. But I have always wanted to say hello."

Do you know what God did? He put us right next to this man on the plane. We had a marvelous time talking with him, and we got to hear how he came to Jesus out of Buddhism. He told us that back when he was a Buddhist, he had always been afraid of flying, but he wasn't anymore. While he was telling us that, he picked up his Bible and held it closely. It was so beautiful to see how much he loved Jesus.

On that same flight, all three of the flight attendants knew Chuck. One of them said, "I've seen you on TV, Pastor Chuck." It was so funny, because the people in front of us were looking to see who she was talking to, and I just knew they were thinking, *Who in the world is that?* I wanted to say, "We're nobody!" I wanted to put a big sign on us that said, "We are nobody but Jesus' ambassadors."

As we were getting off the plane, our new friend said to Chuck, "This is one of the greatest days of my life." Well, we thought it was one of the greatest days of *our* lives to meet him.

WHAT'S YOUR RESPONSE?

Would I exchange my life in Christ for a life in this world, living according to the prince of the power of this world? Never! No matter how often we might stumble and fall, a life lived unto God is still the greatest life you could ever hope to live.

Beloved woman of God, this world is winding down. All you have to do is catch a few minutes of the evening news or glance at a newspaper to know that all the things God prophesied in His Word thousands of years ago are happening. His divine plan is unfolding before our eyes. It is coming to pass just as He said.

Truthfully, it makes me want to shake every Christian awake. I feel like a coach. I want to give everyone a big pep talk. "Listen up! The game is almost over. We're in the last quarter with just a few minutes left, and we are going to win. We know we are, because God's Word has given us the outcome. So give it all you've got! Get out there and run with all your might, with all patience, and with all endurance. Let's do as much praying, loving, and serving as we can. Let's win a big, heavy crown that we can lay at His feet when this is all over." In light of all God has done for us, don't you want this to be your response to Him?

Very early in ministry, Chuck used to teach a lot about doing things that would earn a blessing from God. But then God began to open his eyes. I remember talking with him about this one day and he said, "I'm seeing that it's not about working to receive a blessing. God has already blessed us. We just need to look at all He has done for us and then respond to Him out of gratitude. It's all about our response."

I said, "Oh, that helps me see marriage in an entirely new way."

"How's that?" he asked.

"Well, it's always been a sort of chicken-and-egg question. Does the wife submit to her husband first, and then he loves her—or does the husband love her first and she then submits to him?"

Chuck nodded.

"Well, now I know the answer," I said. "I am just the responder. You love me first, and I respond with submission. So I guess if I am not responding as I should, it is because you are not loving me as you should." With that I smiled and walked out of the room—but he knew I was just teasing him.

When Paul beseeched us in Romans 12:1 to offer ourselves as living sacrifices, he was saying, "Stop and look at all God has done for you. Don't you want to respond to Him by giving Him all you have?"

There's a great deal of work to be done in this world, and not much time left to do it. There's a harvest out there waiting to be gathered.

If we want to be effective in this world, then we need to live to please God. By living to please Him, we become the strongest influence possible to those around us. You cannot become a strong influence for righteousness any other way.

CONCENTRATE AND ELIMINATE

In her book, *Disciplines of the Beautiful Woman,* [9] Anne Ortlund wrote a section about cleaning out your closets and dresser drawers. She used two words that really sum up what we women ought to be doing in these last days—and it doesn't have anything to do with housecleaning. The two words are "concentrate" and "eliminate."

The woman who wants to please God will concentrate on bringing joy to His heart by eliminating anything that clutters her life or her walk with Him.

You know how hard it can be to find something in your closet when it's packed with clothes? Clutter costs us time. You have to push back the hangers and dig and search through all that mess. But when you get rid of the clutter, it's easy to pull out the blouse and skirt you want.

We can clutter up our lives spiritually, too. When we allow too many things to crowd our lives and steal our time, we often miss out on the things we're really supposed to be doing. I want to give you a seven-word exhortation. In your quest to unclutter your life, these seven words will help you to live simply and keep your focus on Jesus. Ready?

"Do not be conformed to this world."

Those seven words come from Romans 12:2.

> And do not be conformed to this world, but be transformed by the renewing of your mind, that you may prove what is that good and acceptable and perfect will of God.

The New Living Translation says, "Don't copy the behavior and customs of this world." *The Amplified Bible* says, "Do not be conformed to this world, this age, fashioned after and adapted to its external, superficial customs." In Barclay's commentary on Romans, he picks up on the idea of fashion.

> "Don't try to match your life to all the fashions of this world. Don't be like a chameleon which takes its color from its surroundings." [10]

Don't let the world decide what you are going to be like. In the Greek, the root word used for "conform" is *schema*, which means an outward form that varies from day to day, from year to year.

DON'T BE CONFORMED

Modesty is one such area where the outward form varies from day to day, from year to year. In the 1920s, if anybody had worn a bikini to the beach, they probably would have been put in jail for indecent exposure. Bathing suits back then actually covered a woman's body. Today, bikinis are the norm.

Words also change over the years. We use words today that we couldn't use twenty years ago. For instance, when I was expecting my children, we did not say "pregnant." You said you were "anticipating" or "expecting." I don't consider myself to be a prude, but it took me a long time to get used to saying "pregnant."

Fashions, of course, vary from day to day, from year to year—sometimes minute to minute. I remember when polyester pantsuits came out and I thought they were the greatest thing ever. I took some polyester pantsuits on a trip to Israel and they didn't wrinkle a bit. It was marvelous! But polyester is no longer fashionable. Today, people like 100% cotton. Do you see how vacillating and unstable this world is? Don't conform to it. Don't be swayed, don't be moved, don't adapt.

KINGDOM DOMINATION

Now, when the Bible speaks about the world, it's not talking about the actual planet, this world created by God. The Bible is speaking of a system of living. The Greek word is *aion*, which means "an age." Don't be conformed to this age, to the things that are going on in your world right now—the behaviors, the moral characteristics, or the value system of this generation. Don't be pressed or squeezed into its mold.

We must remember that there are two kingdoms in existence: the kingdom of light and the kingdom of darkness. God rules one, and the other is ruled by Satan. And the one Romans 12:2 refers to is the world order ruled by Satan.

The Greeks have the word *kata sarka*, which means "a life dominated by human nature at its lowest." That's what the Bible is warning us not to love. Contrast that term with *kata christon*, "a life dominated by Christ," or *kata numa*, "a life dominated by the Holy Spirit." Which kingdom dominates your life today?

Probably one of the clearest warnings against loving the world is found in 1 John 2:15, where John exhorts, "Do not love the world or the things in the world," for when you love these things you show that you do not really love God. That should be enough right there to keep you from loving the world. But John goes on:

> For all these worldly things, these evil desires—the craze for sex, the ambition to buy everything that appeals to you, and the pride that comes from wealth and importance—these are not from God. They are from this evil world itself (1 John 2:16 TLB).

The New King James Bible describes those worldly desires as "the lust of the flesh, and the lust of the eyes, and the pride of life" (1 John 2:16). Those are the same three temptations that Satan brought to Eve in the garden of

Eden (Genesis 3). And he has no new tricks, no new tactics. Still today, Satan is trying to lure women away from God with those same desires.

THE COUNTERFEIT

Why do women fall for those same old tricks? Why do they conform to the world? It happens because they mistakenly think that by conforming to the world's system, their needs will be met and they'll get all the material things they need. But Jesus tells us something different.

> But seek first the kingdom of God and His righteousness, and all these things shall be added to you (Matthew 6:33).

Jesus knew that we needed to be kept from the world's evil, so He prayed that for us.

> I do not pray that You should take them out of the world, but that You should keep them from the evil one. They are not of the world, just as I am not of the world (John 17:15-16).

Did you catch that? You are not supposed to be a part of this present evil world and its lusts, desires, ambitions and goals. You are supposed to be part of the kingdom of light, and look for all of your guidance, information, and values from that far better kingdom.

In his book *Beyond Humiliation*, J. Gregory Mantle describes the world this way:

> "The world has it own prince, its own court, its own council, its own laws, its own principles, its own maxims, its own literature. It is the counterfeit of the church of God, and the Devil 's principal weapon for lowering and poisoning the heavenly life in the individual and the church." [11]

James 4:4 warns very bluntly that if we are friends with the world, we are enemies of God. If we love this worldly system—its immorality, craving for sex, desire for fame, wealth and prestige—then we are enemies of God. That's a sobering thought.

The Living Bible translates it: "You are like an unfaithful wife who loves her husband's enemies." If you love this world system, you are like an unfaithful wife who befriends your husband's enemies.

John actually tells us,

> Do not love the world or the things in the world. If anyone loves the world, the love of the Father is not in him (1 John 2:15).

Too many people think they can have God and have the world too. They think, *I'll pop into church this Sunday, and after that I can do anything I want. I can go out and see any old movie I want and drink all I want, and even sleep around if I want to. I can live any way I please.* Not true! If you want to live that way, the love of God is not in you.

LOVE THE SANCTUARY

I saw someone who I hadn't seen in church for a while, and the subject of church came up. He said, "I don't like to go to church. I don't like to be in the sanctuary. There are too many people in there, and I always end up sitting next to some person chewing gum. It drives me crazy."

I looked at him and I said, "Do you know what you're saying? You are saying that something is wrong with your relationship with God. Because when the love of the Father is within you, you want to be with His people. You want to be in the sanctuary."

I go into our sanctuary and I just feel waves of love. Our church has grown so big now that it's not possible for me to know everybody, but I might know the person sitting next to me, and I always see several others that I know. But it doesn't matter. The love of God and the communion

LOVE NOT THE WORLD

of the Holy Spirit is so strong in that place. I'm always so blessed to be there. I could not even begin to tell you how many times in the sanctuary God has given me the answers I need for life's problems.

I also couldn't begin to tell you how often angry or irritated first-time visitors have come up to my husband after the service and said, "What you just said in your message was about me, wasn't it? My friend told you things about me!"

Sometimes Chuck doesn't even know the friend. Or it's someone he hasn't seen in six months. Chuck just smiles and says, "No, no one told me about you."

That really only leaves one conclusion. They'll think for a minute and then say, "You mean, that was God?"

Chuck would say, "Yes. God had something to say to you today."

Oh, how I love being in God's sanctuary! And I cannot understand how any Christian can feel otherwise.

Paul said, "The world has been crucified to me, and I to the world" (Galatians 6:14). Paul so walked with Jesus Christ that the world was dead unto him. And a dead thing cannot have any grip on you, can it? It can't grab you and pull you. Oh, I long to have the world completely dead unto me with no pull from it at all. I don't want to be conformed to it. I don't want to be squeezed into its mold. I want to see it as God sees it, and I want to be pleasing to the heart of God.

When your spiritual eyes are open to the fleeting, phony, competitive, selfish values of this world, you too will have no love for it. You'll have no desire to be conformed to it or by it. John says,

> The world is passing away, and the lust of it; but he who does the will of God abides forever (1 John 2:17).

CRAFTY AND SNEAKY SATAN

Have you ever stopped to think that all the evil in the world today, all the ugliness, all the heartache, was put into motion because a woman was deceived there in the garden? It worked so well then—do you think Satan has stopped trying to deceive women? He hasn't! He is still pressuring women to conform to this world system.

Most of us would agree that greed, pride, and immoral behavior show a definite love of the world, and an absence of love for God. Those things are obvious. But Satan doesn't always use the obvious things. He's usually more subtle. Genesis 3:1 reads, "The serpent was more cunning than any beast of the field which the LORD God had made." He's still crafty, still sneaky. And because he knows that you might notice a big, obvious attack, he lures you away quietly. He causes you to love some wrong thing just a little bit more today than you did yesterday. And before you know it, you have less time—and less love—for Jesus.

Satan is sneaky, crafty, and subtle. He's also a liar and a deceiver. He tempts you with things that look so desirable and so wonderful that you're convinced you just can't live without them. But that's a deception. It's all part of his plan to destroy you. Remember, "The thief does not come except to steal, and to kill, and to destroy." But what is God's plan for your life? "I have come that they may have life, and that they may have it more abundantly" (John 10:10).

Be aware of Satan's tactics. He is after you like he is after every other woman. And so he will pressure you to conform to this world—especially because you love Jesus. People think it is strange when you don't want to party with them, don't they? They can't understand.

If you work in an office and you don't appreciate their crummy jokes and you walk away, you are a very lonely person in that office. That's the very word one woman used when she was describing her job to me recently. She said, "In my office it is very lonely to walk with Jesus. When they talk about the pleasures of the world and all the stuff they did over the weekend, I'm not interested. And they aren't interested in me. It is lonely." Jesus had a lonely walk to Calvary too, didn't He? He walked all alone.

THE IDEAL WOMAN

Let's look closely at some of the ways the world pressures us to conform to it. First of all, the world sets up a standard for the ideal woman. The world has determined a very specific set of criteria for what makes a woman ideal. She must be young and thin, have a beautiful face and a perfect figure, and be well educated. It doesn't hurt if she's also wealthy and famous. And any woman who doesn't measure up (and who can, really?) is made to feel of little value. But this standard isn't God's—it comes from the prince of darkness. Satan knows that by constantly thrusting this list in front of your face, he can fill you with insecurity. He wants you to feel desperate over these things. He wants to convince you that your life will not be perfect until you measure up to the world's ideal. He whispers those lies to us, and we agree. *If only I had the perfect hairstyle, the perfect figure, the perfect education, the perfect job—then my life would be perfect.* No, it wouldn't.

I've known brilliant women who didn't know God and they were miserable. I once met a woman who had won a beauty pageant. This woman was stunningly beautiful. She had a marvelous marriage to a very wealthy man, and together they had darling children. She had it all—yet she was one of the unhappiest women I have ever met, because she didn't have Jesus. Don't you ever let Satan deceive you into thinking that if only you had it all you would be happy.

GOD'S IDEAL FOR YOU

The world admires its celebrities, but so many of those beautiful people live miserable lives—addicted to drugs or alcohol, jumping from one doomed relationship to another. If they don't die young, they spend the rest of their lives frantically trying to recapture their youth. Eventually, they're all replaced with new beautiful people. It's the way of the world. It's ugly and it will never satisfy.

Have you ever gone into a room wearing pointed-toed shoes when round shoes were the vogue? You really have to walk closely with Jesus not to care about those things. If you are ruled by the kingdom of light, you are free from those senseless worries. You don't have to become anorexic. You don't have to spend money on expensive clothes that go out of style next week. You can be free from *all* of it.

God has a better plan for you. Instead of fretting about whether or not you're measuring up to the world's ridiculous standards, check yourself against God's standards. Ask yourself, *What is God's ideal for me? What qualities and characteristics does He want woven into my life? What does He want me to be like? Is it important to God if I am beautiful? Is it important to Him if I am thin? In what ways would He like me to change?*

When I was a young wife, the Scripture that helped me most was 1 Peter 3:3-4.

> Do not let your adornment be merely outward—arranging the hair, wearing gold, or putting on fine apparel—rather let it be the hidden person of the heart, with the incorruptible beauty of a gentle and quiet spirit, which is very precious in the sight of God.

That kind of deep beauty was seen in the saintly women of old who trusted God. That is God's ideal for you. That is what He wants for you. And you know, it is so freeing.

CLOTHES

For some reason, when I was little my mother didn't think it was important for me to have nice school clothes. I had beautiful clothes for church, but crummy clothes for school. I don't know why she did that, but she did. I also had an aunt who used to sew things for me—sewing some of the strangest looking outfits.

As if that wasn't bad enough, I was a skinny little thing with sore throats all of the time in the fifth and sixth grades. Everybody wore bobby socks, but not Kay Johnson. No, I wore black cotton bloomers that came almost to my knees and showed whenever my dresses moved, and I had to wear heavy, black cotton hose. I would go to school just feeling miserable. It took me years to get over that.

When my parents died I received an inheritance. Do you know what I spent most of it on? Clothes. But when the inheritance was gone, the spending was over. I learned that I had to live on what Chuck made and I couldn't run out and buy new clothes every time the desire struck me. After a while, I wore the same dress Sunday after Sunday, but do you know what? I found such a freedom in it. God released me from that neediness, and it has never clutched me again.

When you walk according to the principles of the kingdom of darkness, anxiety grips your life. A competitive spirit takes over, like a chain that just keeps winding tighter around your body.

Jesus came to set you free. He came to deliver you from all those things that try to press in and conform you to the world's mold. God sets the standard for your life, and when you obey Him and grow into the woman He wants you to be, you will be pleasing to Him. He'll create a beauty in you that will influence everyone you come in contact with. He'll use you to bless and influence your family. God can even use you to be the tool to reach your unsaved husband.

GUARD YOURSELF

On top of all the other pressures already mentioned, the world is pressing women to conform morally. Everywhere you look, the message to women is, "Go out and have all the fun you want. Be as promiscuous as you want—it won't hurt anybody." Don't you believe that. It's a lie right out of the pit. Women were not created by God to live that way. He created us to want love, protection, and caring. When a woman has these brief encounters with men she is only wounding herself emotionally. There's no fulfillment in that kind of life, and you cannot live that way without collecting scars.

Beware of the pressure to conform morally. Guard yourself. When the first evil seed drops in your mind, deal with it right then and there. Don't let anything take root in your mind which would bear harmful fruit in your behavior—and in your life.

We live in a world whose motto is: "Me first. It's my life and I'm going to live it to the hilt." And when that's your philosophy, other people get hurt.

We're living in a culture that doesn't understand or appreciate a woman who chooses to stay home with her children. Now, I know that for some women it's an economic necessity to work outside the home to help put food on the table. I worked a time or two when my children were very little, but I only did it for a short time, and I didn't like it. The moment we could afford it, I quit. Sometimes, you have to work because it's a necessity, but in many cases, it's not. It's just a woman choosing her career or her freedom over being home with her little ones.

SACRIFICES

Staying home is a sacrifice, but it is a sacrifice you will never regret making. I am so glad I was home with my children. To this day all four of my children say, "Mom, it was so nice to come home from school and find you waiting for us." It is awful to come home to an empty house.

We once had next-door neighbors where the mother was always gone and the kids were always alone. Those were the loneliest kids in the neighborhood, and it just broke my heart. My daughter, Cheryl, was the same age as one of the kids and I used to get out in the evenings with the two of them and rollerskate. I almost got caught once when I didn't realize that a church board meeting was going on in the house on the other side of us. I only found out because I saw one of the board members pulling up to the neighbor's house. These were board members from my church! And here I am, the cuckoo preacher's wife, out rollerskating with the kids. I was in such a hurry to get out of sight that I rolled right through my front room, carpet and all, with my rollerskates on.

You have those children such a short time. Be with them, play with them, teach them, and love them. Don't give them over to somebody else who does not love them as much as you do and will not care for them as well as you do. Live without a few things. I know, and it turns out to be a blessing. It really does. Even early in Chuck's ministry, when we didn't have much, we still had so much love. We really enjoyed each other, and enjoyed all the fun things we did as a family. We had each other and we had Jesus and we dwelt in the kingdom of light.

Remember this: fulfillment never comes through pleasing yourself. It comes through walking with Jesus and living to please Him. It comes through sacrifice.

Now, you might be thinking, *Kay, I think I really am walking with Him. I don't think I am at all conformed to the world.* I pray that you're right. But here are a few little checkpoints, just to be sure.

CHECKPOINTS

First of all, what do you really love? If you had to leave your home suddenly, aside from the people you love, what *things* would you hate to leave behind? Your answer to that will tell you what you really love most in your life. Nobody knows but you and Jesus, so be completely honest with Him. Ask God to show you exactly what's in your heart.

Secondly, what activities do you really love doing? When you have some free time, what do you like to do best of all? Now look at that activity and ask if it belongs in the kingdom of light or in the kingdom of darkness.

Up until the time I was eleven, my parents were very spiritually-minded. On Sundays, we did nothing except go to church, and then come home and rest. I could read the funnies in the paper, but I wasn't allowed to work or play or do anything. But then one Sunday, my parents decided we would go to the beach. And on the way there, we had a flat tire. I vividly remember my mom and dad talking together and saying, "This is God's judgment. We've sinned. It's His punishment because we were going to the beach on a Sunday." What that ingrained in my mind was, *On Sunday, I have got to be careful.* Even when I didn't walk with the Lord, I would still feel guilty if I did anything on Sunday.

When I met Chuck, he and his family and I all went to church together one Sunday morning. While driving back to his house, someone said, "Let's go to the beach." I thought, *Oh, the beach. I hope we don't get a flat tire.* But we went to the beach and we had a super time. In fact, Mom and Dad Smith loved to spend most Sunday afternoons walking along the shore together. Watching them, I began to see things differently.

Leisure isn't wrong. Going to the beach is not wrong—even on a Sunday. But the question is whether your leisure activity is something you can do in the light, or something you want to do in the darkness, hoping no one else sees you. Is your free time pleasing to God?

YOUR GREATEST DELIGHT

I would never think to tell you what you can and can't do, unless the activity was sinful. But the Holy Spirit has the right to tell you. And He wants to minister directly to your heart.

What brings you joy and satisfaction? What is your greatest delight? What makes you happy? Is it a material thing, like a ten-carat diamond or a nice new car? Is it a relationship, one that is so important that if that person were out of your life, they'd take all your joy with them? Or can you be happy with just a single verse of Scripture that speaks to your heart?

Job said, "I have treasured the words of His mouth more than my necessary food" (Job 23:12). Think of how we love to eat. I'm especially fond of hot fudge sundaes—gooey, sugary hot fudge sundaes. They're so good they're bad, you know? But no matter how much I like hot fudge sundaes, the Word of God is infinitely more desirable to me. His Word is the joy and rejoicing of my heart. It lifts me like nothing else can on this earth.

Jesus delighted to do the Father's will. I hope you can say it's your delight too.

WHAT ARE YOUR GOALS?

Next, what are your goals? Paul's goal was, "that I may know Him" (Philippians 3:10). He talked about the power of Jesus' resurrection and the fellowship of His suffering, and then Paul added a second goal, "being conformed to His death." That's a real walk with Jesus. No wonder he could say, "The world has been crucified to me, and I to the world" (Galatians 6:14). The world no longer had any hold on him.

David's goal was to bear God's image. He said, "I shall be satisfied when I awake in Your likeness" (Psalm 17:15). Doesn't that sound beautiful? Is that one of your goals today, to awaken in the likeness of Jesus?

Have you ever watched a program or a movie where everyone was so beautiful that you thought you were beautiful too? Then you pass by a mirror and see yourself and you think, *Oh no, I don't look like them after all!* You know, the Word tells us that as we behold Jesus and as we gaze upon Him, we are actually changed into His likeness. We become like Him. We take on His qualities.

THE CRISIS TEST

God loves us so much that sometimes He allows crises in our lives to awaken us to this question: Are you being conformed to the world, or conformed to Jesus Christ? Think about how quickly death brings this issue into focus. For those sitting at the funeral of a loved one, the world's value system suddenly means nothing. For that moment, they catch a tiny glimpse of what life is really all about. Too many people, though, go right back to their old ways when the funeral is over, right after they've had that glimpse of the kingdom of light. They pick up the chains and bind themselves all up again. They could have grown. They could have been freed eternally, but they refused the lesson of the crisis.

I personally believe that every single crisis I've gone through could have been used for my growth had I allowed it. Every one. The longer I've walked with the Lord, the more I've learned to welcome whatever He brings, understanding His purpose. A crisis conforms me to the image of God and it releases the world's hold on me.

A friend of mine is passionate about antiques—so much so that God began to deal with her about it. One day she was praying, "Oh Jesus, I want to love You more than any antique in this whole wide world." She had shared that she discovered a special joy in shopping for an antique but *not* actually buying it. She said sometimes she'd have the money and desire to buy something, but out of her love for Jesus she would say, "Oh, Jesus, I love You more than this antique," and just walk right by.

Now, you might think, *Who loves antiques more than Jesus?* But listen, beloved sister in Christ, misplaced love can be very subtle. We know the first commandment is, "You shall have no other gods before Me," but do we have gods? It can be a person. It can be a possession. It can be a passion. We can be conformed to this world and not even be aware of it.

A saint of old used to pray, "Lord, put a thorn in every enjoyment that is not of You." That's a serious prayer. Only a woman truly determined to please her God would pray that. I hope you will.

Father, we ask first for conviction, that if there is any part of our lives that we have allowed to be pressed and shaped by the world, You would shine Your light on it. And then, Lord, give us the strength and the desire to hand that thing over to You. Free us, Jesus. Release us from the world's hold, and draw us to Yourself. We don't want anything to matter to us more than You.

In Your precious name we pray, amen.

8

RENEW
YOUR MIND

I THINK EVERY CHRISTIAN WOMAN ought to find a spot in her home where she can hang two pictures: one of a caterpillar and one of a butterfly. One is earthbound, the other is free. A butterfly can soar. It can fly. It's not bound by anything on earth because it's been transformed.

God wants to cause a transformation in you. "And do not be conformed to this world, *but be transformed by the renewing of your mind ..."* (Romans 12:2).

The Greek word for "transformation" is *metamorfousthe,* from which we get the English word "metamorphosis." And what do you think of when you hear the word "metamorphosis"? Well, think back to high school biology and you think, *the caterpillar and the butterfly*. Metamorphosis is the transformation from one state to the next, like a caterpillar changing into a butterfly. It implies change.

This same Greek word was used to describe Jesus in Matthew 17:2 when He was transfigured before His disciples on the mountain. *The Amplified Bible* says,

> And His appearance underwent a change in their presence; and His face shone clear and bright like the sun, and His clothing became as white as light.

TRANSFORMED

Transformation should have that same effect in your life. You should be so changed that when the world looks at you, they can see something of Christ in you. Second Corinthians 3:18 tells us,

> But we all, with unveiled face, beholding as in a mirror the glory of the Lord, are being transformed into the same image from glory to glory, just as by the Spirit of the Lord.

The change in us is to be as dramatic and real as the transformation witnessed by those with Jesus on that mountaintop. And it will happen, as the Bible says, "through the renewing of your mind."

I find that so interesting. God could have easily said, "You will be transformed by going to a women's retreat on a mountaintop." After all, Jesus was transfigured while on a mountaintop with just a few of His disciples. I think it would be marvelous if it worked that way for us, wouldn't you? I love the mountaintop experience. And, of course, we do experience transformation during our retreats. How could you not? We're together with other Christian women loving Jesus, we're in the Word the whole time, we're praying, we're seeking God, and we're receiving all sorts of wonderful things from Him the moment we arrive. But this is not the transformation God is speaking to us about through Paul.

In the Old Testament we read about a man named Naaman who was the army commander for the king of Syria. Second Kings 5:1 reveals, "He was also a mighty man of valor, but a leper." All throughout the Bible, we discover leprosy is a symbol of sin.

Elisha the prophet, having compassion on Naaman's plight, instructed Naaman to go dunk himself in the muddy Jordan River seven times, and he would be healed. Naaman did just that, and the Word says, "His flesh was restored like the flesh of a little child, and he was clean" (2 Kings 5:14).

THE RENEWED MIND

Wouldn't that be a wonderful way to be transformed? We could all just make a trek to Israel and dunk ourselves in the muddy Jordan River seven times. We'd get rid of all our sins and experience our transformation. But, no, God wants to bring it about another way—not through some great ritual, but by the renewing of your mind. And in the long run, though that sounds simpler, it's actually much harder than climbing a mountain or jumping in the river, because it requires that we cooperate with the Holy Spirit.

To renew means to make new. When the mind is renewed, it means a complete change in our thoughts, desires, values, imaginations, dreams, meditations, intellectual pursuits, and reasoning that God desires for us to have. It is very different from the world.

We are exhorted in Philippians 2:5, "Let this mind be in you which was also in Christ Jesus." There could not possibly be a sharper contrast between the thinking of this world and the mind of Christ. The mind of the world is self-seeking, envious, lustful, and competitive—all the things that do not please the heart of God. Compare that to the description of Christ's mind in Philippians 2:6-8:

> Who, being in the form of God, did not consider it robbery to be equal with God, but made Himself of no reputation, taking the form of a bondservant, and coming in the likeness of men. And being found in appearance as a man, He humbled Himself and became obedient to the point of death, even the death of the cross.

We see no selfishness here, no competitiveness. Instead, we see an attitude of humility, a willingness to serve, and obedience unto death. This is absolutely alien to the mind of this age.

HOLY SPIRIT COOPERATION

Mind regeneration, which is a work of the Holy Spirit, is accomplished as you present your entire self to God—your physical body, your mind, emotions and will. The renewal of your mind affects your entire being. Something amazing happens to you when the Holy Spirit regenerates your mind. Suddenly, you hate things you once loved. Very often this happens when a person is born again. But as we spoke about in the last chapter, there is constant pressure to conform to the world. Sometimes you go back to those things you once renounced. You need that transformation, that regeneration.

As the Holy Spirit works in your life, you have a part as well. You're to cooperate. Colossians 3:2 exhorts, "Set your mind on things above." *The King James Version* says, "Set your affection on things above, not on things on the earth." The Holy Spirit gives you the power to set your mind on things above, but you have the choice whether or not you fantasize and think about the things on this earth. When you entertain thoughts of, *If I only had this,* or *If I just had him,* or any other "if only" thoughts, your mind is set on earthly things. But God's power is within you—no longer a slave of your passions, nor are you chained to the world anymore. You've been set free from the world. You can choose.

The characteristics of the unregenerate mind—selfishness, envy, conceit, vanity, lust, maliciousness—often describe the woman who has given herself over to the world. This is the woman who has allowed herself to be pressed into the world's mold. It is not enough to be set free by the power of the Holy Spirit. You must submit yourself willingly to God and, as a child of the light, refuse to allow your mind to be conformed or shaped by this world's thinking.

YOU ARE WHAT YOU THINK

Why do you suppose God chose this particular way of transforming us—renewing our minds—instead of sending us to a mountaintop? Proverbs 23:7 reveals, "For as [a man] thinks in his heart, so is he." This particular proverb admonishes the man filled with God's wisdom not to have anything to do with an evil man because it says, "As he thinks in his heart, so he is."

What you think upon, you become. For instance, if you think bitter, mean thoughts, you become a bitter, mean person, don't you? Have you ever started out a day all cheerful and happy, but then a mean thought came into your mind and suddenly your whole countenance changed? You pass by a mirror and see a grumpy, mean woman staring back at you. And you think, *Where did she come from?* The change happened because you first thought it in your mind, and then your face began to reflect it.

Or maybe you have a wonderful, happy marriage and you just adore your husband. But a friend calls you one day, and she's furious with her husband all the way down to the shoes he wore that day. She can't stand him. And what happens? By the end of that conversation you're mad at your husband and you don't like his shoes, either. What a powerful effect the un-renewed mind has on others! As you think, so you are—and you usually end up rubbing off on other people.

DESIRES STIR THE FLESH

The second reason why God chose the mind as the starting place of regeneration is because the original sin began in the mind. It was conceived first in Eve's mind, and then it worked out in her behavior. This is why it's so important to keep our minds under the control of the Holy Spirit.

Often, the desire to do something can start with a stirring in the flesh. For instance, my stomach can start doing funny things and then it relays a message to my brain saying, "I'm hungry." But the decision of whether or not I'm going to eat happens in my mind. Now, I can give in to my stomach. The problem is sometimes we have false appetites, don't we? Have you ever said you were hungry when you knew you really weren't? But we have that chocolate anyway. The mind decided to do it. It is amazing how often we are led by our appetites.

Eve's sin was conceived in her mind. Her surroundings were idyllic. She lived in a place of utter beauty and had all she could want, including an intimate, face-to-face relationship with God. But she indulged Satan when he began talking to her. She listened while he planted doubt about God's goodness and integrity.

I'm afraid there is a little bit of Eve in every one of us—maybe even a lot. The same things that deceived Eve deceive us, and we let it happen. You must always remember that tendency. Always be aware of Satan and his tired, old tactics.

THIRTY-FIVE SECONDS

I think when Eve began her dialogue with the serpent, she probably thought, *This is no big deal. I can handle this little snake. He's hanging from a tree—what can he possibly do?* I can just imagine the scene. Do you do the same? Do you think, *A little conversation with the world won't hurt?* And just like that, you've been deceived into having a dangerous dialogue with this present evil world. You watch that movie, or you go into that bar. You enter into that relationship that grieves the heart of God. All because you thought you could handle it. That's where an unregenerate mind leads you.

Eve's encounter with the serpent caused agony to God's heart and led to the crucifixion of His Son. *The King James Version* records our paradise lost in just 128 words. This is not a long conversation. It probably didn't last much more than a minute. Just out of curiosity, I read the passage as it is written. Do you know how long it took Satan to deceive Eve, bringing all this pain and suffering into the world? Thirty-five seconds. Pretty thought-provoking, isn't it?

It doesn't take hours to conform to the world's system. It only takes a moment. In just that time—an unguarded moment when you've allowed yourself to watch or partake of something you shouldn't—seeds can be planted. And those seeds, if left to take root and grow, can bear fruit that will destroy your life.

You will never be transformed as long as your mind thinks as the world thinks. Be selective about what you put into your mind. If there's a chance that what you're about to watch or do will displease God, then just don't do it. Consider that choice a sacrifice you can offer Him out of your love and gratitude.

TRUTH VERSUS LIES

Thirdly, God chose the mind as the place where transformation begins because that's where we're most under assault by our culture. You can walk up to any newsstand and scan the covers of magazines, and you will find articles aimed at shaping the minds of women. You are told what you should think about marriage, about intimacy, about parenting, your physical health, and your self-esteem. You're told how to wear your hair, stretch a dollar, clean the toilet, save the environment, have a guilt-free affair, and justify an abortion. Whatever the topic, there is a team of "experts" ready to shape your values and modify your behavior. Is it clear that a battle is waging over you? The world wants to dominate you and form you into its image. God wants to free you and make you into His. The thing to remember is that this is not just a battle between two contrary viewpoints. This is a battle between the truth and a lie.

Many years ago a popular women's magazine, written for women between the ages of eighteen and thirty-four, published the results of a survey compiled from 106,000 women. One of the statistics was that one out of every two married women has had an affair. The second statistic was that forty-one percent of those same women said that the affair didn't affect their marriage. Some actually said it *helped* their marriage! Malarkey—it's an outright lie.

That lie gets swallowed whole by those who read it. Among those readers is some sweet little gal who has never had an affair. But she reads that survey and all of a sudden thinks she's missing out on something. And since it says it won't hurt your marriage and might actually help it, why not give adultery a try? Lies, lies, lies—coming straight from the pit. And women are buying and believing them.

Some Christian women believe the world's lies because they've left themselves open to that influence. They've never offered themselves—body, mind, soul and spirit—as living sacrifices unto God; and therefore, they are vulnerable to deception.

If you do not let God renew your mind, you'll let the world reshape your mind—and the world will reshape it to its own liking. Let me ask you: Does the world teach you about morality? Does the world encourage you to walk with Jesus? Does it uphold biblical truths? You know the answer to that—absolutely not.

WE'RE DIFFERENT

The world assaults even our most basic biblical beliefs; for instance, the fact that God created men and women to be different. We have different bodies, different emotional needs, and different roles in marriage. In Ephesians 5:33 we're told,

> Let each one of you in particular so love his wife as himself, and let the wife see that she respects her husband.

Isn't that clear? We have different roles and different responsibilities. Doesn't it stand to reason that we are different? And God made it so. But the world will tell you that the only reason boys and girls grow up to be different is because we "condition" them to be different. And what powerful tool do we use to do this role-conditioning? Toys. We give dolls to little girls and trucks to little boys and that makes them think they're different. I have got to say, those must be some powerful toys if they can make boys become macho and girls become nurturing.

What is the truth? The truth is that God created women to bear children and nurture them. God decided women would be nurturers. But the world wants to override God. "We think men should nurture the children."

Chuck is a marvelous dad. When our children were babies, he loved to pick them up and carry them around the house. His dad was the same way and so are my boys. Changing a diaper didn't bother Chuck a bit. My husband did it, his dad did it, and my boys did it. They are nurturing fathers in the sense that they participated in the care and raising of their children. And I am 100 percent for that. But I do not believe the men are supposed to let the women go out to face this jungle of a world while they stay home to take care of the children. Now, there are cases of sickness or disability where a man can't work and he is forced to stay home, but I haven't personally met one man yet who would rather do that. Men were created by God to go out into the world to work and support and protect their family.

THE MIND BATTLE

There is a warfare waging for control of your mind, and unless you are under the renewing power of the Holy Spirit, you'll be deceived by the world's lies. If you want to see how dark and how dangerous this is, read Romans chapter 1, which describes what happens to those who knew God but didn't acknowledge Him as God.

> Even as they did not like to retain God in their knowledge, God gave them over to a debased mind, to do those things which are not fitting; being filled with all unrighteousness, sexual immorality, wickedness, covetousness, maliciousness; full of envy, murder, strife, deceit, evil-mindedness; they are whisperers, backbiters, haters of God, violent, proud, boasters, inventors of evil things, disobedient to parents, undiscerning, untrustworthy, unloving, unforgiving, unmerciful; who, knowing the righteous judgment of God, that those who practice such things are deserving of death, not only do the same but also approve of those who practice them (Romans 1:28-32).

The thought of being turned over to a "debased mind" is just horrific, isn't it? Doesn't that make you stop and think about the seriousness of this? Some versions say "reprobate mind," which means a mind void of judgment. The people described in this passage can no longer tell right from wrong.

Romans 8:5 describes the warfare between the flesh and the Spirit.

> For those who live according to the flesh set their minds on the things of the flesh, but those who live according to the Spirit, the things of the Spirit.

The choice is very, very clear—and mercifully simple. If you want to bring joy and pleasure to the heart of God, you will set your mind on the things of the Spirit. You will offer your mind to be renewed and transformed.

WHAT'S YOUR PART?

So what is your part in this transformation? First, you must be in obedience to Romans 12:1. You must present your entire self to God so His Spirit can create in you the desires and attitudes that please Him. We cannot have our minds, emotions, and will under the control of the flesh and expect to have a transformed life.

Secondly, find out through His Word what you should be thinking about. There are plenty of Scriptures that will tell you. It would be great to get yourself a notebook and start keeping a list of these verses as you come across them.

One that I love for its simplicity is Colossians 3:2: "Set your mind on things above, not on things on the earth." That's pretty clear, isn't it? It's so much better to contemplate the things of God than to dwell on thoughts of this world.

Philippians 4:8 is a beautiful verse.

> Whatever things are true, whatever things are noble, whatever things are just, whatever things are pure, whatever things are lovely, whatever things are of good report, if there is any virtue and if there is anything praiseworthy—meditate on these things.

This verse has helped me immeasurably. When black and sordid things happened over the years, and my mind would get pulled toward thinking about them, God would stop me and say, "Kay, I don't want you to think about those other things. I want you to put your mind on better things." And He'd remind me of this verse.

There are so many lovely, pure, praiseworthy things to think about. Think on the goodness of God. Think of the parting of the Red Sea and the Israelites walking through the Jordan on dry land. Think about Jesus and what He said to His disciples and all the precious things He did when He was on earth. Think about the day of your salvation, the moments when you've felt God's nearness, and the blessings He's given you. In fact, it would be wonderful to keep a notebook of all these praiseworthy things too!

Joshua 1:8 is a verse with both practical application and a promised blessing. Just before Joshua went into battle—no doubt feeling fearful—God spoke to him, saying,

> This Book of the Law shall not depart from your mouth, but you shall meditate in it day and night, that you may observe to do according to all that is written in it. For then you will make your way prosperous, and then you will have good success.

This is true for you too. If you think on God's Word day and night, God will prosper you. Now, it may not be in the great wealth of this world, but you will be so prospered spiritually that there isn't a possession on this earth that can compare.

Psalm 1:1-3 also has a promise for the one who thinks on the right things.

> Blessed is the man who walks not in the counsel of the ungodly, nor stands in the path of sinners, nor sits in the seat of the scornful; But his delight is in the law of the LORD, and in His law he meditates day and night. He shall be like a tree planted by the rivers of water, that brings forth its fruit in its season, whose leaf also shall not wither; and whatever he does shall prosper.

CAPTIVATE YOUR THOUGHTS

The third step in renewing your mind is to refuse—refuse to fill your mind with things that would displease God's heart. Refuse to think about anything that is contrary to God's will for you. Truthfully, if you are doing step two and filling your mind with all the right things, this step will almost take care of itself. They say that the best way to break a bad habit is to replace it with a good habit. So, in order to make this step easier, go back and do step two.

This step is where some sacrifice is required. When I think of the word "sacrifice," I think about Jesus hanging on Calvary. That's true sacrifice, and it really makes the idea of giving up a TV program or a book or a conversation pale in comparison. It almost seems wrong to use the word "sacrifice" for those things. And yet that's what we need to do. Refuse to put anything in your mind that God wouldn't want in there.

Step four is to ask the Holy Spirit to alert you whenever you begin indulging in wrong thoughts or fantasies. Ask Him to convict you the moment you begin to entertain anything that would displease Him, keeping you from the transformation in your life that He desires. You don't want to continue being a caterpillar. Keep that picture in your mind. Tell yourself, *When I think on these wrong things, I am a caterpillar. When I think on God and the things of God, I am a butterfly.* Wouldn't you rather be a butterfly?

If you find it is a real battle to cease from those thoughts or fantasies, you need to pray fervently. Second Corinthians 10:4-5 says,

> The weapons of our warfare are not carnal but mighty in God for pulling down strongholds, casting down arguments and every high thing that exalts itself against the knowledge of God, bringing every thought into captivity to the obedience of Christ.

That's what we want. We want to bring our thoughts into captivity. And the weapons of our warfare are prayer and the Word of God. Remember this, dear sister in Christ—you cannot help what comes into your mind, but you dare not let it find lodging there.

We want to be convicted, don't we? I don't mean this in a rhetorical way—I am really asking. Do you want to be convicted by God? We recite Psalm 139:23-24, which says, "Search me, O God, and know my heart; try me and know my thoughts; and see if there be any wicked way in me." We say those words, but do we really mean them? Are we bold enough to say, "Know my thoughts, Lord. And while You are looking, see if there is anything wicked in my thoughts, anything that grieves You or brings pain to Your heart."

If our thoughts were put up on a screen for all the world to see, we would probably cringe in shame. And yet God knows every one of our thoughts.

When my son, Jeff, was about two years old, Janette and Chuck Jr. used to say to him, "Jeff, let's play hide-and-seek." And he would just stand right where he was and close his eyes. He thought that if he couldn't see us, we couldn't see him. We're that way with the Lord. Because we can't see Him, we think He can't see us. But He can. Rather than be horrified by that thought, realize that God sees all your flaws and knows all your thoughts, yet He *still* loves you and chooses you for His own! Doesn't that help you to trust Him?

The result of trusting God to cleanse you from all the wickedness that displeases Him is this: you undergo a beautiful transformation. You change from a groveling caterpillar to a lovely butterfly. You gain the freedom to soar, and to captivate others with your God-given beauty. The sight of a delicate, almost weightless butterfly always makes you catch your breath, doesn't it?

THINK UPON GOD

G. Campbell Morgan said, "Fear was the first emotional consequence of Eve's dialogue which led her to sin." [12] I hate fear. I hate it in any form. I don't mean godly fear—an awe, a respect and a reverence for God—I mean the kind of fear that just makes you afraid, the kind of fear that keeps you up at night.

I used to wake up at night terrified there was a burglar in the house. I really don't know how Chuck endured it. He found a cartoon once that showed a burglar who had crept into a house and was stealing the silver. Hearing a noise, the husband went downstairs, found the burglar, and took him by the hand. "Would you please come up and meet my wife?" he said. "She's been wanting to meet you for years." Chuck thought that was pretty funny.

At other times, though, I've been fearful over something real. During some of the darkest trials of our life, I've awakened at night crying out to God. And every time, His Word has come into my mind and I've been filled with peace. I've been able to say, "Oh, thank You, Jesus," and fall right back to sleep.

We need to fill our minds with His Word. When our mind is renewed and we think only upon those things that God wants us to think, we will have peace. Fear will scatter and trust will take its place. And we will begin to joyfully cooperate with the Holy Spirit in all that He desires to do in our lives.

RENEW DAILY

Remember in chapter 6, I shared with you about Reona Peterson Joly, who brought Bibles into Albania. Reona shared her story at one of our church retreats. She detailed the night she was caught giving a Bible to the hotel cleaning woman. She was taken before a group of interrogators, who denied her food and water, and had spent hours badgering her with questions. Early on in the interrogation they told her, "Tomorrow, you die," so she endured that long night of questioning with the knowledge that she had only a few hours to live.

Despite that, Reona felt such a peace. She said, "I didn't gain that peace there in the interrogation room. You know where I got this peace from God? I received it from the Psalms, from my daily devotions. One day I was reading Psalm 23 and verse 4 came off the page."

Yea, though I walk through the valley of the shadow of death, I will fear no evil: for You are with me.

It was there, during her devotional time, that God began preparing Reona in her heart and mind so she could stand in her time of trial. Many mighty men have been broken or brainwashed by interrogators, but God protected Reona's mind through the washing of His Word. And in the end, God delivered Reona from being executed.

When your mind is centered on Jesus Christ, when it is renewed on a daily basis through meditation on His Word, through prayer, through refusing the world's garbage, then in those times of stress and trials and heartache, you too will stand strong, peaceful, and victorious in Him.

I can share these truths, O Lord, under Your anointing, but I can't make anyone walk in it. So I ask that Your Holy Spirit convince us of the truth You've brought forth. Open our eyes to the fact that the world is warring for our minds. Cause us to long daily for renewal, that every choice we make will be in conformity to Your will and Your plan for us.

Transform us, Father.

In Your precious name we pray, amen.

CHAPTER

9

THE HEART
OF WORSHIP

THE STORY IS TOLD ABOUT two angels who came to earth with two great, big baskets. One was to collect all the prayers of the people, and the other was to collect their praises. The angels went to and fro across the earth, and when they had finished their tasks, the basket of prayer was piled high with requests. But the basket of praise was only scantly filled.

If you were to send up baskets of prayer and praise to the Lord today, would your requests outweigh your worship?

Take a moment with me as we enter into the school of worship. Worship is one of the most important actions we will ever do, since worship is a response to the majesty of God. It is recognition of His nature, His attributes, and His mighty deeds. It is an acknowledgment of the lordship of Jesus Christ, an expression of our gratitude and awe in thought, words, song, or deed. It is adoration.

Worship is a loving response to the living God who has made Himself known to us. Right worship embodies a right concept of God. This is so important. A right concept of God ensures that you will follow the right path through life. But if you have a faulty concept of God, you will follow a disastrous course. I have spent more hours on the phone with people who have a faulty concept of God than for any other reason. I'm convinced that every sin in a believer's life can be traced to a faulty concept of God.

THE RIGHT CONCEPT

Going back to the garden again, isn't that how Satan deceived Eve? He planted a faulty concept of God in her mind. He caused her to doubt the goodness of God—and that's a faulty concept if ever there was one. Satan continues to deceive men and women in this way. It is uncanny to me the crazy ideas people have about God.

But a right concept of God will always lead to worship. How I love to see this strength in a person, this ability to ignore her circumstances—or at least set them aside—in order to lift her eyes, heart, and mind toward God. Whether she speaks the words aloud or speaks them in her mind, the cry of her heart is, *Oh God, how I love You! I sit at Your feet to adore and admire You.*

Your concept of God reveals much about you. What you think about God will determine the depth of your prayer life, your sensitivity to sin, and your potential for victory in trials. If you understand that God cares about you and bends His ear to your voice, you will pray differently.

You'll pray as though He's listening—because you know that He is. If you understand that God is holy, omnipresent (everywhere), and omniscient (all-seeing), you'll desire purity in your life. You won't take sin lightly. If you understand that He is omnipotent (all-powerful) and sovereign (over all), you'll lift your head during trials and watch for your victory. You'll leave your problems in His hands, trusting the outcome to Him.

THE SCHOOL OF WORSHIP

I'd like you to sit down with a piece of paper and describe Who you think God is and what you think He is like. You might be surprised at how much you know. I hope that's the case. But you might also be surprised at how little you know about God's character. That's why it's absolutely vital you do this exercise. We want to grow. We want to mature in Christ. The alternative is to remain a kindergarten Christian. But the time for kindergarten is over. It is time to grow up. You can get by with an occasional "Praise the Lord!" and sing a few choruses while you let your mind wander, but you are not worshiping God.

Most false doctrines in the Christian faith spring from ignorance of God. For instance, a person with a right concept of God could not possibly fall for the so-called "prosperity gospel." This false doctrine teaches that God wants you to be rich and healthy, and if you're not, it's because you don't have enough faith. First of all, remember that Jesus, our model, was poor. Don't let anyone tell you differently. No reputable scholar ever argued for a rich Jesus. In Luke 9:57-58 we read,

> Now it happened as they journeyed on the road, that someone said to Him, "Lord, I will follow You wherever You go." And Jesus said to him, "Foxes have holes and birds of the air have nests, but the Son of Man has nowhere to lay His head."

Just that one verse alone dismisses the prosperity gospel. But people want to believe the lies that indulge them. When a person ignorant of Scripture hears, "God wants you to have a Rolls Royce!"—they gobble it up.

FALSE DOCTRINES

Over the years I have watched the devastation this false doctrine has brought people. I've watched while women suffered horrible tragedies and then nearly lost their faith, all because they couldn't reconcile the God of their making with the circumstances they were suffering. Perhaps a loved one was dying, and they believed that if they had enough faith, they could stop the inevitable. They believed they could say the right words in the right way with just the right amount of faith, and they could make God heal that person. But then when the loved one died, doubt and anger rose up against God, and by the time they sat down and asked for counsel, they had nearly lost their faith.

Now, there is truth in believing God for a miracle and there is truth in having faith. God can do anything. He can heal the sick and He can raise the dead. God is not limited in any way, shape or form. But God is also sovereign, and here is where the prosperity doctrine breaks down. This false doctrine refuses to recognize the sovereignty of God. Jeremiah chapter 18 tells us that God is the Potter and we are the clay. If you are His child and walking in the lordship of Jesus Christ, doesn't He have the right to do with your life whatever He wills?

You cannot know how painful it is to have someone come up and announce to you, "I no longer believe in God. He didn't answer my prayers and my loved one died." Chuck has often said that if he could get his hands on those who push this false doctrine, he'd make them stand and face the people whose faith they've destroyed.

I have found that the people who are most victorious in trials are those who know God and know how to worship Him. They are the ones who, when deep trials come, say immediately, "God, I know You are good, and that anything that comes into my life You have allowed." They may grieve, but they accept the trial and grow by it. They don't say, "I am so angry with God." That statement absolutely shakes me to my toes.

How can you be angry with the God Who loves you? Why aren't you angry with the Devil? I have never understood a woman who says, "I am angry with God." I can't fathom having so little fear of God, so little reverence for my Holy Father in heaven, that like a puny little ant on earth I could ever shake my fist in the face of my God Who is unapproachable in His magnificence.

Our God is holy, just, fair, and righteous. He is all-loving. He does what is best for you—every time. And I pray before God today that if you are ever going to be angry, you'll be angry with the Devil who has brought all the sin on us in the first place. Don't ever be angry with my God, please. Love Him, honor Him, magnify Him, exalt Him, but don't be angry with Him.

WORSHIP IN SPIRIT AND TRUTH

Why does God want us to worship Him? Heaven is full of worshipers. In fact, God created angels to worship Him. The Bible proclaims that seraphim and cherubim are flying all over heaven worshiping God and declaring Him holy. It's glorious to read the descriptions of those magnificent beings in Ezekiel, Isaiah, and Revelation. But God wants us to *choose* to worship Him, from our own free will. He seeks those who will worship Him in spirit and in truth.

A Samaritan woman had a life-changing encounter one day at the well where she had gone to draw water. Jesus met her there, and began to tell her about the living water that would satisfy her thirst forever. But then He also told her some things about her past life. "You have had five husbands, and the one whom you now have is not your husband" (John 4:18).

Who was this Man Who knew all about her past? The woman said to Him, "Sir, I perceive that You are a prophet." And then immediately, she turned to the subject of worship.

> Our fathers worshiped on this mountain, and you Jews say that Jerusalem is the place where one ought to worship (John 4:20).

Jesus replied to her—and to us,

> The hour is coming, and now is, when the true worshipers will worship the Father in spirit and in truth; for the Father is seeking such to worship Him (John 4:23).

The Samaritans worshiped on Mount Gerizim, involving the ritual of slaying a lamb. The Jews, though, worshiped in the temple in Jerusalem. It's interesting to me that as the Samaritan woman drew closer to Jesus, the first thing she inquired was, "Where do we worship?" Jesus explained, it is not *where* we worship that counts, but *how* we worship. Is our worship spiritual and real? Do we have the Holy Spirit's help? For God is Spirit, and we must have His help to worship Him in spirit.

God is seeking people who will worship Him in spirit and in truth—not as the angels who were created for just that purpose, and not because we are forced—but because we choose to. He gave us free will. We do not have to worship God. You don't ever have to worship Him, but He seeks those who will. And to think that God would seek my worship blesses me and makes me want to offer Him that worship all the more.

Within the heart of every man and every woman, God has placed an innate desire to worship. In the most primitive tribes and in the most sophisticated cultures, we find this desire to worship. God programmed worship into our being. Everyone worships something. Even atheists worship—they worship their intellect. Anyone who says, "I am too smart to believe in God," is worshiping their own intellect.

WHO WILL YOU WORSHIP?

You do not have a choice as to whether or not you will worship something. You will. But you do have a choice as to whom or what you worship. You can choose something that is created, or you can choose to worship the living God Who created all things.

Worship should be a normal part of our relationship with God. Think about how dull a love relationship would be if you never found a meaningful way to express your love. I think that every wife should ask God on a daily basis, "God, show me a creative way to demonstrate my love to my husband."

Chuck is such a creative man and I always miss him so much when he's traveling. One time he called me while he was away, and at the end of our conversation I said, "I love you." And he said, "I love you, Angel." I immediately thought, *Now what can I say back to him that is comparable to "Angel"?* I still haven't figured that one out, but I'll keep trying. I want to be creative in my expressions of love to him. He's just so good at that!

He's also creative with his notes. When we have to be apart for a time, we leave notes for each other. Chuck writes the zingiest notes you have ever read. They are always very short, but clever, clever, clever. I save every one, because they are just so darling. He used to sign them *Captain*, because I nicknamed him *Captain Zoom Zoom* when he had to fly away so much.

If it's important to be creative in our expressions of love to our spouse, how much more so in our relationship with God. Somebody said that we go to God with our shopping lists, and isn't that true? But maybe we should sit down and ask Him what *He* would like. We could pray, "God, make me creative in my worship of You. I want to worship You in a way that will bless You and satisfy Your heart. Show me what You'd like, Lord."

WORSHIP TOGETHER

Sadly, some Christians don't care a whit about worship. That word "whit" came to my mind, so I looked it up. It means, "the smallest particle possible." Some people don't care a whit about the worship of God. They ask God for help in trouble and to watch over them when they are asleep, but they don't include worship in their prayers. We all know Christians like that. But how cold and indifferent is the bride who cares nothing about adoring her husband or never tells him she loves him. Christians have an abundance of prayer meetings, but not many meetings just to worship. Have you ever gone to a meeting whose sole purpose is to worship Jesus, with no intercession, no petition, no supplication—just worship?

I encourage you to call a few friends together and worship the Lord together, just as Elisabeth and Mary did in Luke 1:39-55. They magnified God, without making any requests of Him. I am amazed at Mary's prayer in that passage. She must have known the Psalms very well to be able to worship God as beautifully as she did.

I always loved the afterglows we held at the little chapel on Church Street. After service we would gather in the first few rows, and we would praise God and sing to Him. One person would speak out praise and thanksgiving, followed by another who would speak out love for

God. Another person would just tell God how marvelous He is. Then we would sing some praise songs. As we sat and were ministered by the Holy Spirit, He always ministered to us.

AN APPOINTED WORSHIPER

I sometimes wish I had been born a few thousand years earlier. In setting up the order of service in the tabernacle and in the temple, God appointed singers to worship Him all day and all night—and that is all they did.

Oh, to be able to just sing and praise God for a few hours at a time, then go home to rest awhile, have a bite to eat, and come back to church to sing and praise God again. And to know that was all you had to do in life! Wouldn't that be marvelous? I think, *Oh Lord, why didn't You have me born then?* But then I think about the wilderness and how unpleasant it had to be to wander for forty years. I might have been one of those complainers, and then look where I would be.

In *Gems from Tozer,* a collection of writings by A. W. Tozer, there's a chapter entitled, "The Missing Jewel of Worship." In this chapter Tozer said, "Man was made to worship God. He can worship Him in a manner no other creature can." [13]

One worship song that always blessed me expresses that very truth. Angels were created to praise God, but they could never feel the joy that our salvation brings. We can worship God the way no other creature can:

Holy, holy, holy is what the angels sing
And I expect to help them make the courts of heaven ring.
But, when I sing redemption's story they will fold their wings,
For angels never felt the joy that our salvation brings. [14]

When we get to heaven I would not be at all surprised to discover that God put that innate desire to worship in us—not because of His great need for our worship, but because of our great need to worship. We need to have our eyes lifted from ourselves and our limitations, and placed squarely on God, Who is all-powerful and sovereign. Worship does that. It reminds us of our insignificance and our helplessness apart from God.

PRACTICAL WORSHIP

On a practical level, how does worship put our problems in their proper place? Let's say I awaken in the morning burdened down with an impossible situation for which I can't see any solution. I'm ready to pray, but instead of rushing into intercession, I begin to worship. "God, You are all-powerful. You spoke and the world came into being." Then I start thinking about that fact. At just a word from God, all the oceans came into being. Light became light—just because God spoke.

I can't fathom that. My mind is too finite to take it in. So I bring it down to a smaller scale and I think about the Pacific Ocean. I will never see the whole Pacific Ocean in my lifetime. And yet, God spoke and the Pacific—all the oceans—came into existence. Not only that, but He spoke and the dry lands came into being—mountains, hills, depths, sky, stars, sun, moon and planets. He spoke. He is powerful enough to do that. And do you know what? My problem suddenly doesn't look so big anymore.

I begin to pray the things I know about God. "Father, You are righteous. You are holy. Your Word tells me You hate sin, and murder, and evil dealings. You hate lying. You hate deceit. You defend and shelter Your children and You are just in all Your ways."

And as I worship, my problem gets smaller and smaller and smaller.

Do you see how worship puts your problem in right proportion to God's power and ability to intervene?

An old saying goes, "What good does it do to tell me you love me, if it isn't the way I need to hear it?" This is the reason why so many marriages are in trouble. The wife says, "Why don't you ever tell me you love me?" and he says, "I bring home a paycheck every week, don't I?" But that's not how she needs to hear "I love you."

What good does it do to worship God if it isn't the way He wants you to worship Him? We are learning how to please the heart of God. So in this area of worship, we want to learn what pleases Him the most.

I once heard Lloyd John Ogilvie, the former pastor of First Presbyterian Church in Hollywood, say during a televised teaching, "My wife's favorite color is purple. What if one day I bought her an orange dress, and she says, 'But you know my favorite color is purple.' And I answered back, 'But I bought this orange dress to tell you I love you.' Now if she hates an orange dress, this isn't going to say 'I love you' to her, is it?" He went on to explain just what we've been discussing—that in our worship of God, we don't want to have the attitude that says, "God, I'm going to worship You, but I'm going to do it on my terms and the way I want to do it."

WORSHIP EDUCATION

In everything that we learn, there is always a step one. The first step in learning how to worship God in a way that would please Him is simply going to the Lord in prayer and saying, "Lord, teach me how to worship You."

Ask God to make you a woman of worship. Literally say those words: "Lord, make me a woman of worship." How it blesses the Lord when we pray His will for us! And it's such a simple thing to just look up and say, "Father, I want to bless You in my worship—will You cause me to do so?"

The second step will take a bit more time. I'd like you to go into a quiet corner someplace with your Bible, a pen, and a notebook. You'll need a concordance too, so if your Bible doesn't have one in the back, buy or borrow one. Turn in your concordance to the word "worship" and look up every scriptural reference you can find. Write those verses—not just the reference, but the entire verse—in your notebook. When you're finished, I want you to do the same thing with the word "praise," and then the word "thanksgiving." You probably won't be able to do this in just one day—probably not in a week. It's going to take a good bit of time, if you do it right, but oh, how it will bless you. And it will turn you into a woman of worship.

Now, some of the Scriptures on worship will be applicable to your worship life, some of them won't. Some of them will talk about the pagan worship of Baal, for instance, but we can learn something from bad examples of worship, as well as good. We can learn what not to do. As you go through all those verses, you will begin to learn what pleases the heart of God. You will learn the importance of obedience in worship, and what God requires and desires.

Take your time as you write out these Scriptures. Let the Holy Spirit imprint these truths upon your heart.

METHODS OF WORSHIP

The third step is to get specific. As you go through these Scriptures—especially in the Psalms—you will see all sorts of instructions or admonitions on worship and praise. In your notebook, create a section called "Methods of Worship." Here you'll begin to list what you learn about specific ways to worship.

To help you understand, let's look at Psalm 95. I particularly like this in *The King James Version*. The first verse reads,

O come, let us sing unto the LORD: let us make a joyful noise to the rock of our salvation.

In terms of method, what is the first thing this psalm teaches about worship? It instructs to "sing unto the Lord." So you'll list, "Sing." What is the second method this verse says? "Make a joyful noise." I don't know if God put that particular instruction in for people who can't sing. If so, that's thoughtful of Him. He's saying to the ones who really can't sing, "You can worship too. You can make a joyful noise." I have sat in church near people who could only sing monotone, but their worship was real and their hearts were precious. Their hearts delighted in making a joyful noise unto the Rock of their salvation. If they blessed me with their courage—and their joyful noise—I know they blessed the Lord as well.

WORSHIP REVEALS TRUTH

As you're going through verses and pulling out the methods you find, I want you to also watch for anything that Scripture tells you about God or about Jesus. This is where faulty concepts of God will drop off and truth will replace them. You will begin to really know God's true attributes—His power, splendor, majesty, justice, and truth. Keep your notebook with you in church. When your pastor tells you something about God, write it down. When you learn something about worship, write it down. Start recording these things, because writing helps you imprint these truths into your brain. Did you know that as you get older, the more you use your brain, the better your brain functions? It's true. So make that brain work. One of Chuck's best friends was a man known as "Daddy Atkinson." At the age of ninety-two, he studied Greek and did very well. So now you have no excuse.

Going back to the first verse in Psalm 95, what does it teach us about God? It tells us that He is the Rock of our salvation. There's a very large, very beautiful rock on the grounds of our conference center in Twin Peaks, California. When I first saw it, I stood and stared in amazement. And then I said to Chuck, "Oh, our Rock of ages! Jesus is our Rock, the Rock of our salvation." He agreed. Even now, every time I pass by that enormous rock, I am reminded that God is the Rock of my salvation. I'm reminded of God's strength and stability. Like that giant rock, you can't move God. He is strong, stable, and immovable. Oh, how I love that!

Verse 3 says that He is a great God. He's not just "a god," as the world would have you believe. He is the One and only God, and He is great. This acknowledgment of God's greatness—seeing Him for Who He truly is, in all His majesty and splendor—is the beginning place of the school of worship. It's where you enter that place of deep worship of God.

Verse 4 says, "He controls the formation of the depths of the earth" (TLB). *The King James Version* says, "In His hand are the deep places of the earth." I was meditating on this and thought, *Where do diamonds come from? Where does gold come from? Where do silver and copper come from?* Most of it comes from mines, which are in the depths of the earth. He controls the formation of the depths of the earth. He causes the pressure that produces diamonds. God does that. Have you ever praised Him for thinking to make jewels and precious metals? Most women like diamonds a little bit, don't they? We like gold, too, because it's so pretty. We have God to thank for those things, because He controlled the formation of the earth.

Verse 5 continues to tell us, "The sea is His, and He made it." No one else did that. No one else can take credit for it. The sea is His. I think of all the people who have spent their lives studying the ocean or searching for the treasures it contains. Do you remember Jacques Cousteau? He knew a lot about the sea, but he had no part in creating it. He didn't have the knowledge to create a single drop. The best he could do was to study the beauty in the sea, but he didn't create it. Only God did that.

The next time you drive by the sea, fly over it, or dip your foot in it, think about the fact that, "The sea is His." Meditate on His might and power. If He can conceive, and then create something that vast, spectacular, deep, and thunderous, is He not sufficient for your situation today? He is. Worship Him.

Verse 6 says, "O come, let us worship and bow down: let us kneel before the LORD our Maker." What method of worship do you find here? "Bow down." Do you know why bowing is an act of worship? It's because bowing down is a sign of humility. It is an acknowledgment that the One on the throne is higher than you. He's greater than you. He's your ruler, your God.

What other method do we find in this verse? "Kneel." I think of kneeling and bowing down as two different things. Bowing down, to me, is having my face almost on the ground. Sometimes when the spirit of worship comes over me and I see my utter nothingness in relationship to the holiness of God, I feel an overwhelming desire to bow low and put my forehead on the floor. Have you ever felt that urge? I hope so. You know, Hindu yogis do this as a form of worship to their false god. It seems so wrong to me that worshipers of false gods are uninhibited, while Christians, who worship the one true God, are often very inhibited in worship. It's something to think about.

Verse 6 also tells us that God is our Maker. He is our Creator. The evolutionists are certainly fighting against this truth. Every time I read something that discounts or ignores God as Creator, it just makes me want to affirm Him all the more. "You, Lord—You are my Maker. You are my Creator. You are the Maker of all things." I think we should say to the heathen world loudly and often, "God is my Creator!"

RESPOND TO KNOWING GOD

Are you beginning to see that worship is so much more than just singing a chorus or saying, "Praise the Lord"? It is your response to knowing God—an outpouring of your love and awe for Him. Whenever you see a mountain or the sea, let your mind go back to this psalm. Tell yourself, "He created that very mountain. He created the sea." It's just a small step from thinking those thoughts to turning them into worship. "Oh, God! How magnificent You are! How beautiful is Your creation. You are the Creator of all things. I exalt You, Lord. I bless Your name."

Psalm 37:5 says that we can trust God to take care of the things we give over to Him. "Commit your way to the LORD, trust also in Him, and He shall bring it to pass." The word *asa* means, "to create something out of nothing." It is the same word used in Genesis where it says, "In the beginning God created." And if you're a woman in a loveless marriage, you need to know that God can create something out of that "nothingness" in your home. Even if there isn't love left between you and your husband, God is powerful enough to take nothing and create love. He can do it. He delights in doing it.

Another method for praising God can be found in Psalm 96:9, which says, "Oh worship the LORD in the beauty of holiness!" *The Living Bible* says, "Worship the Lord with the beauty of holy lives." Did you know that living a holy life is a form of worship to God? Living a sinful life is not worshiping God at all. But just by living a holy life you can worship the Lord.

Psalm 96:12 says, "Praise Him for the growing fields, for they display His greatness" (TLB). When you see a wheat field, do you praise Him for it? You should, for the Word says they display His greatness. Just say, "Oh, God, You are so great! You made the kernel that is put into the ground and produces the wheat that makes our bread. I praise You for Your greatness in this!"

PRAISE WITH INSTRUMENTS

Psalm 98:5-6 instructs us to praise God with instruments—with the harp, the trumpet and the coronets. A friend of mine who plays the piano once told me about being asked to take on an enormous ministry project. She didn't want to do it, but she knew the need was very great, and so God prompted her to say yes. But as soon as she committed to do it, she was filled with fear. She didn't think she could possibly organize it to see the project through. But while she was sitting there fretting, the Lord directed her to sit down at her piano and start worshiping Him. She did. And as she began to play the piano and worship Him, joy began to well up in her heart. A peace came over her, and along with it, a wonder of God. While she sat there worshiping God on her piano, He began laying out a creative plan to complete the project as she worshiped.

You know, I play the piano, but if I hadn't, I would have gone out and bought myself a triangle or something. I am blessed to have great grandkids around, because they have funny little instruments. So I can clap the cymbals, and nobody thinks I am too strange.

I have a tambourine that some sweet hippie girl gave me years ago, and I absolutely love it. The kids used to bring tambourines to church in the early days of Calvary Chapel and they would play them while we all sang. I thought it was wonderful. I have mine at home—but nobody likes to hear it but me, so I have to do it when nobody else is there. Once in a while I'll get that tambourine out and make a joyful noise unto the Lord. He understands.

Psalm 63:3-5 tells us,

> Because Your lovingkindness is better than life, my lips shall praise You.
> Thus will I bless You while I live; I will lift up my hands in Your name.

Here is yet another way of worshiping God. "I will lift my hands." Some people feel hindered doing this in public. They worry that others might look at them funny. If you don't want to do it in church, will you do it in your home? Just stretch out your hands toward God. It is a sign of surrender to Him, and it is beautiful in the eyes of the Lord.

I never really feel like going to a football game, but once I am there and the game starts, I love it. Whenever our team makes a touchdown, I jump up and cheer for them. Don't we all do that? Most of us have at least once in our lives been so excited about something that we've put our hands in the air. But let me ask you, is there anything more exciting and wonderful than God? David was so ecstatic when God gave him victory and he was able to bring the ark of the Lord back to the people, he not only raised his hands, he also danced. That's pretty uninhibited. I have to believe that if I could, I wouldn't just stand on the sidelines and watch the armies of the Lord defeating the armies of Satan, I'd be leading the pack in all that dancing, singing, and jumping up. I'd grab my tambourine for that!

When the miracles come, don't be afraid to raise your arms and praise Him. Don't be afraid to surrender visually to Him that way—whether at church or in the privacy of your own home.

SHE LOVED MUCH

There is so much to learn about the worship of God. I've walked with the Lord over sixty years, and I'm still learning new truths about worship. It takes a lifetime of discovery, a lifetime of response. It takes constant meditation on the wondrous things God has done in your life. I think of the woman in Luke 7:36-50. When she found Jesus at the house of Simon the Pharisee, she stood behind Him weeping, washed His feet with her tears, then wiped them with her hair and kissed His feet, anointing them with fragrant oil.

The Pharisee was startled by this and said to himself, "This Man, if He were a prophet, would know who and what manner of woman this is who is touching Him, for she is a sinner."

Jesus, knowing the man's thoughts, explained her act of worship. He said she did it because her sins had been forgiven. Then He said, "Therefore I say to you, her sins, which are many, are forgiven, for she loved much."

If you have been forgiven much by Jesus Christ, you will love Him an awful lot. Have you been forgiven much? If so, does your love for Him reflect that? Does it spill over into worship? One thing we see in this story in Luke is there's no mention of the woman's embarrassment. We don't know whether she was or not, but I suspect that she wasn't. That's because love covers embarrassment. You can love so much that you just really don't care what people think about you—you've just got to express it. How precious when we can worship Him so freely.

HUMILITY, SUBMISSION, COMMITMENT

Worship requires three necessary elements: humility, submission, and commitment. If all three elements are not there, you are not worshiping. You might be praising God, as in those times when we spontaneously say, "Well, praise the Lord!" but worship requires more than words. Worship includes humility, which signifies God's greatness and your nothingness; submission, which acknowledges His lordship over you; and commitment, which is your declaration of His leadership.

In his book, A. W. Tozer said that worship is comprised of specific factors. First of all, "boundless confidence." He makes the point that "you cannot worship a Being you cannot trust." Next he said comes, "respect for His greatness, and communion with Him ... and then ultimately admiration of His excellency." [15] He said when those things are present, you will naturally be filled with wonder and delight. You will find yourself "captivated and charmed and entranced." I want to spend my life entranced by God, don't you?

The Shulamite woman felt that way toward Solomon. She says,

> I am lovesick ... My beloved is mine, and I am his ... When I found the one I love, I held him and would not let him go ... My heart yearned for him (Song of Solomon 2:5, 16; 3:4; 5:4).

This is a woman utterly captivated. What about you? Are you captivated by the Lord today? Can you say, "Lord, You have captured my heart"?

As the hymn writer said,

> "In our astonished reverence we confess
> Thine uncreated loveliness." [16]

What does astonished, reverent worship do in the life of a person? I'd like to tell you about a woman who really knew how to worship God. I knew her as Mom Smith, but the rest of the world knew her as Maude Smith. And it was during one of the darkest periods of her life that I saw her faith shine the most.

WORSHIP THROUGH TRIALS

One November day, Dad Smith and Chuck's youngest brother, Bill, had flown together down to Victorville, California, in a plane that Bill piloted. Mom Smith, Chuck, and I thought the children would enjoy going to the Orange County Airport to meet the plane, so we went at about

8:00 that night. The kids were jumping up and down, all excited because Uncle Bill was piloting the plane and they couldn't wait to see him and Grandpa Smith fly in. But 8:00 passed, and then 9:00, and then 10:00. Finally, at 10:30 p.m. we decided to go back home. We took Mom back to her house and we went home, but none of us slept all night.

Early the next morning, Chuck was able to get in touch with the Civil Aeronautics Patrol and report that his father and brother were missing. Just a few minutes later, they called us back to say Bill's plane had been found crashed in the hills of Camp Pendleton and it contained two bodies.

Chuck immediately went over to Mom Smith's house. When he walked in the door, he said, "Mom, Dad and Bill have gone to be with Jesus."

And she looked at him and said, "Oh, son, I know. At 4:00 this morning, God awakened me and told me." Then she said, "I got up and knelt down by the side of my bed and I said, 'The Lord giveth and the Lord taketh away. Blessed be the name of the Lord.'"

I watched Mom Smith. I watched her like a hawk. I had never seen anything like that in all my life. The following morning, Chuck went to church and preached—and Mom was right there worshiping. Day after day, Mom continued to worship God. I didn't see any anger. I didn't see any questioning. She never once asked why. Bill was her baby—only twenty-four years old. He was 6' 4" and handsome. He had a way about him that made all the girls fall for him, though he never married.

Mom had a faith and an ability to worship through her grief like no one I'd ever seen, but she was still a woman. Shortly after she lost her husband and son, she moved away from the house. One day, about two months after their death, I was standing with her and I said, "Do you miss the other house, Mom?"

She said, "No, honey, I don't. Every time I walked in the kitchen I could see Bill leaning against the kitchen cupboard talking to me." Then she said, "I am glad I am not there." She grieved, and she sorrowed. She felt the loss deeply. Yet, she worshiped God.

Could you do that, beloved sister in Christ? If you suffered your own deep loss today, would you be able to kneel down by the side of your bed and say, "The Lord giveth and the Lord taketh away, blessed be the name of the Lord"?

I pray that it is so. I pray that you are so captivated by God that you can trust Him through the darkest night.

Father, You are magnificent. You are all that is beautiful, all that is lovely, all that is holy and righteous and good. You are the Creator of the heavens and the earth, and all that they contain. You spoke the world into existence out of nothing, Lord—out of nothing! So we know that You can speak into our own nothingness and create beauty there.

Lord, will You make us women of worship?

We ask it in the name of Jesus, amen.

CHAPTER

10

WALK IN LOVE

WHILE WE WERE IN ISRAEL touring one time, someone spoke harshly to me. I was absolutely devastated by that—really, deeply hurt. Now, I'm not normally a brooder or someone who goes on for a long time carrying sad feelings. When something like this happens, I like to pray about the hurt, find a Scripture that I can apply to it, and then move on to the next thing. But this time, I brooded.

I couldn't help it. I felt so crushed. I tried to think of a Scripture that would cover all that hurt, because I know how powerful God's Word is and how quickly it can release you from those feelings. But the truth is, I had a great fear—giving in to forgiveness immediately.

I simply did not deserve to be yelled at. The person who did this was—and this is awful to say, but true—100 percent wrong. I worried that if

I gave in too soon and forgave them immediately, they wouldn't understand that they're not to speak to me that way ever again. Have you ever been in a situation like that? You think, *I have got to teach this person a lesson.* Partly thinking they need the lesson, and partly thinking, *I never want to be hurt that deeply again.*

Well, I did not handle it well. It took me hours to get over it—a day and a half, actually. On the outside I looked fine, but inside I wasn't. It wasn't until we got back home and I was sitting in church on our first evening study that God began to open my eyes. Chuck was speaking on 1 Peter 2:20. *The Amplified Bible* says,

> [After all] what kind of glory [is there in it] if, when you do wrong and are punished for it, you take it patiently? But if you bear patiently with suffering [which results] when you do right and that is undeserved, it is acceptable and pleasing to God.

I heard that and thought, *Oh, that is what I should have done.*

I was reminded again to continually go over these truths in God's Word, so that when these difficult moments come—and they always come unexpectedly—I'll be ready. I'll have the Word right at my command and I won't brood, fuss, and fret and go down into the valley for a long stay.

Through that verse, the Holy Spirit said, "Kay, when you are buffeted for something, in which you are not guilty, and you accept it with a sweet, loving spirit, that is well-pleasing to Me."

I had been given an opportunity to please God's heart, and I had blown it. Oh, how we need to know God's Word—inside out and every which way! If I had only remembered 1 Peter 2:20 while in Israel, or if I had been freed up enough to let the Holy Spirit bring it to mind, I would have behaved in a way that was pleasing to the Lord. I would have behaved with love—and that always pleases the heart of God.

THE LOVE DEFINITION

How do you define "love"? In the English language, we use that word so casually. As Chuck has said many times to demonstrate this point, "I love my wife and I love peanuts." Now, Chuck is fond of peanuts, but what he feels for them is nothing compared to the love he has for me. And yet we use that word so interchangeably.

The Greeks use four different words to express four specific kinds of love. The first word, *storge,* means "instinctive love." It's the kind of love most mothers have when they first see their brand-new baby. I felt it with all my children and then felt it anew when I saw my first grandson, Bradley, through the nursery window.

The second word, *phileo,* means "brotherly love." It's the love that binds us to our friends. I always say I have lots of best friends, and I suppose most of us do. You can feel *phileo* for many people.

Then we have *eros,* which is "romantic love." This is the kind of love in which two people are drawn together—hopefully in marriage. *Eros* is sexual or romantic love.

The fourth kind of love is *agape.* It is God's love and it is a giving love. *Agape* was manifested in Christ, and it can only be active in us when we are in a right relationship with Jesus and the Holy Spirit is dwelling within us. As Christians, this is the kind of love that should be evidenced by our lives. Apart from Jesus, it's not possible to have *agape* love.

First Corinthians 13:4-7 gives us a beautiful definition of love.

> Love suffers long and is kind; love does not envy; love does not parade itself, is not puffed up; does not behave rudely, does not seek its own, is not provoked, thinks no evil; does not rejoice in iniquity, but rejoices in the truth; bears all things, believes all things, hopes all things, endures all things.

Isn't that beautiful? The kind of love described in this passage expects nothing in return. It is a love that gives.

Let's look more closely at this passage as translated in *The Amplified Bible*. As you read these words, ask yourself, *Does this describe me? Could I put my name in place of the word "love"?*

> Love endures long and is patient and kind; love never is envious nor boils over with jealousy, is not boastful or vainglorious, does not display itself haughtily. It is not conceited (arrogant and inflated with pride); it is not rude (unmannerly) and does not act unbecomingly. Love (God's love in us) does not insist on its own rights or its own way, for it is not self-seeking; it is not touchy or fretful or resentful; it takes no account of the evil done to it [it pays no attention to a suffered wrong] …

Isn't that hard to do? When someone wrongs us, we usually notice. But how beautiful when the love of Jesus is working powerfully in your heart that you take no account of it.

> It does not rejoice at injustice and unrighteousness, but rejoices when right and truth prevail. Loves bears up under anything and everything that comes, is ever ready to believe the best of every person, its hopes are fadeless under all circumstances, and it endures everything [without weakening].

Maybe you don't feel that you could put your own name in place of the word "love" in all those verses. But we can put Jesus' name there, because He is all those things and more.

Because I so desperately wanted this passage to be programmed in my mind, I read 1 Corinthians 13:4-7 every day for a full year. I wanted its truths to permeate my life. So every day, in addition to whatever else I was reading in the Word, I read this passage.

EMOTIONAL HEALTH

No matter what your circumstances are today, if you will allow this kind of love to be worked out through your life—if you forsake bitterness, wrath, anger, malice, revenge, hatred, haughtiness, envy, and jealousy in favor of walking in Christ's love, you will have emotional health you could not have had otherwise. You will be healthy the way God intended you to be. But if you embrace these bitter attitudes they will cause you to be emotionally ill.

Years ago, I went as an observer to a group therapy class in a psychiatric hospital. There were twelve people in the group, and every single one of them had a bitter, unforgiving spirit towards someone else who had wronged them. They probably had a right to their anger, but what good had their bitterness brought them? It had done nothing but land them in a psychiatric hospital. If they had given it over to Jesus and walked in His love—if they had applied Ephesians 4:31-32 to their lives, they could have been out in the sunlight enjoying the beauty of God's creation. Ephesians 4:31-32 reads,

> Let all bitterness, wrath, anger, clamor, and evil speaking be put away from you, with all malice. And be kind to one another, tenderhearted, forgiving one another, even as God in Christ forgave you.

I encourage you to read these verses over and over. Ask God to place His *agape* love in your heart, that it would abound in you. We don't want just a trickle of this love—we want an overflow of His love to all we encounter.

You may have read 1 Corinthians 13:4-7 and thought, *I am not longsuffering. I am not patient or kind.* Ask God to work those traits in you. But understand that they won't come as a one-time gift. As you walk with God and allow His Holy Spirit to flow through you, you will develop these attributes.

I spoke with a lady once who had attended our church. Her marriage was a disaster, in part because her husband was very jealous of her relationship with the Lord. He did not understand it. In fact, he was angry with her for embracing Christianity.

However, as we talked, I detected in this woman an attitude of revenge. Her husband had treated her very badly for a long period of time, and when she found Jesus Christ, it was as if she had a wedge over his head. She told him, "Who needs you? I don't need you anymore. I go to church and get all the fulfillment I need there." She left him home alone, getting angrier, and as she allowed that seed of bitterness to grow, he was quickly becoming hateful to Chuck, the church, Christians, and Christianity.

Now, would *agape* love do that? Would love use salvation as revenge on a husband? That isn't what love does. Love warms hearts. Love draws. Love desires the best for one another.

YOUR MOTIVE TO LOVE

Love must be the motivation behind all we do. The Bible tells us "The heart is deceitful above all things, and desperately wicked; who can know it?" (Jeremiah 17:9). Our motives are not always pure. Sometimes we perform great deeds so that others will notice and tell us how wonderful we are. One way to test your motive is to determine whether or not you care if your great deed is noticed. I have seen people do marvelous things, only to stomp off in a huff because nobody made a comment.

To this day, Chuck doesn't like flowers on the platform in front of the pulpit. Early in his ministry when he was serving in a denomination, different people would donate the flowers each week. But if Chuck ever forgot to thank that person from the pulpit, woe be unto Chuck!

This went on for fifteen years and it escalated. Over time, the flower donors became more competitive with each other. That just made it worse for Chuck, because if he admired one bouquet more than another, he'd hear about it. Finally he said, "I don't care if I never get another basket of flowers in the church." And that was the end of that. No more flowers. It really came down to a matter of motive. If you insist on applause, what is your motive?

In 1 Corinthians chapter 12, Paul talked about some of the spiritual gifts we have been given: word of wisdom, word of knowledge, faith, gifts of healing, the working of miracles, prophecy, the discerning of spirits, tongues, and the interpretation of tongues. Then in the first three verses of 1 Corinthians 13, he deals with the motivation behind our use of those gifts.

I grew up in a church where these gifts were very much in use. As a little girl I was in awe of those who had them—thinking they must be spiritual giants. I thought, *I wish I was closer to the Lord to have those gifts in my life.* Don't we think those things? If we see somebody with gifts of healing, we just assume that they must be deeply spiritual, or they wouldn't have those gifts. It's not true. I have known people who had those gifts but who were motivated by greed, power, or notoriety. I've seen them rise and I've seen them fall.

One of our favorite tour guides in Israel used to be a man who had yet to accept the Lord. I say "had yet" because we had been witnessing to this dear man and his wife and praying for them for years.

Some Christians from another group had come over from the States and during a conversation with our friend, a woman had told him, "I have divorced my husband and left my children because God has called me into the ministry of healing."

Now, our tour guide is very family-oriented. His parents and his wife and children are his whole life. So when we had our next tour, he told us about the conversation he'd had with that woman. He said to Chuck, "That is not God. God did not tell her that. I know that is not God."

Chuck said, "You're right. God doesn't call a mother to leave her children and divorce her husband to have a healing ministry." Even to someone not yet born again, the lack of love on this woman's part was immediately apparent.

WITHOUT LOVE, IT'S NOTHING

It's interesting what Paul has to say about several of the "most desired" gifts. Of tongues, he said,

> Though I speak with the tongues of men and of angels, but have not love, I have become sounding brass or a clanging cymbal (1 Corinthians 13:1).

In other words, without love, I am just noise. I wonder what angels sound like? I think it would be pretty exciting to speak in their language. Yet even then, if the language flowed through me but I had not love, it would all just be noise.

Secondly, Paul spoke about prophecy.

> And though I have the gift of prophecy, and understand all mysteries and all knowledge, and though I have all faith, so that I could remove mountains, but have not love, I am nothing (1 Corinthians 13:2).

Note that he doesn't say *some* faith, or *some* knowledge, or understand *some* mysteries—he said *all*.

I am a mountain-mover in prayer. Truly, I'm not bragging or boasting—it is simply God's work in my heart. I have faith enough to move mountains in prayer. You should have that kind of faith too. Do you know why? Because the Word of God says that if you believe in your heart and doubt not, your prayers can move mountains. But if I move mountains with my prayers and my motivation is not love, it profits me nothing. In fact, I *become* nothing. You would surely think that a mountain-mover would be one of the most valuable people in the body, regardless of their motivation. But they are useless without love.

"And though I bestow all my goods to feed the poor ..." (1 Corinthians 13:3a). We see people who do this, who willingly give away everything they have to feed the poor, and it's pretty hard to find fault with that. Yet what is the motivation behind it?

Lastly, Paul says, "Though I give my body to be burned, but have not love, it profits me nothing" (1 Corinthians 13:3b). Probably the greatest sacrifice is being martyred for Christ. You can go on the mission field and be burned alive or shot before a firing squad, but if your motivation for being there is anything but love for Jesus, you may as well have stayed home. You are of no use in the ministry to the kingdom.

When people use the gifts described in 1 Corinthians 12, we as children of God are to look for the fruit of love in their lives. It is the evidence of the Holy Spirit working in them. "The fruit of the Spirit is love (*agape*)" (Galatians 5:22).

I have seen Christians so driven by their own need for success, power, or money that they would destroy anyone who stood in their way—and use spiritual means to do it. No matter how successful their ministry appears or how spectacular their spiritual deeds, in the end only one opinion will matter. What will Jesus think of their works? Will they be "wood, hay, and stubble" when tried by fire, and no reward is given because they were not motivated by love? (1 Corinthians 3:12-13).

We want our motivation to be pure. As we draw closer to God and our heart beats with His heart, and His desires become our desires, it is only natural that we will want to walk in His love. But we need to be shown in a very practical way how to do that.

COMMANDED TO LOVE

The impartation of God's *agape* love is a mystical thing. It is like the wind—you can't see it; you can only see the results of it. The Bible tells us, "The love of God has been poured out in our hearts by the Holy Spirit" (Romans 5:5). We choose whether or not to walk in that love that He has placed within us.

While instructing His disciples Jesus said,

> A new commandment I give to you, that you love one another; as I have loved you, that you also love one another. By this all will know that you are My disciples, if you have love for one another (John 13:34-35).

It's interesting that Jesus didn't say, "If you move mountains, they will know you are My disciples." He didn't say, "If you speak with the tongues of men and angels, you'll be known as My disciples," or "If you knew all mysteries and had the gift of prophecy, then they will know that you are My disciples." How are people to know that you are a disciple of Jesus Christ? By the love you have for one another. I think sometimes it would be much easier to speak in the tongues of men and angels, or to move mountains through prayer than to love.

I was at a meeting with some of the pastors' wives and I said, "Being a pastor's wife would be great if you didn't have to deal with people." I don't like that I said that. I really don't. And yet, there is truth in that statement. It would be so easy to walk in love if we only had to love ourselves, wouldn't it? It's all the difficulties that come with relationships that make it so hard to walk in love.

If you notice in the Scriptures, Jesus didn't often say, "I command you." But He said it here. He said, "I command that you love one another." That's how strongly He feels about this. He said, "Think about how I have loved you, and then you go and do likewise."

LOVE PRAYS

How did Jesus love them? First, He prayed for them. Speaking of His disciples, Jesus said in John 17:9, "I pray for them. I do not pray for the world but for those whom You have given Me, for they are Yours." Not only did Jesus pray for the disciples who walked with Him during His earthly ministry, He prayed for all those who would come to Him throughout history. "I do not pray for these alone, but also for those who will believe in Me through their word" (John 17:20). Does it bless you to know that Jesus prayed that for you? He did so because He loves you.

I know mothers who don't even love their children and their husbands enough to pray for them every day. Do you know why they don't? Praying is difficult work. It takes time and energy. It takes concern, compassion and caring. That is why prayer meetings are so small. A church can have fifteen thousand people come on Sunday morning, but only twenty-five people will attend an intercessory prayer meeting to pray for other people. It's sad how very few people have an intercessor's heart. It takes the love of Jesus stirring an unquenchable fire within that heart.

I'm convinced that the women who attend intercessory prayer meetings will be some of the most rewarded people in the kingdom of heaven—because their motive is love. It's the love of Jesus Christ burning brightly in their hearts that makes them willing to deny themselves and pray for people. And, oh, the things that are wrought through those prayers! All through the week, things change in the church itself and in the lives of its people because of the prayers lifted up by those intercessors.

One Saturday night a leather-clad, tattooed biker came into our church. While one of our pastors was speaking, the man started walking down the aisle toward him in such a way that the ushers went after him. They stopped the man, brought him outside into our courtyard, and shared

Jesus with him. The man broke down like a baby, accepted Jesus as his Lord and Savior, and said, "I want to be baptized." They took him to the drinking fountain and poured water over him. What a blessing! I'm convinced that the battle for that man's soul was fought in the secret place of prayer, through someone who knows him or through an intercessor who may never know in this life what their prayers wrought.

Prayer takes time, but love provides all the motivation you need. Jesus exemplified that. He loved His disciples, and therefore He prayed for them. He also taught them how to pray.

Are you taking the time to teach your babies how to pray? It is so worth the time and effort you put into it. Some of the sweetest memories I have of my children when they were babies are their prayers. When our daughter Janette was about two-and-a-half, she was praying at the table one night and said, "Lord, bless the good tomatoes and the naughty corn." She hated corn, but loved tomatoes. Then there was our daughter, Cheryl, who, when she was about three, got wiggly in church one morning. As I was carrying her out of the service, she screamed back to the congregation, "Pray for me!" She knew the power of prayer.

Teach your children how to pray. Pray with them, pray for them, and teach them that they can go to God themselves through prayer. Jesus taught His disciples how to pray. In Luke 11:1, one of the disciples said, "Lord, teach us to pray." So Jesus took the time to do that. He taught them how to pray and how not to pray. He taught them the things they were to do when they prayed, and the places to avoid when praying.

LOVE INVESTS TIME

It took time to teach them, but that's one of the marks of love. Love invests time in others. Jesus took His disciples up into the mountains with Him. He put them in a boat on the Sea of Galilee, since the multitudes were pressing in and He wanted time alone with them. Do you exemplify the love of Jesus Christ in your home and in your friendships by taking time with people?

I read an article not long ago about the answers we give that are really to shut people up. Isn't that awful? The article said that when we don't want to take time with others' problems, we give pat answers. "Well, just look unto Jesus." "Keep your eyes on Jesus." If they had been able to keep their eyes on Jesus they wouldn't need us, would they? What they're expressing to you is that they need your help. They need you to take time with them. They need to know you love them. But when that's inconvenient, we pat them on the back and say, "Be fed, be warm, go your way," and we ignore their needs.

It isn't easy to take time with people. When my children were growing up I had a theory that the phone only rang at the most inopportune times. Chuck didn't have an office then, so we had two phone lines in our house—one for home and one for the church. We had hippie kids coming in and out of the house all day and night. We had our own four little ones, and Chuck was gone most of the time. Invariably, the phone would ring right when I was in the middle of mixing up a cake—right at the part where you have to keep beating the batter.

One day while I was mixing up a cake, it wasn't the phone that rang but the doorbell. When I answered it, the boy on the other side of the door said, "Kay, where is Chuck?"

I said, "He is out on calls."

And the boy said, "Well, I just murdered a man."

Another time, when Cheryl was little, she choked on something while I was beating a cake. As I look back, I think the Lord just didn't want me giving my family any more sugar.

Remember, people are always more important than things. We have to be willing to put those things aside. So what if the cake doesn't get baked in time for dessert? People are more important than cake, right? Take time with people. Let the love of Jesus flow through you to them.

LISTENING

I read that a child's sense of worth is formed by the age of three, partially by how much people listen to him or her. I've been around children—and I'm sure you have too—who say the same thing over and over, louder and louder, and do you know why? It's because nobody is listening. Sometimes when my great grandchildren are around and they say, "Grandma, look at this," and I am knee-deep in some marvelous adult conversation with somebody, and I've seen that toy eighty-two times—I'm not very interested in seeing it for an eighty-third time. But then I think of that little heart in front of me, and what he or she is really saying is, "Grandma, let me know that I am important. I just want you, Grandma, to turn your head over this way a little bit and acknowledge that I am special to you." So I look that eighty-third time. And you know, I'm always glad I did.

We all need to know that we are special to someone. Listen to people, even when it's inconvenient, and acknowledge that you hear them.

Author Norman Wright said, "Listen with your eyes. We hear more with our eyes than we do with our ears." [17] There's great truth in that. You can tell a lot about how someone is feeling just by watching them. Watch their eyes. Look for the places of pain on their faces. But use your ears too. Listen to the emotions behind the words. Are they animated, or do they speak with a monotone? Sometimes the ones who speak with a monotone are struggling the most. They're afraid to express their emotions. They're all locked up inside. And then listen with your body. Lean forward and show them that you are intent on what they are saying. Show them that they are the most important person to you at that moment.

Jesus really listened to the disciples. He saw great worth in them and He let them know it. It's like that expression: "Be patient with me; God isn't finished with me yet." Jesus had the patience to spend time and listen to them, and show them what they could become. *Agape* love does that.

ENCOURAGE AND COMFORT

Chuck's dad wrote a note to Chuck's mom once on the program of a ballet they were attending. I still have it tucked away at home. Dad wrote, "Of all the women in the room, you are the most beautiful."

How wonderful to be made to feel so special. We should remind each other as often as we can that others are special. God's Word confirms this repeatedly. In Matthew 10:29-31, Jesus said that God is aware of every little sparrow, and yet you are worth much more to Him. They're not the prettiest birds around; in fact, they're pretty ordinary. But they are special to God. He sees each one individually. And yet you are worth more to Him than any sparrow.

It was *agape* that prompted Jesus to comfort His disciples even before they knew they would need it. Knowing that the hour of His death was approaching, He told them,

> Let not your heart be troubled; you believe in God, believe also in Me. In My Father's house are many mansions; if it were not so, I would have told you. I go to prepare a place for you. And if I go and prepare a place for you, I will come again and receive you to Myself; that where I am, there you may be also (John14:1-3).

He knew they would need that assurance. And He knew they would need peace.

Peace I leave with you, My peace I give to you; not as the world gives do I give to you. Let not your heart be troubled, neither let it be afraid (John 14:27).

He promised to give them a peace that was unlike anything they'd find in the world—a peace that would see them through the coming trials.

Jesus was always encouraging the disciples. I think of how frightened they were when they had gone out on the Sea of Galilee without Him, only to see Him walking on the water toward them during the fourth watch of the night. Matthew 14:26-27 reads,

When the disciples saw Him walking on the sea, they were troubled, saying, "It is a ghost!" And they cried out for fear. But immediately Jesus spoke to them, saying, "Be of good cheer!"

I love that. In the following verses, we read that Peter wanted to try walking on the water too. I think most of us would have considered Peter to be a pain in the neck. He was impulsive, reckless, bold, and in his passion he usually blurted out the first thing that came to his mind. True to form, when Jesus came walking on the water that night, Peter saw Him and said, "Lord, if it is You, command me to come to You on the water" (Matthew 14:28). In other words, "Let me do it too!"

If I had been Jesus, I'm quite sure I would have said, "For heaven's sake, Peter, sit down and quit rocking the boat! You're so impetuous." Then I would have lectured him for standing up in the boat, and for making a fool of himself by asking to walk on water. I would have pointed out the lack of spiritual significance to walking on water and said, "Just because I did it, doesn't mean you have to copy Me." But Jesus has a lot more patience than I do. Jesus said to Peter, "Come."

He beckons you too. Jesus is encouraging you today to get out of the boat and walk on the water. He is! He's saying, "Come on. You can do it. Don't be afraid." Peter *did* walk on the water, for a short time, but then he started to sink. When did that happen? It happened at the point when he became self-conscious instead of Christ-conscious. It wasn't until Peter cried out to Jesus and he took Jesus' hand that he could get up again and walk back to the boat.

Jesus encouraged Peter countless times. One day Jesus looked at unstable, impetuous, spontaneous Peter and called him a rock. Peter—a rock? Jesus said,

> You are Peter [Greek, *Petros*—a large piece of rock], and on this rock [Greek, *petra*—a huge rock like Gibraltar] I will build My church, and the gates of *Hades* (the powers of the infernal region) shall not overpower it (Matthew 16:18 *The Amplified Bible*).

Rocks are stable and steadfast. That's not what comes to mind when you think about the Peter described in the gospels. But then when you read 1 and 2 Peter, you're amazed at the change God brought about in his life. Let that challenge you today. Jesus is inviting you to walk on water.

AFFIRM YOUR LOVE

Ask yourself if, like Jesus, you see the potential in others and then encourage them to be everything they can be. How do you view your husband and your children? Do you look for the best in them, or do you focus on their flaws? If you see your children as loud or interrupting, they will know that. You reflect to your children exactly what you think of them. They catch your attitude. You don't want to be critical of your children. You want to encourage them and look for the best in them.

Agape caused Jesus to feel compassion for His disciples and *agape* also moved Him to give them the assurance they needed. Jesus so often verbalized His love for them. And after He assured them, He told them to love others with that same love.

When we affirm our love for others, it shouldn't be a gushy sentimentality. *Agape* love isn't a one-time, verbal offering. It's a deep love that accepts the other person and keeps on loving—no matter what. This is the love Jesus had for His disciples. John 13:1 tells us, "He loved them to the end." He loved them to the end when they forsook Him. When Peter denied Him. When the rest of them squabbled or doubted. Jesus didn't stop loving them. And only the *agape* love of Jesus Christ at work in your heart can cause you to love others in that same way.

Jesus showed *agape* in very tangible ways. He cooked for His disciples. That really amuses me. I bet it was a gourmet meal, don't you? After His death, the disciples were so discouraged all they could think to do was to go fishing. John tells us,

> Then, as soon as they had come to land, they saw a fire of coals there, and fish laid on it, and bread. Jesus said to them, "Bring some of the fish that you have just caught." Simon Peter went up and dragged the net to land, full of large fish—one hundred and fifty-three; and although there were so many, the net was not broken. Jesus said to them, "Come and eat breakfast" (John 21:9-12).

Isn't that beautiful? Are you willing to cook for someone out of *agape* love like the Lord did? This Man who cooked breakfast for the disciples on the beach is the same Jesus described in Philippians 2:6-8,

> Who, being in the form of God, did not consider it robbery to be equal with God, but made Himself of no reputation, taking the form of a bondservant, and coming in the likeness of men. And being found in appearance as a man, He humbled Himself and became obedient to the point of death, even the death of the cross.

HUMILITY

Jesus had everything in heaven. He was equal with the Father, but He willingly laid all that aside. This One who would eventually be proclaimed King of kings and Lord of lords set aside everything He had in heaven to come to earth—knowing He would be reviled, rejected, scoffed, crowned with thorns, and put to death on a cross. What did He model to His disciples? What example did He give them? This Jesus Who could command the wind and the waves, Who opened blind eyes and unstopped deaf ears, Who caused the crippled to walk, Who cast demons out of people and set the captives free—this Jesus, Who is the King of kings and Lord of lords, bent down and washed their feet—and taught them humility.

I wonder how many people who have these great spiritual gifts in the body of Christ would be willing to bend down and wash someone else's feet? Footwashing today doesn't truly represent what it meant in their culture. In those days it was a genuine act of humility. In a household, it was a servant's task to wash the people's feet as they came in. When churches hold footwashing services today, it's more of a symbolic gesture, but it doesn't require or demonstrate the same degree of humility.

Humility in our culture means taking the lesser place—all the time. It means esteeming others better than ourselves. We are not to feel superior to other people under any circumstance. If we begin to feel this way, God stops us. He reveals Himself to us as He did to Isaiah, who tells us,

> In the year that King Uzziah died, I saw the Lord sitting on a throne, high and lifted up, and the train of His robe filled the temple. Above it stood seraphim; each one had six wings: with two he covered his face, with two he covered his feet, and with two he flew. And one cried to another and said: "Holy, holy, holy is the LORD of hosts; the whole earth is full of His glory!" And the posts of the door were shaken by the voice of him

who cried out, and the house was filled with smoke. So I said: "Woe is me, for I am undone! Because I am a man of unclean lips, and I dwell in the midst of a people of unclean lips. For my eyes have seen the King, the LORD of hosts" (Isaiah 6:1-5).

We need that revelation of God. We need to be reminded continually of His magnificence and His holiness. That's what will work humility in us. And then the *agape* love of Jesus will work humility through us toward others.

As the greatest example of *agape* love, Jesus willingly gave His life on the cross. In that moment, He demonstrated what He had said in John 15:13, "Greater love has no one than this, than to lay down one's life for his friends."

LAY DOWN YOUR LIFE

The willingness to lay your life down for another is the greatest evidence that *agape* love is present in your life. Woman of God, are you living this in your own life? Be honest with yourself. Is it hard for you to put others above yourself? I have to say that I know wives who are not willing to lay down their own lives for their husbands. I know mothers who are not willing to lay down their lives for their children. I know daughters who wouldn't lay down their lives for their mothers. And yet, they profess great love for these people. Well, they may have great *phileo*, and they may have great *storge*, or in a marriage they may have great *eros*, but they don't have *agape*. *Agape* love makes you want to lay down your life for another.

The story is told of a little girl, about six years old, who had a very serious blood disease. The only hope for saving her life was if she had a blood transfusion, but her blood type was very rare. The only person who could be found with the same blood type was her brother, who was just a couple of years older.

Asked if he would be willing to give blood for his sister, he thought for a while, then bit his lower lip and answered, "Yes, I will."

During the transfusion, the boy watched the color return to his little sister's face. As he lay on the table, tears began to course down his cheeks. "Why are you crying?" the doctor asked him. "Your sister is going to live."

This little boy answered, "Yes, but when do I die?" When he made the decision to give his blood, he thought he was giving *all* his blood. He made the choice to die for his little sister.

How many of us have the love of Jesus Christ flowing in our hearts in such measure that we would be willing to lay down our lives for another?

Father, if love is the sign that will prove to the world we are Your disciples, then we need more love. We need a divine transfusion of Your agape love. Have Your way with our hearts, Lord. We surrender to Your Holy Spirit, to do whatever is necessary to break us. Show us our utter emptiness apart from You. Give us that awareness of Isaiah, that we would see You in Your glory and be humbled. Crush the rose petals, that the fragrance of Your beauty might come forth through our lives and we might love as You loved.

Lord, for the woman who is reading this, I pray that You would so infuse her with Your Holy Spirit, and work within her the truths found in 1 Corinthians 13, that she would radiate You with a brightness that overwhelms all she encounters. Let her be a sunny presence in her home and wherever she goes, that the warmth of Your Spirit will flow through her and touch others.

We ask it in Your precious name, amen.

CHAPTER

11

LOVE YOUR ENEMIES

THE ENGLISH WRITER, WILLIAM LAW, said, "There is no principle of the heart that is more acceptable to God than a fervent love to all mankind … because there is no principle that makes us more like God." [18]

Isn't that beautiful? And yet, think of the implications.

"Fervent" is a wonderful word when we think of the *agape* love of Jesus and pleasing God's heart. But then there are those other two words—"all mankind." When we read those two words, we suddenly start making a list of exceptions. And at the top of that list we put "our enemies." Surely, the Lord doesn't mean we need to have a fervent love for them, does He?

He does.

God never asks us to do something that He is not willing to do Himself. And on this topic of loving your enemies, God has already modeled that kind of love for us. The Bible tells us that God so loved the world— that means all mankind, the good *and* the bad—that He gave His only begotten Son for them. God gave Jesus for the entire world. It is up to people to receive or to reject Jesus. He loves the wicked, even those who reject Him—enough to have died for them.

It is as much a law of Christ to love your neighbor as yourself, as it is the law of Christianity to abstain from theft. You wouldn't steal from your neighbor, but sometimes it is awfully hard to love them. And yet it is just as much a command of God.

Remember that we do not love others with God's *agape* love because they deserve it—because they are well-behaved, wise, or virtuous. You do not love people with God's love because of who they are. It doesn't take a *gape* love to love the nice people. With marvelous, sweet, wonderful people, love just flows from you. That doesn't take an act of God's love in your heart.

It is certain, then, that the reason for our being obliged to love people cannot be found in their virtue. But we are still obliged.

If this idea causes turmoil in you, it may be because you're struggling with a difficult person in your own life. Maybe you're wishing this chapter dealt with flowers or birds or something a little less personal. I am too, because whatever topic the Lord gives me to teach, He also tests me—and this chapter is no exception. So I say to you as well as to myself, that though we may never be able to love the difficult people for *who* they are, we are required by God to love them *where* they are. That doesn't mean we condone or approve of their rotten behavior, but it does mean we're to believe the best in them, and show the patient love of God to them.

REPRESENT GOD ACCURATELY

God loves us in order to make us good. His love draws us and changes us. Romans 2:4 asks,

> Or do you despise the riches of His goodness, forbearance, and longsuffering, not knowing that the goodness of God leads you to repentance?

God treats us with kindness and patience in order to draw us to Himself and to repentance.

We gladly accept His kindness toward us, but we're not always quick to show it toward others. Matthew 5:43-46 addresses that:

> You have heard that it was said, "You shall love your neighbor and hate your enemy." But I say to you, love your enemies, bless those who curse you, do good to those who hate you, and pray for those who spitefully use you and persecute you, that you may be sons of your Father in heaven; for He makes His sun rise on the evil and on the good, and sends rain on the just and the unjust. For if you love those who love you, what reward have you? Do not even the tax collectors do the same?

The principle Jesus sets forth in this passage is difficult. But because He tells us to do it, we can be sure there is power available to us to carry it out.

When you don't live according to this principle, Satan gets a foothold in your life. The lack of love toward another person will cause bitterness, resentment, envy, anger, and pride to fester in you.

I read something that said, "The place in your life that has not been given over to Jesus is the place where you are open to Satan's deception." We do hold back, you know. We say, "Lord, I give You all my heart," but then we reserve one little room, one little place that we don't want to give up, and we hope Jesus walks through the house and misses that room. It's in this little secret room that Satan is free to come in and deceive us. If there's a person in your life who is your enemy, and you permit yourself to hold a little bitterness and anger towards that person, that attitude will invade your spiritual life like a cancer cell. Cancer cells don't like to abide alone. They go out and get other cells to clump together with them until the mass just grows and grows. Unless that cancer cell is excised out of the body, it will reproduce itself or it will cause other cells to go astray. Bitterness, strife, and resentment will do the same thing in you. It must be rooted out. The rooting out can hurt, but we must remember that the Surgeon's scalpel wounds in order to heal.

Most of us don't have very many enemies, but all of us have a few. And the truth be told, if you're someone who has never had an enemy, I have to say you're missing out. Actually, enemies are servants of God who are permitted in our lives to help shape us and to give us opportunities to represent God. Enemies give us opportunities that dearly loved ones can't. Some of my greatest lessons in spiritual growth have stemmed from a deep inner struggle to be obedient to the Word of God, in spite of what hurt someone has inflicted upon me.

As hard as it can be to root out those feelings of bitterness with just one or two enemies, think what poor David must have felt. He said, "Those who hate me without a cause are more than the hairs of my head" (Psalm 69:4). Imagine having more enemies than the hair on your head!

The pattern Jesus set forth in Matthew chapter 5 is not easy. It is not possible unless you're walking in His Spirit. It won't happen unless you love and revere Him, and unless you have a hatred for sin and a desire to please God. Unless those things are in place, you will not have the slightest inclination, desire, or ability to obey this Scripture.

What is our natural reaction when someone harms us? We retaliate, or we withdraw from the other person, or we find subtle ways to slander them behind their back. The flesh reacts instinctively. But we need to react in the Spirit, not in the flesh.

Jesus said, "Love your enemies." And our minds go back to 1 Corinthians 13:4-7 and we think, *Yes. I'll put all that into practice. I'll be longsuffering, patient and kind with my enemy.* But then we read, "Bless those that curse you, do good to those who hate you, and pray for those who spitefully use you and persecute you" and all of a sudden, our tune changes. We think, *You have got to be kidding, Lord!* It is against everything in our nature to do those things. But Jesus said we are to do them. And by doing those things we represent God accurately.

I do want to please God and I do want my life to be an accurate representation of Him. Do you? If so, here are ten practical steps we can take to learn how to love our enemies.

STEP 1: ACKNOWLEDGE GOD'S SOVEREIGNTY

Recognize that God allowed this person to bring pain into your life for your growth and to give you an opportunity to represent His love. Now, the *instigator* of this hurtful situation was likely Satan, but God permitted it for a divine purpose.

Joseph was sold by his own brothers into slavery. Yet years later, he was able to say to his brothers, "You meant evil against me; but God meant it for good" (Genesis 50:20). Your enemies might mean to cause you evil, but if you will love your enemies, God will use it for good.

STEP 2: CHOOSE TO OBEY

This is so important I'd like you to affirm it out loud. Say, "Lord, I choose to obey Your Word." I like to affirm my obedient decisions before God, His holy angels, and the "great cloud of witnesses" we read about in Hebrews 12:1. If Satan is lurking around, I want him to hear it too.

STEP 3: AFFIRM YOUR DECISION TO OBEY

After you've verbalized your decision to obey, affirm it in writing. Write, *God, I will walk in Your love towards the one who hurt me.* Writing your decision has a way of bringing your own will into subjection to God's Word. It can help to get you out of your emotional reaction and put you under the Holy Spirit's control again.

Often, when you come to the decision to obey this particular passage of Scripture, you don't feel the slightest bit able to do it. You have no desire to bless that person. In that case, know that the enabling power of Jesus Christ will help you to do it. It has happened to me and I've seen it happen to others who choose to obey.

STEP 4: ASK GOD TO OPEN YOUR EYES AND STAND

Through Jesus, you have the right to use His authority against the work of Satan. But you will only be able to do that if you see where Satan is working against you.

Jesus gave this authority to His disciples. If you are His disciple then these words are meant for you as well.

> Behold, I give you the authority to trample on serpents and scorpions, and over all the power of the enemy, and nothing shall by any means hurt you (Luke 10:19).

This verse is the basis of your authority. When you see that Satan is trying to create more trouble or trying to cause more bitterness in you, stop him. Appropriate the power that God has given you.

STEP 5: TRUST GOD TO DEFEND AND PROTECT YOU

Next to loving your enemies, this might be the hardest thing to do. You want to defend yourself, don't you? You want to speak out on your own behalf and justify yourself. You want to make a phone call or write a letter, or maybe throw a rock through that person's window. What you *don't* want to do is leave your defense in God's hands, but that's exactly what you need to do.

I would like to have a big sign hanging in every room of my house that simply says, "Trust God." That's where Satan most often strikes—right at the point of trust. Isn't that what he did with Eve? He fed her lies until she doubted God.

Never doubt God. Leave your pain in His hands. Leave your enemy in His hands. Trust that He will be your defense.

The Psalms are full of Scriptures that assure us God is our defense and shield. David said, "In God I have put my trust; I will not fear. What can flesh do to me?" (Psalm 56:4). David had many opportunities to put his trust in God, including the situation with his best friend, Ahithophel, who turned on him eventually. This is the friend of whom David spoke when he said,

> For it is not an enemy who reproaches me; then I could bear it. Nor is it one who hates me who has exalted himself against me; then I could hide from him. But it was you, a man my equal, my companion and my acquaintance. We took sweet counsel together, and walked to the house of God in the throng (Psalm 55:12-14).

And if that weren't painful enough, 2 Samuel 15:1-6 records that David's own son, Absalom, turned against him and stole the hearts of the people. One of the saddest scenes in the Old Testament is when David was walking barefoot with his head covered up, weeping, because Absalom was taking over Israel. How grievous this was to David, but he learned to say, "Whenever I am afraid, I will trust in You" (Psalm 56:3).

God has promised to avenge you and He will. God has creative ways of correcting those who have wrongly hurt or persecuted you. If you stayed awake for a week straight trying to dream up ways to open your enemies' eyes to their awful behavior, you couldn't construct anything as creative. Trust Him. God likes to protect you.

> For in the time of trouble He shall hide me in His pavilion; in the secret place of His tabernacle He shall hide me; He shall set me high upon a rock (Psalm 27:5).

Isn't that a beautiful picture? I'd rather be in the secret place, hidden with Him, than out on the frontline fighting my own battle.

Psalm 31:20 talks about this pavilion, but it adds a line that is a great comfort when others begin to slander or backbite you.

> You shall hide them in the secret place of Your presence from the plots of man; You shall keep them secretly in a pavilion from the strife of tongues.

Oh, to be hidden in the "secret place" of God's presence, far from wagging tongues!

If you find you are lacking the desire to trust God, ask Him for that desire. Ask Him for the strength and the faith you need to be able to leave your situation in His hands. He loves when you ask Him for those things, because it means you are recognizing your own limitations.

STEP 6: ASK THE HOLY SPIRIT TO BE YOUR HELPER

In the Greek, the word translated for Spirit is *paraclete*, which means "one who comes alongside to help you." Jesus told His disciples,

And I will pray the Father, and He will give you another Helper, that He may abide with you forever—the Spirit of truth, whom the world cannot receive, because it neither sees Him nor knows Him; but you know Him, for He dwells with you and will be in you. I will not leave you orphans (John 14:16-18).

I think we forget that the Holy Spirit is here to help us. God's precious Holy Spirit is within us saying, "Let Me help you. Let Me strengthen you and fill you to overflowing." But we go along as though we are all alone in the world. We need His strengthening. And we need the love of God, which has been poured out in our hearts by the Holy Spirit who was given to us (Romans 5:5). Remember to ask the Holy Spirit to help you and to fill you with God's *agape* love.

STEP 7: ASK GOD TO CLEANSE UNLOVING EMOTIONS

I love the clean smell of suds in the washing machine. And I miss the days of hanging clothes on the line. If you've never hung your clothes outside on a clothesline, you probably think that sounds daffy. But there is nothing like the fragrance of clothes that have been out in the sun. I think part of the world's ills is due to the fact we don't hang our clothes on the line anymore.

I used to spend a lot of prayer time while hanging clothes on that line. Two of my children were in diapers at the same time, and that meant a lot of time hanging diapers out in the sun. But those diapers would come in as white as the snow, bleached clean and smelling wonderfully. I remember how white my dishtowels would be when I took them off the line at the end of a sunny day. Now I pull them out of the dryer, hold them up, and think how terrible they look.

We need that kind of cleansing in our lives. We need to stand in the sunlight of God's love and allow that heat and bleach and the fragrance of His beauty to flow forth and to reproduce something of His sweetness within us. Feelings of bitterness, hatred, wrath, resentment, and vengeance have no place in your heart. Ask the Lord to cleanse you.

STEP 8: REFUSE TO DO ANYTHING VENGEFUL

Say this aloud: "Lord, I will not do anything vengeful."

Most of us wouldn't launch a fireball at someone's house. We just wouldn't do that. But we don't seem to have any trouble launching a verbal attack. Think of all the clever rottenness the tongue does. We pretend we care about people, but then we make sure we get our little jabs in, little stabs in the back disguised with a bit of syrup.

Don't speak evil. Don't think evil. Don't wish harm to another person. Don't do it! When your thoughts and your attitude are right towards that person, God sees.

> The eyes of the Lord are over the righteous, [He watches what the righteous person does,] and His ears are open to their prayers, but the face of the Lord is against those who do evil (1 Peter 3:12).

When you think evil thoughts and you wish people harm, God sees that too. Make sure you walk in love, to please your Father Who watches you.

STEP 9: FOLLOW JESUS' EXAMPLE

You will not be able to do this apart from Jesus Christ. Only when you have His *agape* love will you be able to love your enemies. Jesus knows how to do that. He modeled that love for us. When He was reviled, He did not revile back. He spoke no harsh or unkind words to those who wrongly hurt Him. If anyone ever had a right to defend Himself, it was our pure, righteous, spotless, sinless Savior. Yet, He did not.

Follow His example. Show incomparable goodness and invincible goodwill to those who hurt you. Love them with *agape* love. When you regard a person with *agape*, no matter what that person has done to you, no matter how he or she treats you, no matter if he or she insults or injures you or grieves you—don't allow bitterness against that person to invade your heart. Continue to seek nothing but that person's highest good. *Agape* love has the power to love those you do not like, and who do not like you.

Within Matthew 5:43-46, Jesus listed the specific actions we are to take in order to love our enemy, and they are all within verse 44:

> Bless those who curse you, do good to those who hate you, and pray for those who spitefully use you and persecute you.

"Bless those who curse you." The word "bless" here means to speak well, not to curse back or slander, but to speak of those things you commend in that person. When cursed by someone, don't use that as an opportunity to tear that person down.

"Do good to those who hate you." Romans 12:17-20 gives us a beautiful picture:

> Repay no one evil for evil. Have regard for good things in the sight of all men. If it is possible, as much as depends on you, live peaceably with all men. Beloved, do not avenge yourselves, but rather give place to wrath; for it is written, "Vengeance is Mine, I will repay," says the Lord. Therefore, if your enemy is hungry, feed him; If he is thirsty, give him a drink; for in so doing you will heap coals of fire on his head."

A lot of people have read that line about the hot coals and thought, *Aha! I'll put a coal of fire on his head—and burn his eyebrows off!* But that isn't what it means. This isn't an act of vengeance, but of love. In many cultures, to give someone a hot coal meant you were helping them to get their fire going. It wasn't like today, where we turn a knob and the stove heats up. Back then if you lost your fire, you were in trouble. So for someone to share their hot coals with their enemy—and not just share one or two, but share a *heap* of them—would be an extreme act of love. This is a tender act, and it would serve to make the other person feel ashamed for the way they've behaved.

Peter wrote,

> Be tenderhearted, be courteous; not returning evil for evil, or reviling for reviling, but on the contrary blessing, knowing that you were called to this, that you may inherit a blessing. He who would love life and see good days, let him refrain his tongue from evil, and his lips from speaking deceit. Let him turn away from evil and do good (1 Peter 3:8-11).

We are called to this tender way of loving, and there's a blessing waiting for you when you do.

"Pray for those who spitefully use you and persecute you." Whenever a situation comes up in which I especially need to give *agape* love, I ask God to show me how to pray. It's not always the same. He gives me new and creative ways to pray concerning each particular issue. I have found it's a good idea to sit before Him with my Bible and a notebook and say, "God, show me how to pray in this situation." What happens is that I start praying for one part of the problem and then another. Sometimes God shows me others who are involved that I didn't even know about. Whatever He brings to my mind, I write it down. Then I pray until I begin to see answers.

In my experience, those who deliberately hurt others are usually in a lot of pain themselves. If you look into their eyes, the pain you see will sometimes break your heart. Compassion fills you. And though you don't know what happened to cause them to act so hatefully, you find yourself feeling love for them. Happy, whole people, whose needs are met in Christ, don't have a desire to hurt others. So when people desire to hurt you, realize they are hurting terribly over something. Pray for God to heal them of their pain and to meet all their deepest, emotional needs.

Pray also for their highest good. The healthier they become spiritually, the less menacing they're going to be, right? So pray for their highest good. How marvelous it would be for God to completely change their outlook. Picture that person smiling—joyful, and freed up to receive love from you and from God.

As you pray for your enemies, something wonderful happens in you— your bad feelings drift away. As you place that person in God's hands, all those negative thoughts are released.

When I'm having trouble with someone, I picture them kneeling before the throne of God. I know I can't imagine what it's really like, but I think about the descriptions I've read about God's throne, with cherubim and seraphim around it, the rainbow behind it, and the sea of sapphire. I imagine the light coming from God, this great light that is a million times brighter than the sun, and I see my dear person kneeling there, worshiping God, and suddenly I love that person! You can't visualize a person in the presence of God and hold bad feelings toward them.

STEP 10: THANK GOD

I heard Jack LaLanne in an interview once. What discipline this man has! At ninety-three, he still rises early and works out at least two hours a day, spending an hour-and-a-half lifting weights, and another half hour swimming or walking. But back when this interview was conducted, Jack was in his sixties—and working out four hours a day. "Ugh!" the interviewer said. "I would hate that!"

Jack LaLanne replied, "Well, I hate it too—but when I think of the results, it makes it worth the effort."

That's true for us too. Good results make the effort worthwhile.

Now, I don't like to confess this before the Lord and all His angels, but I do better in suffering. It shows me those places where I haven't been what I ought to be. It shows me what I'm really like inside. But it's also a way of bringing out something of Jesus in my life, and it puts a desire in my heart to be more like Him.

So when an enemy comes into your life, thank God. Thank Him for bringing that person along. You obviously needed it or He wouldn't have allowed it. He might be testing you. He wants to say, "Here's a person who will behave as My representative in this trial."

In Matthew 5:45 Jesus added, "That you may be sons of your Father in heaven." *The Living Bible* says, "In that way you will be acting as true children of your Father in heaven." The world is watching you, and they will know you belong to God by the way you treat your enemies. Isn't that beautiful? It's not easy to do, but the result is worth it. If you keep relying on the Holy Spirit, and continue to give over your feelings to Him, in the end you will have a beautiful offering to God.

I once struggled with a painful situation for over a year. I remember pounding my pillow and saying, "God, I cannot walk in love with that person! You've seen what they've done … I can't do it."

The Lord answered back, "Yes, you can, Kay. You can love them as I love you."

"I can't, Lord!"

"Yes, you can."

I would stay in my room and struggle in prayer until I'd feel something of the love of God. Just a little bit. But then a few days later, I would see that person again and I would think, *Ugh!* All those bad feelings would rush right back. So I'd go back to the bedroom, back to my prayer closet, back to the Bible. At the end of a year's time, God gave me victory, but it required that willingness to struggle.

Sometimes it happens immediately. He just infuses you with His love and you don't have to do all ten steps. But sometimes it takes longer. It takes a lifetime of work.

I saw a plant expert on TV once who had this scraggly, stringy, arrowhead plant. She said, "Do you know how to make this plant beautiful?" She showed how to take all the little stringy, hanging vines and wind them around the plant inside the pot. Then you pin them down with hairpins, and every so often you plant them down into the soil. When you do that, do you know what happens? It bruises or breaks open the skin of the plant, and everywhere that it's bruised, cut, or hurt, it produces new roots. The result is a fuller, more beautiful plant.

Some of us are like little scraggly plants, but God wants to make us full, lovely, and healthy. So He trims and He winds and He pins. In the process, we're cut and we're bruised and we're broken. But the result is worth the pain. Out of that suffering, He creates a beauty that reflects *His* beauty. And it makes the watching world want to know Him too.

Father, teach us to walk in Your Calvary love, that we could love our enemies as Jesus loved the world, and died for it. We are scraggly plants, Lord, and You are the Master Gardener. Have Your way with us, Father. Where we need bruising, bruise us. Where we need cutting, cut what needs to go. Take from us the haughtiness and conceit that keeps us from loving with Your love. Give us Your eyes so we can see the ones who hurt us as You see them, and love them with Your agape love.

It's in Your precious name that we ask it, amen.

12

EVERYTHING UNTO JESUS

IT'S ALMOST IMPOSSIBLE IN THIS society to get through a day without being bombarded by images of the beautiful woman. As mentioned before, the world sets a standard through books, magazines, television, and movies that is impossible for women to attain. But should you even want to reach it? Not if you want to please Jesus.

As we will see in our study, His design of beauty clashes sharply with the world's idea. What He values is not what the media values. And His opinion is the only one that matters.

AN ACT OF LOVE

> Then, six days before the Passover, Jesus came to Bethany, where Lazarus was who had been dead, whom He had raised from the dead. There they made Him a supper; and Martha served, but Lazarus was one of those who sat at the table with Him. Then Mary took a pound of very costly oil of spikenard, anointed the feet of Jesus, and wiped His feet with her hair. And the house was filled with the fragrance of the oil. But one of His disciples, Judas Iscariot, Simon's son, who would betray Him, said, "Why was this fragrant oil not sold for three hundred denarii and given to the poor?" This he said, not that he cared for the poor, but because he was a thief, and had the money box; and he used to take what was put in it. But Jesus said, "Let her alone; she has kept this for the day of My burial" (John 12:1-7).

Scholars and commentators debate whether this Mary is the sister of Martha or if it is Mary of Magdalene. We can't know for sure. Most expositors think she was not Mary Magdalene, because that woman was born in Magdala. But it's possible. One reason why some believe it is Mary Magdalene is because we know from Luke's gospel that this woman was forgiven much.

My own thinking is that this woman is Mary, the sister of Martha and Lazarus. Martha and Lazarus were both there with Jesus. John's gospel mentions them in verse 2 of that passage, and then mentions Mary in verse 3. So it seems likely that this Mary is the sister of Martha and Lazarus.

We don't know very much about this woman. We don't know, for instance, how old she was. We're not told whether or not she was beautiful. It's almost certain that she had very little importance in her day and in that society. As far as what the Bible tells us, there was nothing about Mary that would make the world look at her and say, "Oh, what a marvelous woman!" She isn't mentioned because of her great talent, her surpassing beauty, her fame, or anything else our society would think was important to be remembered. This woman is remembered for one thing: her glorious act of love for Jesus.

HER COURAGE

The fourteenth chapter of Mark gives us a few more details about the events of this night. The variation is slight, but it gives some interesting information.

And being in Bethany at the house of Simon the leper …

Bethany was about two miles from Jerusalem. The fact that this passage says Simon was a leper tells us that he had obviously been healed or he could not have had people in his home. Lepers, considered to be unclean, couldn't be near other people.

As He sat at the table, a woman came having an alabaster flask of very costly oil of spikenard. Then she broke the flask and poured it on His head. But there were some who were indignant among themselves, and said, "Why was this fragrant oil wasted? For it might have been sold for more than three hundred denarii and given to the poor." And they criticized her sharply. But Jesus said, "Let her alone. Why do you trouble her? She has done a good work for Me. For you have the poor with you always, and whenever you wish you may do them good; but Me you do not have always. She has done what she could. She has come beforehand to anoint My body for burial. Assuredly, I say to you, wherever this gospel is preached in the whole world, what this woman has done will also be told as a memorial to her" (Mark 14:3-9).

I would think it took a lot of courage for Mary to walk into that room. For one thing, the room was full of young men. Jesus was just thirty-three when this happened. The disciples were likely all younger than He. Simon the leper was probably the oldest man there because he may have been the father of Judas Iscariot. But all the rest of them—Jesus, the disciples, Mary, Martha, and Lazarus—were most likely young.

I can imagine that the scene was probably lively with noise and activity. Martha, no doubt, was busy bringing in dishes and serving as she usually did. Reclining around the table, Jesus and the disciples talked as they ate. At one point, the disciples began arguing about which of them would be the greatest in heaven. And then into the room walked Mary, carrying the costliest possession she had.

HER FOCUS

I believe Mary had an awareness the disciples didn't yet have. They were so interested in Jesus establishing an earthly kingdom—and then giving them prominence—that they really didn't understand much about His crucifixion or His resurrection. We read that even after the resurrection, it wasn't until Jesus began to expound upon the Scriptures from the prophets all the way through to their present time that they began to understand.

But Mary wasn't focused on an earthly kingdom, or her place in it. She was focused on Jesus. This precious woman loved to sit at Jesus' feet. It's one of the secrets of Mary's life, and probably the reason why she sensed something more. I don't know if she sensed sadness in Jesus or if, when He talked about the crucifixion and the things He was about to go through, she heard Him with her heart and understood. But she knew.

Mary had walked into that room and ignored all the men in it—except one. Standing before Jesus, she broke the box in her hand and she anointed Him with the oil it contained. The gospels Matthew, Mark and Luke give us a complete picture of what she did. Both Matthew and Mark wrote that she anointed His head, and Luke said she anointed His feet. I love that. It was a complete anointing of love.

Her beautiful act earned her great criticism from the others in the room. The Bible says the disciples were filled with indignation, and murmured together. Judas spoke out openly against her gesture.

Isn't it strange how an act of love towards Jesus could so incense one of His disciples? But we know the one incensed was the one who betrayed Him.

Jesus, though, looked at Mary, looked around at the others and said,

> Assuredly, I say to you, wherever this gospel is preached in the whole world, what this woman has done will also be told as a memorial to her (Mark 14:9).

HER EXPRESSION

It's not possible for us to do what Mary did. She was right there with Jesus. She had the chance to talk with Him face to face, to walk with Him, to literally sit at His feet, and then to anoint Him with her ointment and her tears. What a blessing to have been with Jesus while He walked on the earth. But we can still have the heart of Mary. We can learn from Jesus just what made her gift so beautiful.

Jesus made three strong statements about Mary. The first one is found in Mark 14:6, "She has done a good work for Me." *The Amplified Bible* says, "She has done a good and beautiful thing to Me."

I would like that to be said about me concerning my Lord, wouldn't you? Wouldn't you like Jesus to look down upon you and say, "She's done a good thing for Me, a beautiful work. She has anointed Me, and worshiped Me, and blessed Me. She's poured out her heart of love and praise and adoration unto Me." I can't think of anything I'd rather hear.

The second statement that Jesus made is one I pray the Holy Spirit will impress on your heart. "She has done what she could" (Mark 14:8).

You know what it's like to love someone so deeply that you just have to express it. From the depth of your being, you want to say, "I love you!" But it's not enough to just say it. It's not enough to write it on a greeting card. A regular gift won't do it. You realize a love that great is only going to be expressed one way: through a great sacrifice.

I think that's what happened to Mary. She spent a lot of time watching Jesus and learning from Him. She walked with Jesus, ate meals with Him, sat at His feet, and listened as He taught. She wept with Him over the death of her brother, Lazarus—and then watched in astonishment as He called Lazarus out of the tomb and brought him back to her. All of those things taught Mary to love Jesus, and love Him so greatly that she had to find a way to express it.

HER MINISTRY

As Mary mused about how to show her love to Jesus, she thought of the idea to bring her precious spikenard ointment to Him. I'm not sure she realized she was about to anoint Him for His burial, but with her alabaster box of ointment in hand, she headed to the house of Simon. The cost of this spikenard or "nard" (as it's more properly called), was equivalent to a year's wages in that particular time. It was the costliest thing she possessed, and therefore the only thing that could express her heart.

Some have suggested that the spikenard was Mary's anointing oil for her own burial. In that culture, your parents might give you this embalming ointment to be kept aside for your death. Or if you could afford to do so, you bought it yourself. But however you came to have it, spikenard would be your most-prized possession.

When Mary reached Jesus and stood before Him with her gift, the Word tells us that she broke the alabaster box in order to pour the contents on the feet and the head of her Lord. I love that she had to first break the box. Brokenness always implies sacrifice.

As the box was broken, the entire house was filled with the fragrance of Mary's deed.

And that is true of us. As our lives are broken before the Lord, a fragrance comes forth from us that nothing else could produce.

Mary gave her costliest possession. But that's not all. She took the very thing that was her greatest glory, and she laid it at the feet of Jesus. In fact, she used it to wipe His feet. Paul writes in 1 Corinthians 11:15 that a woman's hair is her glory, her pride, and joy. Mary laid her glory at the feet of Jesus, and used it to bless Him.

Thirdly, Jesus said of Mary, "She has come beforehand to anoint My body for burial" (Mark 14:8). No one knows for sure if Mary really understood that Christ was going to be crucified. But she did have a sense that something was happening to Him. Living in a small town like Bethany, she would have perceived the antagonism of the Pharisees and the hatred of the people toward Jesus. However much she knew, because of her love for Jesus, Mary wanted to minister to Him.

HER SENSITIVITY

I want to be like Mary. I want to be so attuned to Jesus that I sense when others have a need. I want His concern to be my concern. Sometimes we're so glib and disinterested in the people we meet—where they are and what they're going through—that we pass by without seeing their need. And we miss an opportunity to minister to them.

Mary had that sensitivity within her. I pray that we will too. As an unknown poet once said, "Lord, give me eyes that I may see, lest I, as people will, should pass by someone's Calvary and think it just a hill."

We too often pass by someone going through great sorrows, someone standing on their own *Golgotha*, and all we offer them is, "Hi! Good-bye! Love you!" We say we love them, but we don't take the time to show it. But Mary took that time. We need to do the same.

One February night many years ago, after evening service had ended, I got up right away and headed for the door. As I often did, I had driven my own car to church so I wouldn't have to wait for Chuck. On that particular night, I was thinking how glad I was that I had driven my own car because I was very, very tired. My daughter Janette was a kindergarten teacher at the time and still had to go home to prepare all her lessons for the next day. She was also terribly tired, so she too decided to go home right away with me.

As Janette and I started out the door, we saw our dear friends, Tony and Mary, standing there. "What are you doing?" they asked.

We said, "Oh, we're going home. We're just zonked!"

But they said, "Oh, come and have a bite to eat with us!"

I said again, "Oh boy, I am so tired. I really ought to go home." Janette agreed. "I've got so much to do." But suddenly, the strangest thing happened. Both Janette and I felt a tug to go with them. To this day, I cannot explain it. We just knew we were supposed to go.

That was the last time we saw Tony well. The next morning he had a stroke, and less than two weeks later, he went home to be with the Lord. I've thought so many times that if Janette and I had put our own will first, we would have missed out on a precious time—one of the sweetest, most tender memories I have. But because the love of Jesus was flowing through us and we wanted to do what Jesus wanted us to do, we were receptive to His voice. When He said go, we went. And I'm so glad we did.

The time Mary spent at the feet of Jesus granted her an understanding to His mind and His heart. She wanted to please Him—and she did. She pleased Him because she did what she could.

YOUR TIME

Mary offered the costliest thing she possessed. Assuming you don't have a box of spikenard hidden away somewhere, what else do you own that is costly? I have a suggestion. I suggest that your time is your costliest possession.

We spend twenty-four and a half hours a day pleasing ourselves! If you looked at a normal day and added up the time you spend in your prayer closet, the time you spend studying God's Word, and the time you spend worshiping, I think the average woman spends about fifteen minutes alone with Jesus. There are prayer intercessors here and there—women who are so committed to Jesus that they are purposeful about the time they spend with Him—but most Christians, sadly, give Him only the leftovers of their time.

Caitlyn, Janette's daughter, was a precocious little girl as a toddler. When she was three, if you asked Caitlyn if she was a Christian, she'd say, "No." Nobody in the Smith family had ever done that before—and I hope she's the only one that ever does! It really bothered me and I would get after Janette. A typical mom, I'd say, "Janette, are you teaching her to pray?"

"Yes, Mom!" she'd reassure me. Caitlyn could rattle off three or four Bible stories from memory. She knew all about the loaves and the fish, and she could tell you about the man who was lowered through the roof to be healed by Jesus, but she absolutely did not want to be a Christian.

Well, I had said everything I knew to say to the child. I gave her my best messages and nothing worked. Her mommy and daddy tried. Grandpa talked to her—and who's better than Grandpa to talk about these things? But nothing worked.

I thought, *Why, surrounded by all these Christians, doesn't Caitlyn want to be a Christian?* So I began to pray. I said, "Lord, will You somehow show our Caitlyn what it means to be a Christian? Give her that desire. She probably doesn't know too much of what she's saying, but break down that little stubborn spirit that refuses to acknowledge You."

A few weeks after I prayed that, Caitlyn and her cousins, Bradley and Vanessa, were at our house for dinner. We all sat down at the table and held hands to pray, but Caitlyn didn't bow her head and she wasn't going to pray for her dinner. This really upset her cousins. So I said to Bradley and Vanessa, "Well, Caitlyn doesn't pray because she's not a Christian."

Bradley and Vanessa's mouths went into little O's and they said, "She's not a Christian?"

I said, "No."

That little rebellious Caitlyn said, "No, I'm not a Christian."

So Vanessa, who was six at the time, popped up in her chair, and said, "If you're not a Christian, you love the Devil!"

Well, that hit Caitlyn. She said, "I don't love the Devil!"

"Oh, yes, you do if you're not a Christian!" Oh boy! Did the Lord give Vanessa the right thing to say!

Bradley jumped into the conversation. "If you don't love Jesus then you love the Devil. Christians love Jesus!"

Do you know what Caitlyn said? "I'm a Christian." Immediately she wanted to be a Christian.

Of course, the adults had to come in on it then to be sure that Caitlyn had good understanding. "Well, Bradley, how did you become a Christian?"

He said, "I asked Jesus to forgive me of my sins and asked Him to come into my heart."

Then we asked, "Vanessa, how did you become a Christian?"

Caitlyn was all ears, let me tell you. And from that day on she has been a Christian. She even graduated from Bible college.

It took awhile for Caitlyn to pray for meals. But whenever her mother would sing, *Jesus Loves the Little Children*, Caitlyn would sing along with her. And when Janette would sing the verse that says, "Jesus died for all the children, all the children of the world. Red and yellow, black and white, they are precious in His sight. Jesus died for all the children of the world." Caitlyn would say, "Mama, that's sad." She understood, even at three, that Jesus died for her. Of course, Janette wouldn't leave on that sad verse. She'd end with, "Jesus lives for all the children!" Then Caitlyn would say, "That's happy, Mama!" Their little minds are so active, and they understand far more than we realize. You can instill these truths in them right from the beginning.

DO WHAT YOU CAN

I pray that as you've been going through this chapter, the Holy Spirit has been impressing on your heart the statement Jesus made in defense of Mary: "She did what she could." Do you want to do what you can for Jesus? Do you have a desire to bless Him as she did? If so, I have some thoughts for you. These are practical ways you can focus your mind on Jesus, and on all that He has done to make you His own.

First, read all four accounts of Jesus' suffering and crucifixion in the Bible. Here are the references: Matthew 26-28; Mark 14-16; Luke 22-24; and John 12–20.

Next, I want you to read Isaiah 53, which gives a prophetic description of His suffering. The people who crucified Jesus thought they were doing God a favor. They felt that Jesus must have done something very, very wicked to be judged by the high priest and punished by God. Verse 3 of this passage says, "And we hid, as it were, our faces from Him." They turned their faces when they saw His suffering—but it wasn't because of the horror of His suffering—the people who loved Him saw His suffering—the others turned away because they thought He was evil. They didn't know that He was wounded for our transgressions and bruised for our iniquities. They didn't know that the chastisement for our peace was upon Him, or that the stripes that He bore on His body through the scourging and the whipping post were for us.

How painful that must have been for Jesus. I think one of the worst things that can happen to you when you're suffering is to be misunderstood. That makes it doubly painful when you're already hurting badly.

Now with His sacrifice fresh in your mind, I want you to think of one thing you can sacrifice for Him. Maybe your friends invite you to lunch and you dearly want to go. Sacrifice it. Say, "Jesus, I love You more than lunch with my friends. I'd rather spend that hour with You." Then do it. Spend that time in fellowship with Him.

THE COST OF YOUR SALVATION

When you read passages like Matthew 27:28-31, read it with your heart. Don't just skim by the words. Skimming robs you of the impact these words should have. Read this slowly, and remember that Jesus went through this for you:

And they stripped Him and put a scarlet robe on Him.

They took our sinless, precious Lord—Who had done nothing but bless them, revive their sick, open the eyes of their blind, and heal their lame—and they stripped Him and put a scarlet robe on Him.

When they had twisted a crown of thorns, they put it on His head …

Who could have conceived of that kind of torture? That probably wasn't planned. Likely, someone just got a spontaneous idea while they were beating and torturing Him. "Won't this be great? He said He's King of the Jews, so let's make Him a crown!" I have some thorns at home that are supposedly the same kind that were used to make His crown. They're three to four inches long, and very sharp—and every time I look at them it breaks my heart to imagine them piercing the head of my Savior.

… and a reed in His right hand.

They gave Him the reed to denote a scepter. "Aha! Since You're the King of the Jews, here's Your scepter!"

And they bowed the knee before Him and mocked Him, saying, "Hail, King of the Jews!" Then they spat on Him …

To be spat upon was the greatest insult in the Eastern culture.

… and took the reed and struck Him on the head.

Think about this: they took the reed they had just placed in His hand, and they hit Him on His head. Each blow must have driven those thorns deep into His scalp.

And when they had mocked Him …

Have you ever been mocked? If you have, you know how awful it is. I hate to be mocked. Most people do. It's a terrible thing to make fun of someone, to laugh at them and to make them feel worthless and horrible.

… they took the robe off Him, put His own clothes on Him, and led Him away to be crucified.

This hurtful passage is just one of many that describes the torment Jesus went through. I want you to read it and think about it. Meditate on it. Let your heart be filled with an awareness of the cost of your salvation, the price that Jesus paid to redeem you out of Satan's hand.

Then I want you to behold Him. To behold means to gaze intently. When Jesus came to be baptized and John saw Him for the first time, he said, "Behold! The Lamb of God who takes away the sin of the world" (John 1:29). Jesus is the Lamb of God, Who is without spot or blemish.

Lambs are sweet, gentle animals. When they are led to slaughter, they go without making any sound. That's what Jesus did. Behold the Man of Sorrows, and think about His agony and His suffering.

Listen to His cries from the cross. "My God, My God, why have You forsaken Me?" (Matthew 27:46). To be forsaken of God is to be separated from Him—and to be separated from God is hell itself. Jesus was forsaken of God, and separated from His Father—and all because He took our sins upon Himself. Can you imagine what it would be like to be forsaken of God? And yet Jesus suffered that for us. He suffered that for you. Hear His cry again and again, and listen with your heart.

I believe that if we thought more about the suffering of Christ, we could not sin so easily. If we meditated on what it cost Him to purchase our salvation, we could not live as carelessly as some do.

Let the magnitude of what Jesus endured for you motivate you to love Him more fervently, to do what you can to bless Him, and to live in such a way that you bring pleasure to His heart all the rest of your days.

Father, I ask that by the power of the Holy Spirit, You make Your suffering real to us. We know that in the battle for our souls, Satan fights hard to keep us from looking at Your suffering and realizing the cost You paid for our redemption. We can't look on the cross and take in the magnitude of the pain You felt there without being changed. So cause us to look, Father. Cause us to behold. We want to be changed. We want to live in the light of the cross, motivated every moment of our lives by the great sacrifice You paid there.

In Jesus' name we pray, amen.

13

PRAISE AND FEAR THE LORD

I READ A QUIZ THAT asked, "How well do you know your mate?" If you could answer all the questions correctly, that meant you knew your mate really well. If you could only answer ten correctly, I guess that meant you had some work to do.

Some of the questions were tricky for me. For instance, "What is his favorite color?" The answer to that is: it depends. If you ask Chuck, he'll say, "Well, it depends. If I'm looking at the sky, I like blue. If I'm eating pudding, I don't want blue pudding." It's hard to nail him down.

"What is his favorite food?" It's hard to nail Chuck down on that one too. Others weren't so hard. "What is his favorite song? Where would he like to travel if he could go anyplace in the world?"

But then they got a little tougher. "What living man does he admire most? What's his favorite time of the day?" I had never even thought to ask Chuck that before. And then there was, "What does he like best about you?" And right after that one, "What does he dislike about you?"

I know a lady whose husband dislikes her laugh—actually, he hates her laugh because it is so loud. For years he'd make little comments about it and she'd just ignore him. But then finally he couldn't take it anymore and he told her in some pretty strong terms that he could not stand her laugh.

I want to know what Chuck dislikes—but not really. I really don't want to know. I don't want him to dislike anything about me at all. To find out would be painful.

KNOW GOD

If someone were to ask you what pleases God, would you have an answer? Could you tell that person what displeases God? The real question is, how well do you know God? Knowing God is critical if you want to live a life that is pleasing to Him. In fact, it's very difficult to please someone you don't know very well.

In this chapter, we're going to learn how we can know God through His Word. We're going to study Psalm 34 to find out what it teaches about pleasing God.

> I will bless the LORD at all times; His praise shall continually be in my mouth. My soul shall make its boast in the LORD: the humble shall hear of it and be glad. Oh, magnify the LORD with me, and let us exalt His name together (Psalm 34:1-3).

What is the first thing we learn about pleasing the heart of God from these verses? What are we supposed to do? We're to praise Him! I love when we can have that freedom of the Spirit and we can rejoice in the Lord with abandonment. One of my greatest fears is that we will lose the spirit of worship. It's easy to let our minds wander when we're singing. Our lips sing, "I love You, Lord, and I lift my voice," but our minds are way out in the fields someplace. God wants us to focus on Him and praise Him with freedom. If you feel like lifting your hands as a sign of love and surrender, do it.

I will bless the Lord at all times.

When do we praise Him? At all times and continually! *The Living Bible* says, "I will praise the Lord no matter what happens."

My soul shall make its boast in the Lord.

This is a good reminder that we're not to boast in ourselves or in other people, but only in the Lord.

The humble shall hear of it and be glad.

The Hebrew word translated here as "humble" means discouraged and afflicted. When the discouraged and afflicted person hears you praising God and thanking Him, it will lift their heart. I don't mean you're supposed to run around saying, "Glory, glory, glory! Hallelujah, hallelujah, hallelujah, praise the Lord!" No! You're to praise Him specifically for the wondrous things He has done.

We once met a woman at the Maui airport. We didn't know her, but she heard Chuck's big, hearty laugh from two counters over and came over to say hello. She recognized his voice from hearing his radio program in Seattle. And as we stood talking, she said, "I have to share with you what happened yesterday." She said she had been at the beach all day and had lost her diamond wedding ring. She didn't realize it for three hours, but when she did, she decided to go back to the beach and look for it anyway.

Well, even as she stood there telling us the story, I thought, *Three hours?* I've lost car keys on the beach, never to see them again. To go look for something as tiny as a wedding ring, forget it.

But as she continued her story she said, "I prayed all the way to the beach, and when we got there, we looked around for a minute, and then all of a sudden, I saw something bright and glistening in the sand. I thought, *No way.* But it was! It was my ring."

And then she said something so beautiful. She said, "My husband gave me that ring the first time, but God gave it to me the second time. And every time I look at it, I'll be praising Him."

Now, I'm telling you that story because those are the specific deeds we need to be sharing with people. Instead of just running around yelling, "Praise the Lord! Praise the Lord!" why not praise Him specifically for the many wonderful things He does?

When people hear those kinds of praises, their faith is increased and their wonder of God grows tremendously. As your soul boasts in the Lord, that discouraged person will say, "Hey, if He did that for her, He can do it for me!"

MAGNIFY GOD

The humble shall hear of it and be ... glad (Psalm 34:2).

What? Glad! What are discouraged and afflicted people like? They're down. They're disheartened. Their countenance is sad. The thoughts in their minds are depressing, and oh, how Satan loves to put a spirit of depression on us. But when you talk to someone who has the joy of the Lord flowing through her and she's praising Him and giving thanks for what He's done, what happens to you? Your spirit is uplifted.

Let your boast be in the Lord. *The Living Bible* says, "I will boast of all His kindness to me" (Psalm 34:2).

Psalm 103 speaks about God crowning us with His lovingkindness and tender mercies. What does a crown denote? It means authority and kingship. When God puts a crown of His tender mercies and lovingkindness upon you, you can face the world with authority and confidence.

> O magnify the LORD with me, and let us exalt His name together (Psalm 34:3).

I have loved the times when I've exalted the Lord together with my friends, thanking Him beforehand for the things we know He's going to do for us at a retreat, or just praising Him for all the wonderful things He's done for us in the past. He is so worthy of our praises.

> I sought the LORD, and He heard me, and delivered me from all my fears. They looked to Him and were radiant, and their faces were not ashamed. This poor man cried out, and the LORD heard him, and saved him out of all his troubles. The angel of the LORD encamps all around those who fear Him, and delivers them. Oh, taste and see that the LORD is good; blessed is the man who trusts in Him! Oh, fear the LORD, you His saints! There is no want to those who fear Him. The young lions lack and suffer hunger; but those who seek the LORD shall not lack any good thing (Psalm 34:4-10).

We please God by trusting Him. If you mark your Bible like I do, you could put brackets around verses 1-3 and write, "Pleasing God by praising Him," then put brackets around verses 4-10 and write, "Pleasing God by trusting Him." Some people think it's terrible to write in your Bible and others think it's wonderful. I love my Bible, and if the Lord inspires me with something, I put it right next to that verse. Chuck does that too. I have hearts, arrows, exclamation marks, and all kinds of things written in there. Sometimes I'll just write, "Wow!" I'll often write the date beside a note, especially when God gives me something to help me through a trial. Often I'll see a note from long ago and think, *Oh, boy. June 14, 1977. That was a wowie of a day, but God met me and He did such and such …* and I remember how He gave me that particular verse and how I stood on the authority of His Word and watched His deliverance come to pass. What a blessing!

FAITH REPLACES FEAR

> I sought the Lord and he heard me and delivered me from all my fears (Psalm 34:4).

Fear is the opposite of faith. It is basically unbelief. When you are filled with fear, you're saying you do not believe God. Reading the newspaper or watching the evening news can fill us with fear. I think if you can get through an issue of *Time Magazine* without asking the Lord to remove your fear, you're doing pretty well.

David wrote this psalm after he fled from Abimelech. While hiding in the territory of the Philistines, he was terrified that Abimelech would capture and kill him. So do you know what David did? He drooled and carried on and acted crazy in front of the king. Not the most regal behavior from the man whom God had anointed to be king over Israel, is it?

David writes that he sought the Lord and was delivered from all his fears after his crazy behavior. Why he didn't do it beforehand, I don't know. But don't we often do a lot of crazy things before we remember to seek the Lord? By the time we turn to God, we are praying from a point of fear rather than from a place of trust.

I remember several years ago being down on my knees praying about a situation, and I began by saying, "Oh Lord, would You …" and before I could go any further, I stopped and realized I was filled with fear. I was afraid God wasn't going to move in my situation. The Holy Spirit began to impress on my mind that I needed to trust God instead of praying all tensed and bottled up and scared. So I released it to the Lord. I said, "Lord, I trust You. I trust Your hand in this. Thank You for taking my fear. Thank You that what You promised in Your Word You will do." Be sure you're not praying from that point of fear. If you feel fear in your heart, ask God to replace it with trust.

One of our retreat speakers, Ramona Jenson, gave a beautiful definition of unbelief. She said, "Unbelief is the darkroom where we develop our negatives." And how are negatives destroyed? With light! When the light of the knowledge of Jesus Christ and the truth comes in, the negatives are destroyed. If you're in the darkroom today, filled with fear, that isn't God's plan for you. Trust Him and watch your fears vanish.

> They looked to Him and were radiant, and their faces were not ashamed (Psalm 34:5).

I love how *The Living Bible* phrases verses 4 and 5:

> For I cried to Him and He answered me! He freed me from all my fears. Others too were radiant at what He did for them. Theirs was no downcast look of rejection!

Again, your trust or your fear will have an effect on the people around you. Years ago while traveling home from Israel, someone made a bomb threat against our group. We didn't know it until we were in the airport in Copenhagen. We were instructed to go through security, but not told that it was due to a bomb threat. When news came of the threat, a woman came to me and said, "You are in a very dangerous position." One hundred-and-fifty people were going through security at that moment, and not one of them knew why. As soon as the woman informed me, I immediately went to prayer. Afterwards, when everyone found out, people said to me, "You knew, but you didn't show it. You looked so happy." I was able to look happy because I *was* happy. God gave me peace, and helped me to trust Him. Fear is contagious, and like chickenpox, it spreads fast. If I had looked or acted fearful, others would have been fearful too.

CRY OUT TO GOD

> This poor man cried out, and the LORD heard him, and saved him out of all his troubles (Psalm 34:6).

David was not poor in material things. He was poor in spirit. He was down, he was brokenhearted, and he cried unto the Lord. God heard him and saved him out of *all* his troubles. That's a good word to underline in your Bible. God saves you out of <u>all</u> your troubles. Now, that doesn't mean that if you're in a very difficult marriage, when you go home tonight, God will have your suitcases packed, a new home, a new husband, and a new life waiting for you. That's not the way He does it. Instead, He gives you the peace, strength, grace, wisdom, and faith to walk through the fire and come out the other side unharmed.

Look again at verses 4 and 6. Note that in verse 4 David said, "I sought the LORD," and in verse 6 he said, "This poor man cried." David showed a deliberate, earnest seeking of God. It pleases God when we seek Him from the very bottom of our heart, when we say, "God, if You don't deliver me, there is no hope! Come, Lord, and deliver me!" He will. He will deliver you out of all your troubles.

> The angel of the LORD encamps all around those who fear Him, and delivers them (Psalm 34:7).

This is a verse that has comforted me many, many times. I recommend that you memorize it. Just knowing that God has put His angels around you can be the difference between being terrified and being at peace.

Many years ago, Chuck left for a trip that would have him gone for several days. Cheryl and Brian were going on the trip too, and all the rest of our children were grown, so I was going to be alone in the house.

Before they left, Cheryl said, "Mom, you ought to get the machete out." We'd been given a machete during a ministry trip to Guatemala. I just laughed when she said it, but that night, just before bed, I heard her words again. "You ought to get the machete out." And I thought, *What if the Lord put that thought in my mind?* So I got the machete out and I put it right by my bed. That doesn't sound too brave, does it? I really wasn't afraid, but I didn't want to be foolish. Maybe it was the Lord.

I went right to sleep without any trouble Sunday night and then again on Monday night, because before bedtime I reminded myself, "The angel of the Lord encamps all around those who fear Him, and He delivers them."

Tuesday night, I went right to sleep. But around midnight I awoke to see that the hallway light was on. I knew I hadn't left it on. I thought, *Somebody's in the house.* Chuck wasn't due back until the following night, and everybody else was gone. I thought, *Maybe Greg and Janette dropped by for a visit.* But it was midnight! Who would come by for a visit at midnight? So I started praying. "Oh Lord, You've got to do something!" Then I thought, *Is it time for the machete?*

About that time I heard the front door open and close and I thought, *This is it, Kay!* In my bravest voice, I yelled, "Who is it?"

This big voice answered back, "It's me!" It was Chuck!

But right away, I thought, *That can't be Chuck. Chuck's not due home until tomorrow. That's not Chuck! That's not his voice! I know his voice— and that's not him!* So I said, "Who?"

He said again, "It's me!"

And then I knew it was him. I was so relieved. He had come home a night early. Interestingly, he told me that the last thing Cheryl said as he got out of the motorhome was, "Dad, be careful of that machete!"

I'll tell you, I used to be a woman who could not have stayed home alone. I had the most horrifying nightmares as a child. I would wake up screaming and my dad used to run in the room with a crowbar, thinking somebody must be in my room. My bedroom had French windows, and my parents had to put all kinds of locks on them for me. I still had horrible nightmares even after Chuck and I were married. The first few years, I used to dig my nails into Chuck's arms when I'd wake him up and scare the life out of him. Finally, I realized through a Scripture just like this that there was fear someplace deep inside me. I knew that God could deliver me, so I asked Him to—and He did. I praise Him for it! "He gives His beloved sleep" (Psalm 127:2).

When the Word tells us, "The angel of the LORD encamps all around us," this is not talking about floaty, little creatures with flapping white wings. God's angels are mighty. Remember what Elisha's servant saw when he prayed that his spiritual eyes would be opened? The Word tells us, "The LORD opened the eyes of the young man, and he saw. And behold, the mountain was full of horses and chariots of fire all around Elisha" (2 Kings 6:17). As Elisha said in verse 16, "Those who are with us are more than those who are with them." This is true for you and for me. God has placed His chariots of fire all around to protect us.

A. W. Tozer wrote that two types of people dwell on the earth: those who live in a world inhabited by spiritual beings, who walk and talk with God and whose prayers God answers; and those who live in a material world full of cars and planes—a world where they walk with their feet solidly on the ground. [19] We each choose which world we want to live in. I want to be one who endures "as seeing Him who is invisible" (Hebrews 11:27). When things get hard, I want to remind myself that I'm a pilgrim and a stranger in this world. My citizenship is elsewhere.

The word "encamps" literally means that the angel of the Lord "pitches his tent" around you. Isn't that a reassuring thought? In these dark days, these last days, God wants you to know that.

TASTE AND SEE

Oh taste and see that the LORD is good (Psalm 34:8).

One of the hardest things in the world is trying to get a baby to taste something they don't want to taste. Chuck would get so frustrated when he had something really yummy on the tip of his spoon and he'd offer it to one of the children and they wouldn't take it. They'd shake their heads and tighten their lips as if he was offering them green beans. And Chuck would say, "Just try it! It's good! Take just one taste!" That's what the Lord is saying to you today. "Oh, taste and see that the LORD is good; blessed is the man who trusts in Him." *The Amplified Bible* says, "Blessed (happy, fortunate, to be envied) is the man who trusts and takes refuge in Him" (Psalm 34:8). Try trusting in God and see how it blesses your life.

We met a girl from Colorado when we were in En Gedi. Standing there together, we struck up a conversation and I asked her why she had decided to visit Israel.

"Oh, I suppose I'm just seeking truth," she said.

"Well, do you believe there's a God?" I asked.

She said, "I'm seeking to know."

So I said, "Ask Him to reveal Himself to you. He will." When we parted she said she would. I walked away thinking, *Oh, taste and see.* I pray that she did.

RESPECT GOD

> Oh, fear the LORD, you His saints! There is no want to those who fear
> Him. The young lions lack and suffer hunger; but those who seek the
> LORD shall not lack any good thing (Psalm 34:9-10).

The kind of fear spoken in verse 4 is a terrorizing fear. But the fear
in verse 9 is completely different. As defined by commentaries, it is
profound reverence, awe, honor and respect. My own definition of
the "fear of the Lord" is recognition of Who and what He is. It's an
acknowledgment that He has the right to your life—you're His servant
and He can do whatever He wants.

In an age where refinement and manners have been shoved aside, one
tragic result is a terrible disrespect of God. With that disrespect has also
come a dishonoring of His holiness and a casual attitude towards sin.
But Proverbs 8:13 says, "The fear of the LORD is to hate evil." Proverbs
16:6 says, "by the fear of the LORD one departs from evil." If you are
walking in deliberate sin today, you do not have the fear of God in your
heart and you cannot claim Psalm 34:7. That verse clearly applies
only to those who fear the Lord.

Does it grieve your heart when you sin? Praise God! It should hurt you
badly to grieve the One Who loves you so dearly that He gave His Son
to die on a cross for you. His fear must be in your heart if you are to
hate evil and depart from it. You cannot please God and love sin. You
just can't.

Joy Dawson shares about women who come to her and confess that
they are involved in an affair. They say, "Oh, pray for me! I'm just so
bound. Pray for my release." So she would pray and then they would be
released. But after a couple of months, they'd be back. "I'm in bondage
again! It's a new person—will you pray for me?" Joy said she finally got
to a place where she said to them, "I will not pray for you anymore. You

have a love for that sin or you wouldn't keep repeating it. You have to pray that God will give you a hatred for that sin."

If you keep committing the same sin over and over, don't say, "Oh, I'm so weak. I don't know how I got into this." That is a lie from Satan. You love the sin. You do not have the fear of God in your heart that would make you hate that sin. God will give you a hatred for that sin if you ask Him, because He is faithful. But you must ask Him.

I am personally fed up with hearing of that sin in the body of Christ. The chief characteristic of God is holiness. What do the seraphim and the cherubim sing around the throne? "Holy, holy, holy." And our holy God is coming for a holy bride.

First John 1:6 reads, "If we say that we have fellowship with Him, and walk in darkness, we lie and do not practice the truth." What does it mean to walk in darkness? It's like trying to walk through a pitch-black room—you bump into things. You get a lot of bumps and bruises trying to walk without the light of His guidance—injuries that you wouldn't have gotten if you'd walked in the light. We lose that light when we break fellowship.

Sin breaks fellowship with God. The results are both tragic and plenteous. One of the first results of broken fellowship is the loss of joy. You can't have real joy apart from fellowship with the Father.

Wise judgment is also lost. The person who has lost the fear of God and a hatred of sin will twist or misquote Scripture or will just stop talking about God or the things of God altogether. Oh, how much lesser our lives are when we lose the fear of the Lord!

Come, you children, listen to me; I will teach you the fear of the LORD (Psalm 34:11).

I cannot stand it when people refer to God as "the Man upstairs," or "the Guy in the sky." That's so irreverent! Can you imagine approaching the Creator of the universe, the One Who sits on the sapphire throne, the One who created you and Who blesses you continually, and greeting Him so glibly and carelessly?

We come to the throne of grace boldly, but not rashly. We enter His presence with deep love and with the utmost reverence. Only those ignorant of His true beauty and majesty could refer to Him as "the Man upstairs."

KEEP YOUR LIPS FROM EVIL

Continuing in Psalm 34, David lists three specific things we are to do.

> Keep your tongue from evil, and your lips from speaking deceit (Psalm 34:13).

The fear of the Lord begins with our mouth and our tongue. If you have the fear of the Lord when you start to say something you shouldn't, you'll feel a nudge. The Holy Spirit will say, "That doesn't please Me. Don't say that." We can be so careless with our tongues. Many times while in a group of friends some juicy bit of information has come into my mind, and I've started to say, "Oh, did you hear ..." and before I can go any further, the Holy Spirit will say, "No, Kay."

And I'll think, *Oh, but I want to tell it!*

But then I hear, "If you have My fear in your heart and you want to please Me, you won't tell it."

So I stop and I say, "I can't tell it."

Then of course everyone says, "What?!"

The Lord is teaching me now not to say even the first few words, "Oh, did you hear ..." He wants to stop me before I even say that much, so that my dear friends don't have to suffer through their curiosity.

Keep your tongue from evil. We all know bad things about people. Everybody does. But don't speak it. Gossip hurts so terribly. Even if it's said carelessly or meant humorously, it can still wound deeply.

Obviously, if we are keeping our lips from evil, we are watching what we say. We're not swearing, we're not saying ugly things about a situation, we're not being negative, and we're not programming fear into others. Ask the Lord to help you be sensitive to how you use your tongue. Say, "Lord, would You just tap me on the shoulder any time I speak evil?"

... and your lips from speaking deceit (Psalm 34:13).

Some versions use the word "guile" in place of "deceit." In Psalm 32:1-2, David said, "Blessed is he whose transgression is forgiven, whose sin is covered. Blessed is the man to whom the Lord does not impute iniquity, and in whose spirit there is no deceit." The woman who keeps her lips from speaking deceit is a happy, blessed woman.

I read something once that said you could tell if someone is feeling hostile toward you because they'll give you a compliment with a barb in it. A long time ago I went to a convention with a suitcase full of old clothes. We didn't have money to buy new clothes, so I just brought the same clothes I'd been wearing for several years. A woman came up to me and said, "I really like that dress. I liked it last year when you wore it too." At the time I didn't recognize that she was being hostile toward me. I just knew I had a wounded spirit. Be sure there's no guile in you, or deceit.

Depart from evil and do good ... (Psalm 34:14).

God will show you what "departing from evil" means to you. Some things are obvious and apply to all believers, but others are individual. When God puts a searchlight on our lives, our hearts are often broken. But that's a wonderful thing if it leads to repentance.

A man who was saved at Calvary Chapel began sharing Jesus with his wife. After a time, she also decided to accept the Lord. He told her, "Now you must ask God for forgiveness of sin and you must repent."

The woman, who was in her early forties, said, "I honestly don't have anything to repent. I've lived a very good life." But he persisted and told her she just needed to pray and ask God to show her what she needed to repent. She did, and when she told me the story later, she said, "I wept for three days." Isn't that beautiful? Some of us would probably have to repent a lot longer than three days.

Are you courageous enough to ask God to put His searchlight on your life? I urge you to ask Him. Let Him show you those things you need to depart from. Then repent and do good! It isn't enough to stop doing evil—we need to start doing good. Like most mothers, mine had all kinds of platitudes and little sayings. One of her favorites was, "Idle hands are the Devil's playground." She was so worried about that, in fact, she kept my days filled with chores and piano practice.

Do whatever God would have you to do. Just ask Him! He is so inventive, there's no end to the things He can come up with. He'll have you say a kind word to one person, or write a note to another. He'll have you make a call to brighten someone's day. He'll have you pray for another, or bake a cake to bring to someone else.

PURSUE PEACE

Seek peace and pursue it (Psalm 34:14b).

When I read that verse, I can't help but remember back to one time, years ago, when picketers lined the front of our church property. They had taken issue with something Chuck taught out of the Bible—and they had all these awful signs that read, "Blind leaders of the blind," and

"Chuck is a wolf in sheep's clothing," and other horrible things. We had to drive past those picketers every time we went to church. I'd see those signs and I would just become enraged.

Chuck and I drove in one Tuesday night for church, along with Cheryl and Kristyn, who was a baby at the time. As we came down the street, there they were. I became furious all over again. I knew I had to pray. So when Chuck got out of the car, I turned it around and drove it up to the entry where they were all walking back and forth with those awful signs. Cheryl and I sat there and prayed and prayed and prayed. And then I rolled down my window to say something to them, and one of the Charles Manson look-alikes called me "honey!" So I rolled the window up and we went back to praying.

My spirit was so troubled over that. I thought, *How dare they do this? How dare they hinder people who are coming to worship God?* But as I was praying, God brought to mind this very verse: "Seek peace and pursue it."

The more I meditated on that verse, the more peaceful I felt. In fact, God brought me to such a peaceful place that the next time we drove by the picketers and I read those awful signs, I was able to smile along with Chuck. I had confidence that God would take care of it.

When people do hurtful, aggravating things, our natural instinct is to defend ourselves or set them straight. But that usually just causes everything to escalate. Instead, we want to bring peace into the situation. One translation of this verse says, "Work at it." It can be work to bring peace to a situation, but it's what God would have us do.

Read the rest of this psalm and think about these beautiful promises.

> The eyes of the LORD are on the righteous, and His ears are open to their cry. The face of the LORD is against those who do evil, to cut off the remembrance of them from the earth. The righteous cry out, and the

LORD hears, and delivers them out of all their troubles. The LORD is near to those who have a broken heart, and saves such as have a contrite spirit. Many are the afflictions of the righteous, but the LORD delivers him out of them all. He guards all his bones; not one of them is broken. Evil shall slay the wicked, and those who hate the righteous shall be condemned. The LORD redeems the soul of His servants, and none of those who trust in Him shall be condemned (Psalms 34:15-22).

As you've read through this chapter, it's likely that the Holy Spirit has been speaking to you about something specific. Maybe you're not trusting Him. Maybe you're having trouble controlling your tongue. Maybe there's a great deal of strife in your relationships, and you haven't been working to pursue peace. Or maybe there is a persistent sin that you truly don't want to let go. God wants to free you. Be honest before Him and confess whatever He's shown you. Great blessings await those who fear Him. Let Him bring you to that place of praise, that place of godly fear.

Father, a battle is being waged over Your bride. I pray for all those who have lost their reverence for You. I pray for those who have an issue with gossip. I ask, Lord, that You would free those who feel trapped by an immoral sin and who do not want to give up their love of it. Deliver her, Lord. Give her hatred for that sin. Show her that You are ready to cleanse her and make her new.

I pray for those with fearful hearts this day. Would You open their eyes to see Your chariots of fire all around them? Help them to know that You reign! Remind them that You hear their cry and see their poverty of spirit, and that You want to deliver them out of all their troubles if they will just partake of that trust.

We love You, Lord, and we praise You for Your faithfulness, Your goodness, and Your grace. Teach us how to please You with the life You've given us.

In Jesus' precious name we pray, amen.

14

PARABLE OF
THE SOWER

DO YOU KNOW WHAT I'D like to see hanging just inside the front door of our church, and every church? Right at eye level, where people can't help but notice it, I'd like to see four framed pictures displayed side by side—images that tell the parable of the sower as told by Jesus in the gospels. If people could be reminded of those four different soils every time they walk through the doors of the church, they might better prepare their hearts for the Word.

I'm sure we've all known Christians who started out well. They attended Bible studies faithfully, and every time you saw them, they just glowed with the light and love of Jesus. But over time they became dull and apathetic. That one who was so alive in Jesus now has no patience when you try to share a Scripture. There's just no life left. They have no interest in God or in the things of God.

But we've also known Christians who have continued to blossom and grow in their faith. Like the sun going forth in her glory, these believers become brighter and brighter as they sit under the teaching of God's Word. What a joy they are. How they please the heart of God!

Why do some Christians whither away while others bloom and grow? It's so important to know. It's important to have an understanding of why this happens, and to search ourselves to make sure we're receiving God's Word on good ground. We don't want to be in that company that grows cold or turns back or is unprepared for the coming of our Lord Jesus Christ. We want to be fruitful Christians, pleasing God in the time that's left.

THE PARABLE

Let's look at what Jesus said in Mark chapter 4:

> And again He began to teach by the sea. And a great multitude was gathered to Him, so that He got into a boat and sat in it on the sea; and the whole multitude was on the land facing the sea. Then He taught them many things by parables, and said to them in His teaching:
>
> "Listen! Behold, a sower went out to sow. And it happened, as he sowed, that some seed fell by the wayside; and the birds of the air came and devoured it. Some fell on stony ground, where it did not have much earth; and immediately it sprang up because it had no depth of earth. But when the sun was up it was scorched, and because it had no root it withered away. And some seed fell among thorns; and the thorns grew up and choked it, and it yielded no crop. But other seed fell on good ground and yielded a crop that sprang up, increased and produced: some thirty-fold, some sixty, and some a hundred." And He said to them, "He who has ears to hear, let him hear!"

... And He said to them, "Do you not understand this parable? How then will you understand all the parables? The sower sows the word. And these are the ones by the wayside where the word is sown. When they hear, Satan comes immediately and takes away the word that was sown in their hearts. These likewise are the ones sown on stony ground who, when they hear the word, immediately receive it with gladness; and they have no root in themselves, and so endure only for a time. Afterward, when tribulation or persecution arises for the word's sake, immediately they stumble. Now these are the ones sown among thorns; they are the ones who hear the word, and the cares of this world, the deceitfulness of riches, and the desires for other things entering in choke the word, and it becomes unfruitful. But these are the ones sown on good ground, those who hear the word, accept it, and bear fruit: some thirty-fold, some sixty, and some a hundred" (Mark 4:1-9, 13-20).

This parable is the key to all the kingdom parables that Christ taught. If you mark in your Bible write, "Key to Parables" in the margin next to this passage.

Can you see the four pictures right there in the entryway of the church? One would reveal an evil spirit coming in to snatch away the Word as it is being sown. One would portray seeds falling on hard, rocky soil. A third would expose seeds being sown in a plot of thorny thistles, which so clearly will grow up and choke that good seed. And the last picture would show seed scattered over good, rich soil.

Jesus used this parable to teach about four different heart conditions and how the seed, the Word of God, is received in each. Jesus used parables frequently. Parables are stories that illustrate truth. Unlike an allegory, which sometimes requires you to really study it to find the point, the beauty of a parable is that the truth it teaches can be caught instantly.

When I read this passage, my mind goes right to Israel and to that rich farming area which surrounds the Sea of Galilee. I can imagine what Jesus might have seen from the boat as He spoke to the multitude gathered on the shore that day. Perhaps as He sat there, His eye caught sight of a sower just beyond the crowd, walking slowly through his fields, sowing his seed. Maybe when Jesus decided to use a sower to illustrate His teaching, He did so knowing that as the multitude later turned to leave, they would catch a glimpse of that sower, and this lesson would be further imprinted on their minds.

Back in biblical times, the people in Palestine were well acquainted with sowing seed. It was an agrarian society. Most of them were farmers themselves, or at least they saw farmers constantly working in the fields. These people knew that soil was the key to successful crop growing. If you start with the wrong kind of soil, the seed will never grow or produce.

THE SOWER, THE SEED, AND THE GROUND

So when Jesus said, "Behold, a sower went out to sow," the crowd instantly understood the setting of His teaching. They didn't understand the heart of the message yet, but they understood the parameters of the story.

Jesus began by introducing the sower and the seed. "The seed is the Word of God" (Luke 8:11). The sower is anyone who sows that seed—whether it's a pastor, a radio teacher, a writer, or someone simply sharing God's Word. Seeds, of course, are sown into the ground. And Jesus begins to describe the different types of ground that God's Word falls on. This is anyone who hears the teaching of the Word—whether it's someone sitting in a sanctuary on Sunday morning, or listening to a teaching on the radio or TV, someone reading a book that is explaining a truth from God's Word, or listening to a friend explain the Bible. In its simplest terms, the seed is God's Word. The sower is anyone who teaches God's Word. And the ground depicts the heart of a person that hears God's Word.

THE WAYSIDE HEART

The first ground that Jesus described was by the wayside. The sowing illustrated here is simple scattering. It's just as if you wanted to plant wildflowers, but you didn't want to plant them seed by seed. You do what they call broadcast sowing. You just take the seed in your hand and throw it. I often think about that when Chuck is preaching. He's scattering the seed of God's Word through the congregation in our sanctuary and then out over the radio broadcast and on the Internet, where thousands and thousands of people hear it.

Now, not everyone who hears the Word broadcast in this manner is like the wayside. Some, as we will discuss later, have hearts that are ready to receive the Word. They listen to a teaching and they draw the seed deep down. But with others, the seed stays right at the surface, on hard ground—soil that was not prepared ahead of time. Luke tells us what happens when seed lands on hard ground. "It was trampled down and the birds of the air devoured it" (Luke 8:5). Birds and fowls are always a sign of evil. Mark 4:15 says that, "Satan comes immediately and takes away the word that was sown in their hearts."

The wayside heart is not prepared. Matthew says these are the people who do not understand what has been sown (Matthew 13:19). This is why it's so important when you bring someone to church who is not yet born again to pray for them ahead of time and ask God to give them understanding. Satan waits like a vulture. He doesn't want that seed to fall on good soil. So pray that God will prepare the soil. Ask Him to give that person a tender heart for the Word to fall upon.

How can you tell if someone is "wayside ground"? There are several indicators. The first is a general lack of interest. You've probably tried witnessing to them and they show no interest in eternity and don't care at all about prophecy. They may come to church with you, but they're glad when it's over and they leave with the same "live and let live" motto they came with. They're not changed at all by an encounter with the Word of God. Again, it's so important for you to prepare the ground ahead of time through prayer.

The second indicator with wayside ground is that the seed of the Word falls on a closed mind. These people are deaf to God's truths because they choose to be deaf. Very often they feel a prejudice toward God as a result of humanistic education. I've been so grieved to watch over and over again the damage ungodly educators can do to young minds, those who used to believe in God and walk closely with Jesus. They leave college with a degree and a head full of vain philosophy, which has closed them off to God and the things of God. They've been prejudiced against God. With these, you must pray for God to remove the blindness so they see how they've been indoctrinated against God.

A third indicator of hard ground is the indifferent person. Indifference is not the same thing as a lack of interest. The one who lacks interest doesn't care at all. The one who is indifferent has an interest in God, but is just not ready to do anything about their relationship with God today. They put it off. "One of these days I'll get to it," they say. But the truth is, they feel they can get along fine without God. And even when tragedy comes or life becomes unbearable, instead of turning to God, they turn to their favorite crutch—alcohol, drugs, therapy, or the occult. They try anything they can that will keep them from yielding to God.

Other people are simply not teachable. They already know everything and there's nothing left for them to learn. "Oh, I've studied the Bible," they say. Or they may go so far as to claim, "I know God's Word backwards and forwards!"

My son-in-law, Brian, tried to minister to a ninety-two year old man in a convalescent home. This man was very bitter. When Brian attempted to share what Ephesians 4:31 said about letting go of bitterness, the man got angry. "I know God's Word!" he yelled.

"If you know God's Word, then you know you can't be bitter," Brian said. But before he'd even finished the sentence, the man started punching him! He didn't stop with one punch, either. He punched Brian three times. Brian said, "I got kind of tired of that—it hurt."

Some people are wayside ground because they are afraid of the truth. Have you met these people? They're the ones who stop you when you talk to them about prophecy. "Don't tell me that!" they say. "I don't want to know anything about it. It's too scary!" These people are terrified of the truth. But we who walk with Jesus know that the truth sets us free.

Still others are hardened ground because they have an immoral character. They worry that if they come to Christ they will have to change their lifestyle, and they don't want to do that because they love their sin.

I've known many women who are suffering because they married men like this. Some of these women knew very well they were marrying immoral men, but they believed they could change them. Others believed men who said, for the sake of love, "Oh, yes! I will accept Jesus," but their conversions weren't real. That's a word of caution for single women. Choose your husbands carefully. If you marry an immoral man, you will suffer from that choice.

Consider this list carefully. If you are trying to witness to people in your life, be sure to precede that witnessing with prayer. Ask God to show you the true condition of their heart and to prepare the soil to accept the Word as you speak it forth.

THE STONY HEART

The second kind of soil Jesus described was the stony ground. He told us that when the seed fell on this stony ground, it sprang up quickly, but because the ground had so little soil, the roots couldn't go down deep, and they withered away under the scorching sun (Mark 4:5-6).

My heart just breaks over these people. If you've walked with Jesus very long, you've met them too. They're the ones who come to church and say, "Oh, this is truth! Praise God—this is so wonderful!" They embrace everything they hear with great enthusiasm. But when the lows hit, they want out. They are shallow Christians. They never take time to really study God's Word. They know nothing of discipleship, or of denial, or of abiding in Christ. Therefore, they know nothing about walking in love—or pleasing God. They endure for a short while and then they wither up.

Unfortunately, the body of Christ today is full of these superficial believers. The Word falls and hits rock and just lies there. At the beginning it may have looked like they had a big growth spurt, but without good soil and without the living water, they eventually scorch and wither away. How sad this is—and how unnecessary. God has given us everything we need to flourish, grow, and remain green and healthy.

These unstable Christians eventually succumb to affliction. When trouble comes in the form of temptations, persecutions, illness or loss—they can't stand. Like plants put in soil too shallow, they flop over to one side or the other. They become angry with God and turn away, or they become offended at the truth of His Word.

We need to pray some good soil into the lives of these unstable Christians. Not only are they a danger to themselves, they stir up trouble within the body. Every new craze that comes along excites them, and they pull others along with them. They understand nothing about the life of Jesus. They can't fathom serving others or suffering for the sake of the gospel. They're open to every wind of doctrine, and they do what they can to spread those heresies to others.

I call these people "circuit-riding Christians" because they're always running around in circles, chasing one strange thing after another. Wherever fire has popped up, they run to see it. But big fires have a way of turning into embers in no time.

Christians planted deep in good, rich soil know the truth, and they recognize lies. But those planted on rocky soil have no discernment at all.

THE THORNY HEART

The third soil Jesus described was the thorny ground. I like to think of this ground as being covered with thistles or even weeds. It's possible that the seed sown here fell on good ground initially, but that ground was also covered with thorns.

As a woman who is serious about seeking God and living to please Him, I would suggest that you meditate on Mark 4:19 frequently and use it as a checkpoint for your life. This verse is speaking about the person who has heard the Word and even received the seed into the deep places of her heart, but that plant began to get choked out in very slow, very subtle ways.

> And the cares of this world, the deceitfulness of riches, and the desires for other things entering in choke the word, and it becomes unfruitful.

Riches and a desire for things are not necessarily bad things in and of themselves. But they are things that have the potential to preoccupy us and to take priority over the things of God. As more attention is spent on these things, less attention is paid to Jesus. The result is a gradual spiritual decline as riches and desires crowd out Christ. These people may still attend church, but the Word begins having less effect on their lives.

The New Living Translation says it this way,

> The seed that fell among the thorns represents others who hear God's word, but all too quickly the message is crowded out by the worries of this life, the lure of wealth, and the desire for other things, so no fruit is produced (Mark 4:18-19 NLT).

UNFRUITFUL

It couldn't be much clearer, could it? The thorns come in and choke out the fruitfulness. I know how true this is, because it is my own testimony.

My parents had brought me up in the things of the Lord, but when I was thirteen, they bought a ranch and we would visit on the weekends. At first, we still attended church very regularly. We'd drive out to the ranch on Saturday morning, stay all day, but come back Saturday night so we could be in church on Sunday. After a while we started going out to the ranch on Friday night, and drive back Saturday night. Then we started driving up Friday night, staying through Sunday morning, and come back just in time for church Sunday night. And of course, it wasn't too long before we began going up and staying the entire weekend and missing church altogether.

I was thirteen when we stopped going to church, and for seven years, that was our lifestyle. But then when I was twenty, we were involved in a horrible, horrible accident on the way home. I believe God permitted that accident as a wake-up call. It was His chastening hand upon my parents because they'd completely crowded Him out of their lives. We had stopped everything. We had no church attendance, no Bible study, no prayer, no spiritual influences whatsoever.

As a result of our lifestyle, I became so disillusioned with spiritual things that by the time I was eighteen, I did not believe in God at all. I had been brought up in the Word as a child, but watching my parents turn away from God had disillusioned me to the point where I no longer believed. I remember visiting a church around that time and just crying because I wanted to believe so badly, but I just couldn't get past my parents' lifestyle. All the things they had always taught me to be evil, they were now doing.

At eighteen I started college, and that's all I needed to push me over the edge. My teachers all embraced humanistic philosophies. As they would stand before our class laughing at God and tearing down the things of God, I'd think, *They're right. There's nothing to Christianity.* I was completely disillusioned.

If you've been among thorns, you will not bear fruit. Thorns will choke out your fruitfulness. Between the ages of thirteen and twenty, my parents bore no fruit in my life. Every bit was choked out.

It makes me so sad to look back at that time, and to see how my parents began. They had loved Jesus so intensely that they both enrolled in a Bible school. It's how I came to live in their home. My mother decided to open up her home to minister to babies and little children when their own parents couldn't keep them. She thought, *Oh, what an opportunity to pray over each baby, each little child!* The court would bring children to her and she would keep them for a certain period of time until the people got their lives straightened out and could have their children back. My biological mother dropped me off one day and just never came back.

I praise God for the first eleven years He gave me in that home. But oh, what a tragedy those remaining years were as the thorns slowly crept in. Be aware that good soil produces good fruit, but good soil also produces sturdy weeds. And weeds always seem to grow much faster and so much more abundantly than good plants. When you're a good plant sown among thorns, you might have a blossom here or there. You might witness to someone you meet and produce a tiny bit of fruit, but there won't be abundant fruit that Jesus wants in your life. Like a neglected garden, weeds and bugs slowly take over and the beauty and fruitfulness are choked out. And it happens so slowly and so subtly that we often don't realize it's happening.

THE NEED TO WEED

An unfruitful Christian is not living to please God. We need to weed constantly. We need to get our priorities straightened out, and put God and the things of God first in our lives.

So what are the thorns and weeds as Jesus describes them? The first weed He mentions is "cares of this world." Some of those might be, "What shall we eat? What shall we drink? What shall we wear?" Clothing, in particular, is a problem for many women. Isn't that an awful problem? I'll be so glad when I'm clothed in my white robe, and I never have to wonder ever again what to wear!

Meal planning can be a care of the world. How much time do you spend worrying about putting a good meal together? I remember one time right before our big summer church picnic when I was just busy, busy, busy. In the back of my mind, I kept wondering about what I should bring to the picnic, since we had a big group with us—at least fifteen or twenty. But I also had several speaking engagements to prepare and teach. I could have really used a clone or two that week! All week, right in the middle of my planning or studying, I'd think, *What am I bringing to that picnic? And I can't forget paper plates ... and Chuck will want me to bring this ...* and I'd have to pull my thoughts off of the picnic and get them back on my lesson. But then the Holy Spirit spoke to my heart and reminded me to put first things first. So I said, "All right, Lord, I'm going to do those things first that You're requiring of me. And I'll trust You with the menu planning for the picnic."

Cheryl came over a few days later while I was studying for my *Joyful Life* teaching and she said, "Mom, what are we going to bring to the picnic tomorrow night?"

I said, "Let's take about five minutes and think about it." And in that time, God gave me the menu, down to the last pickle.

DIFFERENT WEEDS

What shall we eat, what shall we drink? I have found when I put Jesus first in my life, He helps me overcome this "care of life." All I have to do is say, "Lord, would You help me figure out the menu for dinner tonight? I need two vegetables ... which two vegetables, Lord? What kind of salad? What kind of salad dressing?" And He will do it! Just as He promised in Matthew 6:33, if we seek Him first, all the rest will be added to us.

Anxious thoughts of any kind are thorns in your life because they crowd out fruitfulness. Time you could be spending in prayer, you spend laboring instead over what you're going to put in or on your body. It isn't pleasing to the Lord and it chokes out your fruitfulness for Him.

Finances are often one of the "cares of this world." "How am I going to pay the bills?" I know what it means to struggle like that, but it's unfruitful to fret over bills. When your mind is full of anxious worries over finances, it's hard for God's Word to penetrate through those weeds. You must give that care to Him and trust that He will provide for you. You must delight yourself in Him first, and watch as He takes care of all your needs.

For a single woman, one of the cares of this world can be the question of how long it will take for God to send someone your way. "When, Lord? When will You bring the right man into my life?" For a married woman it could be, "Lord, why did You ever send this man into my life?" That's bad! Don't let your thoughts go there. That's definitely a thorn. Don't let the weeds of discontentment choke out your fruitfulness. As in all things, place your marriage in God's hands and seek to serve and love Him first.

God has a plan for your life, and His timing is perfect. He's methodical and orderly in all He does, and not a sparrow falls to the ground without Him knowing. Every hair on your head is numbered. He knows the name of every star in the sky. You can't even count them all because if you try, you'll forget where you started. Just stare at all those shimmering dots and let the thought sink in, *God has named them all!* Not only did He name each star, He flung them into space with His hand.

Chuck was teaching about this one Sunday morning, and it was one of those times when I was tracking what he said, that I jumped ahead. The Holy Spirit was guiding me right to a beautiful thought. Chuck started to say, "And the same Hand that created the world and flung the stars across the sky …" and in my heart I was thinking, *I get it! I get it!* I had to poke the person next to me and finish Chuck's sentence—" … is the same Hand that helps us!" I was so excited! God is there and He is ready to help us with every problem, every concern. The One Who created the world can put order in our lives and solve all our problems if we'll just put Him first.

Why in the world would anyone want to put the cares of this life—mere thorns and thistles—before God? But we do. God has given to us "all things that pertain to life and godliness" (2 Peter 1:3), and yet we choose to sit down among the thorns. Isn't that quite a picture?

Jesus next spoke about the deceitfulness of riches. Do you know why riches are deceitful? It's because they make you think you can be satisfied. But there's not a jewel in the world that can permanently satisfy you. You could have the largest of diamonds, rubies, sapphires, amethysts, and turquoise ... but there's not a jewel anywhere that can bring the deep satisfaction our hearts crave.

I have watched people become rich. They started with little and they slowly accumulated wealth, and as they did, they slowly turned from Jesus. Their interest in possessions crowded out their interest in God. That's the deceitfulness of riches. Psalms warns us, "If riches increase, do not set your heart on them" (Psalm 62:10).

My advice to women is this: live as simply as you can. Chuck and I live simply. Our home was already fifteen years old when we bought it and it's unpretentious and perfect for us. I wouldn't want anything different. From time to time, we've had people to our home and I can tell by their expressions that they thought we ought to be living differently. Maybe they expected a bigger house with more lavish furnishings. But we live a happy, simple life. God told me long ago, "Kay, you're right where I want you to be. I want you to keep your life simple. I don't ever want your possessions to possess you."

The third thing that Jesus said could come in and choke out the Word is "desires for other things." *The King James Version* states this as, "lusts of other things." We tend to think of lust in a sexual connotation, but lust simply means strong desire. Anything you desire above God is a lust.

Again, I want to caution the single women for a moment. The anxiety some single women feel about marriage, that strong desire to find the perfect mate, can be a lust in your life. If that desire is stronger than your desire for God, then it will surely choke out your fruitfulness. Wait upon the Lord. Keep loving and serving Him. Trust Him. If He intends you to be married, He'll bring the right man to you.

THE BEST HEART

And now with the hard shallow soil, the rocky soil, and the thorny soil behind us, we can turn to the best kind of soil. As my kids would say when they were young, "The very *bestest* of all."

> But other seed fell on good ground and yielded a crop that sprang up, increased and produced: some thirty-fold, some sixty, and some a hundred (Mark 4:8).

Oh, that's the kind of life I want! I want all the nutrients that are in the soil to produce an abundant crop in me. That's God's will for my life, and for yours too.

Right outside our kitchen window there is a beautiful gardenia plant. It's special to me because it takes me back to the first night I met Chuck. Back then, the style was to wear your hair on top of your head and arrange flowers in the bun. That's how I was wearing my hair the first night we met, and the flowers I wore were gardenias.

On our twenty-fifth anniversary, Chuck brought me a gardenia plant and planted it right outside the kitchen window. Our anniversary is June 19, and every year in June my gardenia plant blooms. Some mornings from the kitchen I'll catch the scent coming in my window and I just want to run outside and draw in big lungfuls of that beautiful smell. How fragrant and wonderful they are!

I also love the flowers they have in Hawaii—plumeria, carnations, and white ginger blossoms. They're so beautiful and so fragrant. Once when we were there, they added an exotic flower to our leis, and wherever we went, people near us would breathe in and say, "Oh, that smells so good!"

That's how I want my life to be. I want it to be so fragrant with Jesus, that anyone who comes near me will pick up that wonderful fragrance and want it for her own. It makes me think of perfume. Whenever I smell something really fragrant, I ask, "What's that you're wearing?" Some people will tell you but some refuse. They want to keep it their own little secret, like it's a precious family recipe.

As Christians, we want to share the secret of our beautiful fragrance. It's Jesus. When the seed of God's Word falls on good soil and is bathed by the sun—and in the Son—it produces healthy, fragrant plants out of your life. And we want to share that with others, that they too might become a fragrant plant before Him.

A QUALITY CROP

John 15:8 tells us, "By this My Father is glorified, that you bear much fruit."

Do you want to live pleasing to Jesus? Then you've got to have the Word of God planted in good soil. When you're sitting in service on a Sunday morning, listen to your pastor. Don't let your mind drift to fifteen different things, or even one other thing. Be focused on the Word of God. Say, "Lord, I want to hear from You today. You have anointed my pastor to teach and I'm going to listen and receive all that You have for me this morning, that I might bring forth much fruit for You."

The quality of our crop comes through yielding. As William Barclay said in his commentary on the book of Matthew, "The fate of any spoken word depends on the hearers." [20] Take heed to what you hear. Focus your heart. Ask God to plow deeply and plant His Word within you. Yield to Him.

All through our study of pleasing God, we've encountered choices. And this is no exception. When God sends out His Word, through His messenger to you, He puts a choice before you. You can let it fall by the wayside where Satan will come and snatch it away. You can let it fall on rocky soil where it will scorch and wither away. You can let the cares of this life choke it out. Or as a woman who loves God and wants to please Him, you can make the only wise choice. You can take it in and let God's Word take root in your heart, where it will bloom and grow into a thing of beauty.

Our prayer is simple, Lord. Plow up the ground of our hearts that the soil there would be soft and pliable and ready for Your Word. Keep us humble and teachable. Remind us that we can trust You with all our needs, all our concerns, that our minds would be freed to focus only on You.

You are all-beautiful, Father. You satisfy like nothing on earth could possibly do. Your fragrance is lovely and pure, and we want to be like You. So have Your way with our hearts, Lord. Plant Your Word deep within us, that we will grow to be women who please You and who draw others by Your beauty.

In Your name we pray, amen.

CHAPTER

15

REMEMBER

I HEARD GAIL MAYS TELL a story about a little girl named Erica, who, along with her Sunday school class, memorized Colossians 3:20. After church that afternoon, Erica recited her verse to her mother: "Children, obey your parents in all things, for this is well pleasing to the Lord." She then wrote it out and put it on the refrigerator, and repeated her verse all afternoon and evening, making her mother very proud.

But the next morning when her mother told her to go make her bed, Erica said, "No."

"What about that memory verse?" her mother asked.

To which Erica replied, "I just have to memorize it. I don't have to do it!"

I think a lot of us are like that. Sometimes our attitude about God's Word is, "I just have to hear it. I don't have to do it." But that's not what the Lord wants. He wants us to hear, remember, and do.

I once read that scientists were working on a chemical that would help you to learn faster and retain what you learn better. And my first thought was, *I want gallons of it!* Who wouldn't want to pick up information more quickly and retain it longer?

One reason why our capacity for memory is so important is that our judgments and future actions are based upon our past experiences. If you're careful when you're cooking around the stove, it's likely because you've been burned. There is no pain like a burn. At first you don't quite feel it. Then you really feel it, and then three hours later it's excruciating. You don't have to go through that crazy pain very often to learn to be careful.

Remembering can protect us and remembering can make us stronger. When we look back on God's goodness and care for us, our faith is strengthened. And likewise, when we fail to remember His goodness and care, our faith is replaced with anxiety.

God is pleased when we remember. In fact, the word "remember" is mentioned over 300 times in the Bible. He tells us to remember because He knows that when we're mindful of His nearness—when we stop to ponder the fact that God, the Creator, Who is all-powerful and all-knowing, is right here with us—we are more careful to walk in obedience. And when we remember that He sacrificed His Son for us and has adopted us as His own, we respond with a desire to please Him. How could you not? I've asked myself so many times, *Could I give my son for someone else's sin?* And I know that I could not. The realization of what it cost God to redeem us always causes a response of love and gratitude.

REMEMBER GOD

Before we talk about the specific things God wants us to remember, we need to talk about the things He wants us to forget. It was Paul who wrote in Philippians 3:13, "Forgetting those things which are behind...." God wants us to forget those things that make us feel guilty and condemned. If anyone knew about having a guilty past, it was Paul the apostle. He had a lot of forgetting to do. Remember that it was Paul who consented to the death of Stephen, who is considered to be one of the first Christian martyrs. It was Paul who hunted down Christians and pulled them from their homes and forced them to blaspheme Jesus Christ or face death.

Not only did Paul need to forget his past sins, he needed to forget his past achievements. Paul came from an impressive lineage and was a brilliant, well-educated man. But neither his lineage, nor his intellect, nor his fame mattered as much as Jesus. Paul said,

> But what things were gain to me, these I have counted loss for Christ. Yet indeed I also count all things loss for the excellence of the knowledge of Christ Jesus my Lord, for whom I have suffered the loss of all things, and count them as rubbish, that I may gain Christ (Philippians 3:7-8).

Some things aren't worth remembering. But some are. What are some of the specific things God wants us to remember? For one thing, we're to remember God's wonderful works to us. Psalm 103:2 says, "Bless the LORD, O my soul, and forget not all His benefits." The psalmist then goes on to list some of God's marvelous works:

> Who forgives all your iniquities, who heals all your diseases, who redeems your life from destruction, who crowns you with lovingkindness and tender mercies, who satisfies your mouth with good things, so that your youth is renewed like the eagle's (Psalm 103:3-5).

This psalm then talks about His patient, merciful character, and the fact that He has cast our sins as far as the east is from the west. Next, it paints a picture of His majesty and His creative power. This is a beautiful psalm, and one that should be read over and over.

MEMORIES

A lot of us keep photo albums. My daughters have put together at least a dozen for me over the years, and I have boxes of pictures at home. Many are photos of our trips to Israel, but most are of my children. I love my children's baby pictures. When I get them out and look at them, memories flood my heart. I don't ever want to forget how they looked or how they acted when they were little. Looking at those pictures brings it all back to me. That's why we take pictures, isn't it? We take pictures so we will not forget the wonderful memories of the past. We keep journals for the same reason. I love looking back in my journal and remembering all the important things that have happened in our lives and in the lives of our children.

Most women do one or both of those things. We compile photo albums and we keep journals. But how many of us keep a journal of the great things God has done for us? How many of us have ever written down one miracle that God has performed for us personally? We think we'll always remember His blessings. But without writing them down, many will be forgotten.

I think that as an act of worship, and to bless the heart of God, you should begin to keep a journal of all the things He does for you. Even if you just write out a few words in the day, get in the habit of capturing those memories. Not only would this please God, it would also give you strength when a crisis comes. When you look back and remember how God met you in this trial or that painful experience, you'll be filled with faith to believe that He'll meet you in this current crisis too. But if you don't write these things down, you will forget.

THE NEXT GENERATION

Another form of remembering is sharing God's wonderful works with the next generation. If you have children, you must teach them the good things God has done. If you don't have children of your own, you still should be sharing these things with the next generation. Our children should know how God delivered the children of Israel out of bondage and led them through the Red Sea. They should know about Jonah and the big fish. They should certainly know about the cross. You must teach everything you can about what God has done to deliver them.

After the children of Israel had crossed over the Jordan River and into the Promised Land, God commanded the priests to take stones from the river and build a memorial, so that in years to come when the children would see the stones and ask, "What do these stones *mean* to you?" (Joshua 4:6), the older people could say, "Oh, that was when God got us through the Jordan on dry land."

Whether you choose to remember God's deeds in a journal or some other way, you should have your own memorials to Him. And then when your children say, "What's that for? What does that mean?" you can answer, "That's where God did this for us. That's where God performed this miracle."

God came up with a specific way for the children of Israel to stop every year and remember His mighty acts on their behalf: He established three annual feasts. "Three times you shall keep a feast to Me in the year" (Exodus 23:14). These three main feasts were the Passover, the Feast of Pentecost, and the Feast of Tabernacles (or the Festival of Booths).

Chuck and I have been in Israel during the Feast of Booths, and it's a fascinating thing to see. Following God's instructions in Leviticus, the Jews build small, temporary booths or shelters in their yards.

You shall dwell in booths for seven days. All who are native Israelites shall dwell in booths, that your generations may know that I made the children of Israel dwell in booths when I brought them out of the land of Egypt: I am the LORD your God (Leviticus 23:42-43).

God wanted them all to remember—not just the first generation, but all the generations that were to follow. If they weren't reminded year after year, they would forget that the children of Israel once lived in booths.

God is very definite about the instructions for these booths. They are to be at least ten cubits high, but not more than twenty cubits. One cubit is roughly eighteen inches long. The booths are usually built up against the house, which gives them a back wall for shelter. They must be frail, meaning that you can't build something sturdy enough to dwell indefinitely. They have a door in the front and a thatched roof that is often made of tree branches or reeds. The roofs must have an opening in them so that those inside can look up and see the stars, but it must cover enough so that there is more shade inside than sunlight. This is a reminder to them that as the children of Israel wandered in the wilderness, God's protection kept the sun from smiting them by day.

Technically, the Jews are required to eat all their meals in their booth, or *sukkah*, and sleep within it during the seven nights of the feast, although most do not sleep in the booths anymore.

Is this not a beautiful tradition? And the symbolism is so applicable to us as Christians. Your family might love to have their own Feast of Booths to remember God's deliverance and provision. Not only could this be an opportunity to teach them more about Jesus, but it would draw your family together too. What child would not want to eat and sleep in a homemade structure?

God used the Feast of Booths to remind the Israelites of three specific things. These are reminders for us as well. The first is found in Leviticus 23:43: "I brought them out of the land of Egypt."

GOD'S DELIVERANCE

You need to constantly remember that you were brought out of the kingdom of darkness when you accepted Jesus Christ. As were the children of Israel, we are so prone to forget. Once they began wandering in the wilderness, they started lusting after the food they had enjoyed in Egypt. Why? Because they did not remember the bondage of Egypt. They forgot that they had been beaten and enslaved.

Satan loves this tactic. He will often remind us of some pleasurable sin we once participated in before we knew Jesus. Satan tries to make us miss the world. But we can only do that if we forget the bondage we were in and all the suffering we endured while in darkness.

One of the great joys I have is listening to our pastors' wives speak. Those women who came to us as young girls back in the early days of Calvary Chapel have grown to be such beautiful, godly women—and all with such a passion for Jesus. Not long ago, while I was sitting at one of our pastors' wives' retreats and I heard some of them speaking, I couldn't help but think back to their husbands' conversions, and praise God for the work He has done in their lives.

When Sharon Ries spoke, I thought of Raul before he came to the Lord. He was an angry, ungodly man, filled with hatred and bitterness. He was a man who, in Vietnam, had developed a taste for killing. But that was before Jesus delivered him.

Then when Cathe Laurie spoke, I thought of Greg's troubled childhood and youth, and how he had turned to drugs to fill his emptiness. But that was before he met Jesus.

When Sandy MacIntosh shared her testimony of how God restored her marriage to Mike after their divorce, I remembered meeting Mike in those early days. He had taken LSD with Timothy Leary before he came to God, and truly believed that half of his brain was blown off.

Listening to Gail Mays, I thought about how her husband, Steve, had shown up at one of our early Christian communes disheveled, drugged out, and carrying a gun.

Seeing Karyn Johnson reminded me of her husband, Jeff, who had been an infamous drug dealer in Downey.

These men were changed by Jesus. All are used powerfully by Him today. Each has a tremendous ministry, reaching and influencing thousands of people in their communities and across the world—through crusades, rallies, and radio broadcasts. Each is a testament to God's deliverance and redemption.

As we remember God's great works of deliverance, praise begins to well up in our hearts. Just as the Jews are reminded of their deliverance out of Egypt, we should be reminded of our deliverance out of sin. We were slaves just as they were. Before we met Jesus, we were slaves to the kingdom of darkness.

GOD'S PROVIDENTIAL CARE

The second thing the Feast of Booths reminds the Jews of is God's providential care for them in those forty years in the wilderness. This is another thing Satan tries to strip from our memories. He doesn't want us to remember God cares for us. When we forget that, we become anxious and fretful. We feel hopeless because we can't see any way out from our problems. We mutter and complain.

It's amazing to read of the specific ways God provided for the children of Israel while they were in the wilderness. Did you know their shoes didn't wear out? Not one pair in forty years! Did you know Moses' eyesight didn't dim? He was one hundred and twenty years old, and the Bible says, "His eyes were not dim nor his natural vigor diminished" (Deuteronomy 34:7). Chuck used to walk all over the house searching for his glasses saying, "Lord, You kept Moses! He didn't need glasses! I love You too, Lord … why won't You keep my eyes from dimming?" I remind him he's out of the wilderness, that's why!

How we need to remind ourselves of God's beautiful provision. I'm trying to write down even the smallest of things, because I don't want to forget even one moment of God's care for me.

I remember one time when Chuck and I were supposed to meet with authors, John and Elizabeth Sherrill. Just before we were to see them, Chuck had to take a very sudden trip. As he was walking out the door, he asked me to call the Sherrills and let them know what had happened, and see if we could meet the following week instead.

Well, I didn't have the foggiest notion how to get in touch with the Sherrills. But I didn't want them to drive here for nothing, and I didn't want Chuck to feel bad about having to take his trip, so I did what I could. I tried getting a phone number from our church office. That number led to another number, and then another. When I ran out of ideas, I prayed, "Lord, unless You do it, there's no way I can get in touch with these people. Will You help?" And do you know what happened? At almost the same instant the Sherrills called the church office. Just like that. By the time Chuck got home, everything was beautifully arranged and we met with them and had a marvelous time in God's plan.

Now, some would look at that and say it was a coincidence. But I know better. I know that it was just one of many times when God provided just what I needed, just *when* I needed it.

Sometimes God's provisions are a little more dramatic. One time I awoke at four o'clock in the morning thinking that somebody was downstairs in our house. What had awakened me was the sound of our doorbell chimes gently ringing. It wasn't the same sound as when someone rang the bell. We had chimed doorbells at the time and they would not ring unless they were physically bumped from inside the house or someone hit the button from the outside. Well, I heard a gentle ring, a sound that could only have been made if somebody had brushed by them. And that wasn't all. I heard several other slight noises downstairs and I knew somebody was there.

I had a dilemma. I wanted to wake Chuck up, but he's one of those types who awakes noisily. I knew he'd say, "What, what! What's the matter! What's going on!" and that would tip the intruder off. I thought, *That burglar will hear Chuck and he'll know right where we are. And then he'll come up here and get us!* So I just lay there and I started praying. "Help, Lord, help! I know somebody's there!"

Then I heard more noises—real noises. I heard one of the downstairs doors squeaking as it was being pushed open. So I prayed harder. "Oh, God! You've got to help us fast!"

And do you know what happened? Our phone rang—at four o' clock in the morning! It was someone from the church who needed Chuck to come to the hospital. The minute Chuck answered the phone I jumped up and threw on all the lights upstairs! And as soon as I did, I heard the front door open, so I knew that the person had left. They left because they knew we were awake. To this day I believe they thought we probably had a burglar alarm downstairs and the phone call was from the police, alerting us.

That was God's providential care. Only God could cause the phone to ring at just the right moment.

So many times, especially in our early years of ministry, God provided in the most practical ways. When we didn't have a cent for food, God would send provisions for us. One of my memories, which is actually kind of funny now, is one Saturday night when I was just a few weeks from giving birth to Chuck Jr., I'd been cleaning house all day and had on the ugliest dress you can imagine, and my hair was going every which way. At the time we lived in a big room walled in by big concrete blocks, which I had tried to pretty up with curtains. And we were flat broke.

Around nine o'clock that night, I heard a knock on the back door. Chuck opened it while I hid myself behind this little drape that I had hung to separate our bedroom from the living area. Peeking out from the side of the curtain, I saw a couple standing there, and a gorgeous Cadillac just beyond them in the driveway. They said they wanted to get married. Their pastor was out of town and they didn't want to wait, so would Chuck do it? Chuck asked them a lot of questions before finally agreeing to marry them. And then he said the most awful thing. He said, "Kay, come be a witness."

I was mortified! I had to come out from behind the curtain and join the cleaning man from the church whom Chuck had called to be the second witness. Of course this woman was gorgeous herself and dressed in a beautiful outfit. And there I stood in my ugly dress and my hair standing every which way. But as they left, the man shook Chuck's hand and slipped him a hundred-dollar bill! They drove off before we could do anything about it. We just stood there praising God for His providential care. That hundred dollars got us through almost a month, I'll tell you!

What I want to tell you is this: Chuck and I are not special. We're not! God wants to care for you just as He has cared for us over and over again. He only asks that you believe He is capable and believe He is willing to provide for all your needs. Like the Israelites who build their yearly booths, you need to build a booth in your heart—a memorial to remind you of God's goodness toward you.

TEMPORARY DWELLINGS

Lastly, God asked the children of Israel to make the booth frail, even shakeable, because He wants to remind us that we are in a temporary dwelling. Our bodies are nothing more than tents. This physical body can be amputated, mutilated, or destroyed. But our spiritual bodies cannot be touched.

A woman I met was telling me that in the affluent area where she lives, nearly all the women she knows have had "little eye tucks" and "little facelifts" and a lot of other little this and thats. I'm sometimes amazed at all we do in an attempt to keep our bodies gorgeous and in shape. We scrub 'em, we paint 'em, we polish 'em, we perfume 'em, we adorn 'em, we feed 'em and we starve 'em! Worst of all, we base our self-worth on how other people react to them. Don't we?

Think of those times when you've had to rush out to the store looking a little less than your best, only to have the clerk act rudely to you. Don't you automatically think, *If I had just combed my hair and put some make-up on, she would have been nicer to me.* That's not to say that there's something wrong with trying to look your best. I don't mean to imply that. But it's extreme when you feel completely awful about yourself— then it's a problem.

Women are so prone to this. I've known women who hate their noses, and women who hate their chins. I never much liked mine either, come to think of it. And I used to have a gap in my front teeth before I discovered that little dental rubber bands could pull them together. It worked and I was happy and I forgot about it. But back in junior high school, before I discovered those dental bands, I was walking down the hall toward my locker and some boys whistled at me. It was obvious that they were whistling at me, but when I walked up to my two friends who were waiting at my locker for me, I acted like I didn't know. I said, "I wonder who they were whistling at?"

One of my friends said, "Oh, they were whistling at you. You know, you're pretty cute except for that gap in your teeth."

After that every time I laughed, I covered my mouth. That's what our society and our culture and even some of our friends do to us sometimes.

TRUE BEAUTY

We place such a high value on such a temporal body. It's not eternal—it's just a tent. When we remember that, we're freed from all those awful thoughts that torment us—thoughts like, *I'm not gorgeous,* or *I'm getting old.* It no longer matters, because there's something better to live for. There's a higher purpose for our lives. Instead of worrying about how well our tent is holding up, we can turn our focus to the beauty within. As Peter said,

> Do not let your adornment be merely outward—arranging the hair, wearing gold, or putting on fine apparel—rather let it be the hidden person of the heart, with the incorruptible beauty of a gentle and quiet spirit, which is very precious in the sight of God (1 Peter 3:3-4).

Every woman wants to be beautiful, but not every woman concerns herself with her inner beauty. And yet this is the only beauty that is incorruptible. Every external thing we do to our bodies will be lost in the end as this tent of ours is destroyed. But we have the opportunity right now to develop a gentle and quiet spirit which is so valuable in God's eyes.

If you feel you have no balance in this area, that your time and attention is all spent on outward adornment and you have none left to give to your inner beauty, then ask God for balance. I am very deliberate about this. I want that "hidden person of the heart" to get twice as much attention as my outer body. So if it takes me ten minutes to get my make-up on or to comb my hair, I try to spend at least twenty minutes adorning my heart. I try to be mindful that "the things which are seen are temporary, but the things which are not seen are eternal" (2 Corinthians 4:18).

Doesn't an incorruptible body sound wonderful? No aches, no pains, no funny chins or noses. What a relief it will be to finally change into that perfect body God has designed for us! I sometimes look up with longing and think, *Is today the day, Jesus? Is this the day You will come back for me?*

Beloved sister in Christ, I pray that God will impress these lessons on your heart, that they would forever change the way you view your life. I pray that God will show you His great love for you, and bring to remembrance all the times when He delivered you and provided for you. I pray that you will remember how fleeting your life is—that it is but a fog, a vapor. But even more so, I pray that you will recognize your purpose for being. With the life that you've been given, you have an opportunity to serve the God Who loves and cares for you—the God Who saved you. In the days that you have left, you can live purposely with His pleasure in mind. You can order your life in such a way that it blesses Him and pleases His heart.

And I ask this for you in Jesus' precious name.

Amen.

FOOTNOTES

Chapter 1

[1] George Herbert, *Teach Me, My God and King*, 1633.

Chapter 2

[2] E. May Grimes, *The Quiet Hour*, 1920.

Chapter 4

[3] Frederic William Faber, *O Soul of Jesus, Sick to Death*, 1849.

[4] Roy Hession, *The Calvary Road*, (CLC Publicaions, 1980).

Chapter 5

[5] Brother Lawrence, *The Practice of the Presence of God*, (1958, 1967 Fleming H. Revell, published by Spire Books).

[6] Charles Austin Miles, *In the Garden*, 1912.

[7] Mary Stevenson Zangare, *Footprints in the Sand*, 1936, © 1984.

Chapter 6

[8] Reona Peterson Joly, *Tomorrow You Die*, (YWAM Publishing, 1997).

Chapter 7

[9] Anne Ortlund, *Disciplines of the Beautiful Woman*, (W Publishing, 1984).

[10] William Barclay, *The Letter to the Romans*, (Louisville, KY: Westminster John Knox Press, 2002).

[11] J. Gregory Mantle, *Beyond Humiliation: The Way of the Cross*, (1896), (reprinted by Kingsley Press, 2004).

Chapter 8

[12] G. Campbell Morgan, source unknown.

Chapter 9

[13] A.W. Tozer, *Gems from Tozer*, (Camp Hill, PA: WingSpread Publishers, 1979).

[14] Johnson Oatman Jr., *Holy, Holy Is What the Angels Sing*, 1894.

[15] Tozer, *Gems from Tozer*.

[16] Fredrick William Faber, *The Holy Trinity*, 1871.

Chapter 10

[17] Norman Wright, source unknown.

Chapter 11

[18] William Law, *A Serious Call to a Devout and Holy Life*, (1728), (Published by J.Barker, 1845. Original from the University of Michigan), pg. 206.

Chapter 13

[19] Tozer, *Gems from Tozer*.

Chapter 14

[20] William Barclay, *The Daily Study Bible: The Gospel of Matthew*, Volume 2, (Edinburgh: Saint Andrew Press, 2001), pg. 69.

BOOK RESOURCES BY

Kay Smith

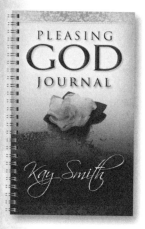

New!
THE PLEASING GOD JOURNAL

Designed to accompany the *Pleasing God* book by Kay Smith. Perfect for personal or group Bible studies for women.

9781597510868

New!
PHILIPPIANS

A complete and in-depth Bible study by Kay Smith.

160-page book
9781597510806